Lecture Notes in Computer Science 3307

Commenced Publication in 1973
Founding and Former Series Editors:
Gerhard Goos, Juris Hartmanis, and Jan van Leeuwen

Christoph Bussler   Suk-ki Hong
Woochun Jun   Roland Kaschek
Kinshuk   Shonali Krishnaswamy
Seng Wai Loke   Daniel Oberle
Debbie Richards   Amit Sharma
York Sure   Bernhard Thalheim (Eds.)

Web Information Systems – WISE 2004 Workshops

WISE 2004 International Workshops
Brisbane, Australia, November 22-24, 2004
Proceedings

 Springer

Volume Editors
See next page

Library of Congress Control Number: 2004114700

CR Subject Classification (1998): H.4, H.3, H.2, C.2.4, I.2, H.5.1

ISSN 0302-9743
ISBN 3-540-23892-1 Springer Berlin Heidelberg New York

Springer is a part of Springer Science+Business Media

springeronline.com

© Springer-Verlag Berlin Heidelberg 2004
Printed in Germany

Typesetting: Camera-ready by author, data conversion by PTP-Berlin, Protago-TeX-Production GmbH
Printed on acid-free paper   SPIN: 11353928   06/3142   5 4 3 2 1 0

Christoph Bussler
National University of Ireland
Digital Enterprise Research Institute (DERI)
University Road, Galway, Ireland
E-mail: chris.bussler@deri.org

Suk-ki Hong
Dankook University
College of Business and Economics 147
Hannam-ro, Yongsan-gu, Seoul, Korea 140-714
E-mail: skhong017@dankook.ac.kr

Woochun Jun
Seoul National University of Education
Dept. of Computer Education
Seocho Dong 1650, Seocho Gu, Seoul, Korea
E-mail: wocjun@ns.snue.ac.kr

Roland Kaschek
Kinshuk
Massey University
Department of Information Systems
5301 Palmerston North, Private Bag 11 222, New Zealand
E-mail: r.h.kaschek@massey.ac.nz; Kinshuk@ieee.org

Shonali Krishnaswamy
Seng Wai Loke
Monash University
School of Computer Science and Software Engineering
900 Dandenong Rd, Caulfield East, Victoria 3145, Australia
E-mail: {Shonali.Krishnaswamy;seng.loke}@infotech.monash.edu.au

Daniel Oberle
York Sure
University of Karlsruhe, Institute AIFB
76128 Karlsruhe, Germany
E-mail: {oberle, sure}@aifb.uni-karlsruhe.de

Debbie Richards
Macquarie University, Department of Computing
NSW 2109, Sydney, Australia
E-mail: richards@ics.mq.edu.au

Amit Sharma
Software Engineering Technology Labs
Infosys Technologies
Electronics City, Hosur Road, Bangalore, 560100, India
E-mail: amitdce@yahoo.com

Bernhard Thalheim
Kiel University, Computer Science Institute
Olshausenstr. 40, 24098 Kiel, Germany
E-mail: thalheim@is.informatik.uni-kiel.de

Editors

The editors of the volume are in this order: Christoph Bussler, Suk-ki Hong, Woochun Jun, Roland Kaschek, Kinshuk, Shonali Krishnaswamy, Seng Wai Loke, Daniel Oberle, Debbie Richards, Amit Sharma, York Sure, Bernhard Thalheim

Christoph Bussler
Affiliation: Digital Enterprise Research Institute (DERI)
Address: National University of Ireland, Galway, University Road,
                      Galway, Ireland
Email: chris.bussler@deri.org

Suk-ki Hong
Affiliation: Dankook University, College of Business and Economics
Address: 147, Hannam-ro, Yongsan-gu, Seoul, Korea 140-714
Email: skhong017@dankook.ac.kr, skhong017@naver.com

Woochun Jun
Affiliation: Dept. of Computer Education, Seoul National University
                      of Education
Address: Seocho Dong 1650, Seocho Gu, Seoul, Korea
Email: wocjun@snue.ac.kr

Roland Kaschek
Affiliation: Massey University
Address: Dept. of Information Systems, Massey University
                      5301 Palmerston North, Private Bag 11 222
Email: R.H.Kaschek@massey.ac.nz

Kinshuk
Affiliation: Massey University
Address: Information Systems Department, Massey University,
                      Private Bag 11-222, Palmerston North, New Zealand
Email: kinshuk@ieee.org

Shonali Krishnaswamy
Affiliation: Monash University
Address: School of Computer Science and Software Engineering
                      900 Dandenong Rd, Caulfield East, Victoria 3145
Email: Shonali.Krishnaswamy@infotech.monash.edu.au

Seng Wai Loke
Affiliation: Monash University
Address: School of Computer Science and Software Engineering
                     900 Dandenong Rd, Caulfield East, Victoria 3145
                     Australia
Email: Seng.Loke@infotech.monash.edu.au

Daniel Oberle
Affiliation: University of Karlsruhe, Institute AIFB
Address: D-76128 Karlsruhe, Germany
Email: oberle@aifb.uni-karlsruhe.de

Debbie Richards
Affiliation: Macquarie University
Address: Dept of Computing, Macquarie University, NSW 2109,
                     Australia
Email: richards@ics.mq.edu.au

Amit Sharma
Affiliation: Software Engineering Technology Labs, Infosys Tech-
                     nologies
Address: Electronics City, Hosur Road, Bangalore, India-560100
Email: amitdce@yahoo.com

York Sure
Affiliation: University of Karlsruhe, Institute AIFB
Address: D-76128 Karlsruhe
Email: sure@aifb.uni-karlsruhe.de

Bernhard Thalheim
Affiliation: Kiel University, Computer Science Institute
Address: Olshausenstr. 40, 24098 Kiel, Germany
Email: thalheim@is.informatik.uni-kiel.de

WISE 2004
Workshop Chair's Message

I would like to welcome you to the Workshop Proceedings of the 5th International Conference on Web Information Systems Engineering (WISE 2004), which took place in Brisbane, Australia. As in previous years, workshop proposals were invited continuing the tradition of workshops in conjunction with the WISE conference.

Originally four workshop proposals were accepted. During the workshop organization it became apparent that WISE 2004 would be served best by combining these four workshops into two, allowing a better and wider coverage of topics while avoiding a too segmented workshop program.

The workshop titled 'Intelligent Networked and Mobile Systems' organized by Woochun Jun, Suk-ki Hong, Daniel Oberle, Debbie Richards, and York Sure covered the areas 'Ontologies for Networked Systems' and 'Advances in Mobile Learning.' The workshop with the title 'Web Information Systems' organized by Roland Kaschek, Kinshuk, Shonali Krishnaswamy, Seng Wai Loke, Amit Sharma, and Bernhard Thalheim addressed Web applications and Web services.

I would like to thank all authors who submitted and presented papers at the workshops for their hard work. Also, I would like to thank all attendees of the workshops for their engagement at the workshops as well as at the conference, as they together with the authors represent the WISE community. The workshop organizers did a great job in organizing the workshops, including the paper selection and proceedings preparation. It was a pleasure cooperating with them putting together the workshop program; thank you for that. Last, but not least, I'd like to thank the WISE conference organizers for their efficient support of the WISE 2004 workshop program.

September 2004   Christoph Bussler

Intelligent Networked and Mobile Systems
Workshop Chairs' Message

The international workshop "Intelligent Networked and Mobile Systems" consisted of two main tracks:

- **Ontologies for Networked Systems (ONS)**, and
- **Advances in Mobile Learning (AML)**

Track ONS: Ontologies provide a shared understanding of a domain of interest to support communication among human and computer agents, typically being represented in a machine-processable representation language. Thus, ontologies are seen as key enablers for the Semantic Web. Recently the convergence of paradigms such as those currently being monitored in the areas of the Semantic Web, Web Services, Agents, Peer-to-Peer networks and Grid Computing requires multidisciplinary approaches and cooperation. This workshop was designed to bring together researchers and practitioners from the mentioned areas and to act as a platform for discussions on experiences and visions.

Track AML: Mobile Learning is the use of mobile or wireless devices for learning on the move. Mobile learning aims to improve levels of literacy and participation in education amongst young adults across all nations. It makes use of young people's interest in their mobile phones and other handheld communications/entertainment devices to deliver exciting and unusual learning experiences and related messages. The aim of this workshop was to invite researchers from various fields to present and discuss their ideas on mobile learning.

The workshop was held in cooperation with two prominent networks of excellence and was meant to act as a focal point for joint interests and future collaborations:

- **Knowledge Web:Realizing the Semantic Web**, European-funded network of excellence, see http://knowledgeweb.semanticweb.org/ for further details
- **ARC Research Network for Next Generation Web Technologies**, Australian research network – Intelligent Applications Through the Semantic Web, see http://www.comp.mq.edu.au/research/semantic/ for further details

Your organization committee,

Track ONS	*Track AML*
Daniel Oberle	Prof. Woochun Jun
Debbie Richards	Prof. Suk-ki Hong
York Sure (contact)	

Acknowledgements: The workshop was supported by the EU funded projects Knowledge Web (IST-2004-507482) and SEKT (IST-2003-506826).

Web Information Systems
Workshop Chairs' Message

Engineering Web information systems (WIS), apart from meeting functional require-ments, in particular needs to focus on the quality of the systems to be provided. This quality in the end will be crucial regarding acceptance of new technologies such as Web services. Putting a stronger emphasis on system quality also is a consequence of the increased awareness of this issue among those who care for systems development.

WIS comprises both general Web applications and Web services in particular. Con-sidering WIS from a holistic perspective may help to account for this diversity. Such a perspective should encompass both quality at the engineering and development level and quality at the operational level. It thus is essential for quality to pervade through the development, the management and the use of Web information systems. The desired quality aspects need to be considered and interrelated for a systematic technology-based approach to the construction of high-quality Web information systems. In addition, qual-ity at the operational level becomes significant for service-oriented systems. At this level, the focus is on the levels of service quality that the Web application provides for quality aspects such as performance, scalability, availability, and reliability. It becomes a bench-mark to differentiate services and providers. Quality of service forms the underpinning for a broad spectrum of Web service activities such as selection, scheduling, pricing and specifying service level agreements. If economic feasibility is a major development goal then quality-related decisions in design and implementation need to focus on sys-tem usage. This involves taking note of a number of different system characteristics and methods, techniques, and tools for dealing with these characteristics. Fruitfully applying the mentioned holistic view requires integrating into a reasonably coherent conceptual framework the knowledge already obtained regarding WIS. This is the task that was set out by the FIPWIS workshop: to look at competing and complementary approaches to WIS issues. To tie things together, to identify and stick to what is good and fruitful and to improve what is not satisfactory. The focus of the WQW workshop was on the oper-ational quality levels of Web services in particular. The responses to the calls for papers of WQW and FIPWIS were not so numerous as to justify running both workshops as separate events on one-day duration bases. Furthermore, given the holistic perspective that needs to be taken when dealing with the quality of Web information systems, it became evident that the two workshops could meaningfully be integrated. The same went for the other WISE 2004 workshops.

All WISE workshops were supposed to add to the benefit of attending WISE 2004 by broadening the spectrum of the papers provided. It thus was decided to merge the four intended WISE workshops into two. WQW and FIPWIS immediately found that idea attractive and merged into WOWIS (Workshop on Web Information Systems). The present volume contains the papers that were independently peer-reviewed and selected by the FIPWIS and the WQW program committees. In both cases 50% of the paper submissions were accepted.

Roland Kaschek and Shonali Krishnaswamy

Organization Committee

Christoph Bussler
    Digital Enterprise Research Institute (DERI)
Suk-Ki Hong
    Dankook University, College of Business and Economics
Woochun Jun
    Dept. of Computer Education, Seoul National University of Education
Roland Kaschek
    Dept. of Information Systems, Massey University
Kinshuk
    Advanced Learning Technologies Research Centre,
    Information System Department, Massey University
Shonali Krishnaswamy
    Monash University
Seng Wai Loke
    Monash University
Daniel Oberle
    University of Karlsruhe, Institute AIFB
Debbie Richards
    Dept of Computing, Macquarie University
Amit Sharma
    Software Engineering Technology Labs, Infosys Technologies
York Sure
    University of Karlsruhe, Institute AIFB
Bernhard Thalheim
    Kiel University, Computer Science Institute

Program Committees

Workshop on Intelligent Networked and Mobile Systems (INMS)

Ontologies for Networked Systems (ONS) Track

Andreas Abecker, Research Center for Information Technologies (FZI), Karlsruhe
Andreas Eberhart, University of Karlsruhe
Boualem Benatallah, University of New South Wales, Sydney
Jos de Bruin, University of Innsbruck
Jürgen Angele, Ontoprise GmbH
Heiner Stuckenschmidt, Vrije Universiteit Amsterdam
Lawrence Cavedon, Stanford University
Leon Sterling, University of Melbourne
Michael Sintek, DFKI Kaiserslautern
Oscar Corcho, iSOCO
Philippe Cudre-Mauroux, EPFL Lausanne
Valentina Tamma, University of Liverpool
Jian Yang, Macquarie University, Sydney
Ryszard Kowalczyk, Swinburne University of Technology, Australia

Advances in Mobile Learning (AML) Track

Christos J. Bouras, University of Patras, Research Academic,
    Computer Technology Institute, Greece
Jo Coldwell, Deakin University, Australia
Le Gruenwald, University of Oklahoma, USA
Zhigeng Pan, Zhejiang University, China
Youngbum Park, Dankook University, Korea
Ilkyeun Ra, University of Colorado at Denver, USA
Daeyoung Seo, Korea Polytechnic University, Korea
Timothy K. Shih, Tamkang University, Taiwan
Sean Siqueira, Catholic University of Rio de Janeiro, Brazil
Li Yang, Western Michigan University, USA

Workshop on Web Information Systems

Fragmentation Versus Integration – Perspectives of the Web Information Systems Discipline – (FIPWIS) Track

Vladan Devedzic, University of Belgrade, Yugoslavia
Klaus Jantke, DFKI Saarbruecken, Germany
Roland Kaschek, Massey University, New Zealand
Kinshuk, Massey University, New Zealand
Stephen Liddle, Brigham Young University, USA
Heinrich C. Mayr, University of Klagenfurt, Austria
Gustavo Rossi, La Plata National University, Argentina
Demetrios Sampson, University of Piraeus, Greece
Yuzuru Tanaka, Hokkaido University, Japan
Bernhard Thalheim, University of Kiel, Germany
Alexei Tretiakov, Massey University, New Zealand

Web Services Quality (WQW) Track

Gustavo Alonso, ETH Zentrum, Zürich, Switzerland
Rashid Al-Ali, University of Cardiff, United Kingdom
Boualem Benatallah, University of New South Wales, Australia
Luigi Buglione, GUFPI-ISMA, Italy
Rajkumar Buyya, University of Melbourne, Australia
Jorge Cardoso, University of Madeira, Portugal
Fabio Casati, HP Labs, USA
Lawrence Cavedon, CSLI, Stanford University, USA
Coral Calero, University of Castilla-La Mancha, Spain
Oscar Diaz, University of the Basque Country, Spain
Heiko Ludwig, IBM, USA
Massimo Meccella, University of Rome, Italy
Michael Maximilien, IBM and NCSU, USA
Aad van Moorsel, HP, USA
Barbara Pernici, Politecnico di Milano, Italy
Mario Piattini, University of Castilla-La Mancha, Spain
Andry Rakotinarainy, CARRS-Q, Australia
Shubhashis Sengupta, Infosys Technologies Ltd., India
Leon Sterling, University of Melbourne, Australia
Bala Srinivasan, Monash University, Australia
Jian Yang, Swinburne University of Technology, Australia
Arkady Zaslavsky, Monash University, Australia
Liangzhao Zeng, IBM, USA

Table of Contents

Short Papers

Workshop on Web Information Systems Track1: Fragmentation Versus Integration – Perspective of the Web Information System Discipline (FIPWIS)

Track2: Web Services Quality (WQW)

Workshop on Intelligent Networked and Mobile Systems

Track1: Ontologies for Networked Systems (ONS)

A Framework for Semantic Grid Service Discovery

Fei Liu, Fan-yuan Ma, Ming-lu Li, and Lin-peng Huang

Department of Computer Science and Engineering, Shanghai Jiaotong University,
Shanghai, P. R. China, 200030
{fliu, ma-fy, li-ml, huang-lp }@cs.sjtu.edu.cn

Abstract. Grid computing provides key infrastructure for distributed problem solving in dynamic virtual organizations. It has been adopted by many scientific projects, and industrial interest is rising rapidly. Compared with traditional single computer system, effective service locating in Grid is difficult because of huge amount and wide-area distribution of dynamical services. This paper presents a new Grid framework that discovery services through the overlay network based on Grid service description semantic vectors generated by Latent Semantic Indexing (LSI) [1]. This framework uses WSRF as its base architecture and regards each Grid node as a register node to publish service that enables it has better scalability. Comparing with other Grid services discovery techniques those are based on simple keyword matching, our framework has better accuracy for it considers the advanced relevance among Grid descriptions.

1 Introduction

Grid computing technologies enable wide-spread sharing and coordinated use of networked resources [2]. Grid evolve around sharing of networks, computers, and other resources. They provide support for services, which are distributed over multiple networked computers known as clusters. Because Grid computing is service oriented computing, service discovery is important for Grid. A service in this context may be defined as a behavior that is provided by a component for use by any other component based on a network-addressable interface contract (generally identifying some capability provided by the service). A service stresses interoperability and may be dynamically discovered and used. According to [3], the service abstraction may be used to specify access to computational resources, storage resources, and networks, in a unified way. How the actual service is implemented is hidden from the user through the service interface, hence, a compute service may be implemented on a single or multi-processor machine. However, these details may not be directly exposed in the service contract. The granularity of a service can vary, and a service can be hosted on a single machine, or it may be distributed.

Owning to these characteristics, traditional centralized service discovery services are difficult to be used in Grid. So we propose a new Grid framework that discovery services through the flat, fully decentralized overlay network. Most of Grid service discoveries are based on simple keyword matching, ignoring advanced relevance between queries and Grid descriptions. The service discovery in this paper is based on Grid description and queries semantics vectors generated by Latent Semantic

C. Bussler et al. (Eds.): WISE 2004 Workshops, LNCS 3307, pp. 3–10, 2004.

Indexing (LSI). A semantic discovery process relies on Grid service description, containing high-level abstract descriptions of service requirements and behavior.

The rest of this paper is as follows. Section 2 discusses related works. Section 3 introduces the Latent Semantic Index and Section 4 proposes the Grid service discovery framework based on semantic overlay networks. We conclude in Section 5 with lessons learned and future work.

2   Related Works

Service discovery has played a crucial role in the evolution and deployment of distributed systems. Early distributed systems comprised collections of components (e.g. client/server or object-oriented) that were implicitly linked through function names, or linked through TCP/IP-based host and port addresses. Federated domain name servers (DNS) simplified and abstracted the use of these numeric addresses by providing a registry-based mechanism for locating the hosts. JINI [5] used a similar approach as part of its Java-based distributed infrastructure. Classes exposed and published their interfaces as proxy objects with a JINI discovery service. By searching for a given class-name, matching proxy objects could then be retrieved and invoked, which would in turn invoke the remote service. Whilst providing a mechanism whereby services could easily be added, removed or replaced within a system, this approach was based on an assumption that there was a shared agreement about what a given service type was called (i.e. its class name) and that there was an agreed and well defined interface. Other distributed technologies support similar principles, including DCOM, Corba, XPCOM, etc.

Web Services extend the idea of JINI services by relaxing several assumptions. Built upon web technologies, Web Services are declared in XML and utilized Web-based protocols to publish and retrieve XML documents. The Simple Object Access Protocol (SOAP) [6] provides a transport mechanism to shuttle XML content between services or applications. The Web Services Description Language (WSDL) [7] explicitly defines the interface of a service. By adhering to these definitions, services can be produced that automatically publish WSDL descriptions that in turn are used to define the content of SOAP messages, and thus simplifying the development of interoperable components.

However, in order to utilize these published services, developers must first locate them. Unlike JINI, Web Services do not belong within well defined class hierarchies, and thus it is not feasible to locate services through class labels. Instead, the UDDI service directory [8] provides a mechanism whereby service providers can register information about themselves, such as physical address, contact phone number, etc; the types of business they are involved in; and references to the service descriptions. UDDI registries provide this information in response to white-pages queries (i.e. given the name of a service provider, what are its detail) and yellow-pages queries (i.e. what service providers provide services that belong to a given pre-defined service type). Based on a set of queries, developers are able to browse through a list of service descriptions to locate a desired service. However, little support is provided for searching for a service based on a capability or user defined data.

Technical Models (tModels) support the specification of additional attributes that can be associated with objects stored in the UDDI repository. In their most common mode of use, tModels provide a fingerprint that are defined globally across a UDDI registry and refer to a technical specification adhered to by a particular service binding template. The other use for tModels is as expressions of particular identifier or classification namespaces that can be attached to business entities, services, or binding templates. Additional information can be associated with such tModel references within a UDDI entry, thus allowing metadata to be associated with these entries. The Open Grid Services Architecture (OGSA) [9] was created to define a base framework of services to achieve interoperability between different Grid implementations. Though, OGSA provides interoperability and defines discovery of services between different Grid domains, semantic matching will provide a much better service discovery.

3 Latent Semantic Indexing (LSI)

Literal matching schemes such as Vector Space Model (VSM) suffer from synonyms and noise in description. LSI overcomes these problems by using statistically derived conceptual indices instead of terms for retrieval. It uses singular value decomposition (SVD) [10] to transform a high-dimensional term vector into a lower-dimensional semantic vector. Each element of a semantic vector corresponds to the importance of an abstract concept in the description or query.

Let N be the number of description in the collection and d be the number of description containing the given word. The inverse description frequency (IDF) is defined as

$$IDF = \log[\frac{N}{d}] \tag{1}$$

The vector for description Do is constructed as below

$$Do = (T_1 * IDF_1, T_2 * IDF_2, ..., T_n * IDF_n) \tag{2}$$

Where T_i takes a value of 1 or 0 depending on whether or not the word i exists in the description Do. The vectors computed for description are used to form a description matrix S. Suppose the number of returned description is m, the description matrix S is constructed as $S = [S_1, S_2, ..., S_m]$. Based on this description matrix S, singular value decomposition (SVD) of matrix is used to extract relationship pattern between description and define thresholds to find matched services. The algorithm is described as follow. Since S is a real matrix, there exists SVD of $S : S = U_{m \times m} \sum_{m \times n} V_{n \times n}^T$ where U and V are orthogonal matrices. Matrices U and V can be denoted respectively as $U_{m \times m} = [u_1, u_2, ... u_m]_{m \times m}$ and $V_n = [v_1, v_2, ..., v_n]_{n \times n}$, where $u_i (i = 1, ..., m)$ is a m-dimensional vector $u_i = (u_{1,i}, u_{2,i}, ..., u_{m,i})$ and $v_i (i = 1, ..., n)$ is a n-dimensional vector $v_i = (v_{1,i}, v_{2,i}, ... v_{n,i})$. Suppose $rank(S) = r$ and singular values of matrix S are: $\beta_1 \geq \beta_2 \geq ... \geq \beta_r \geq \beta_{r+1} = ... = \beta_n = 0$. For a given threshold ε $(o < \varepsilon \leq 1)$, we choose a parameter k such that $(\beta_k - \beta_{k-1})/\beta_k \geq \varepsilon$. Then we denote $U_k = [u_1, u_2, \ldots u_k]_{m \times k}$, $V_k = [v_1, v_2, \ldots, v_k]_{n \times k}$, $\sum_k = diag(\beta_1, \beta_2, \ldots \beta_k)$, and $S_k = U_k \sum_k V_k^T$. S_k is the best approximation matrix to S and contains main information among the description. In this algorithm, the descriptions matching queries are measured by the similarity between them. For measuring the descriptions similarity based on S_k, we choose the ith row R_i of the matrix $U_k \sum_k$ as the coordinate vector of description i in a k-dimensional subspace:

$$R_i = (u_{i,1}\beta_1, u_{i,2}\beta_2, \ldots u_{i,k}\beta_k) \quad i = 1, 2, \ldots, m$$

The similarity between description i and query j is defined as:

$$sim(R_i, R_j) = \frac{|R_i.R_j|}{\|R_i\|_2 \|R_j\|_2} \tag{3}$$

4   Grid Service Discovery Framework Based on Semantic Overlay Networks

The framework proposed in this paper has three layers. From Fig. 1 we can find it contains user layer, semantic overlay network layer, service layer. Users use nature language to descript what they want to queries those will be transformed to query semantic vectors. The query semantic vectors will be transmitted to the register nodes which hold the register information about Grid services which semantic vectors is the highest similar to the query semantic vectors. So our framework has better accuracy for it considers the advanced relevance between descriptions and queries.

4.1   User Layer

How to deal with the denotation of user query is the most important problem in user layer. The users using the Grid services are various, so deploying a uniform namespace in user layer is impossible. The mechanism we propose allows users to utilize nature language to descript their command. In our framework, these descriptions will be transformed to semantic vector use LSI mentioned in section 3.

4.2   The Semantic Overlay Network Layer

We construct semantic overlay networks based on CAN [11] overlay network and WSRF [12]. So the service semantic vectors are generated by WSDL using LSI. Each node in our framework is regarded as register node. Our design centers around a virtual d-dimensional Cartesian coordinate space. This coordinate space is completely

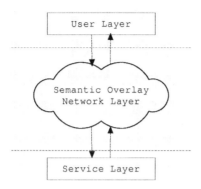

Fig. 1. The three layers of the framework

logical and bears no relation to any physical coordinate system. At any point in time, the entire coordinate space is dynamically partitioned among all the nodes in the system such that every node owns it individual, distinct zone within the overall space.

This virtual coordinate space is used to store $(s1, s)$, $s1$ is the service semantic vector and s is service address. Service semantic vector is mapped onto a point P in the coordinate space. The corresponding $(s1, s)$ pair is then stored at the node that owns the zone with which the point P lies. After node A receive query q, it uses LSI to transform q to service semantic vector SV. SV can be regarded as a point P_1 in d-dimensional Cartesian coordinate space. If the point P_1 is not owned by node A or its immediate neighbors, the request must be routed through our framework until it reaches the node in whose zone P_1 lies.

Routing in our framework works by following the straight line path through the Cartesian space from source to destination coordinates. Each node in our framework maintains a coordinate routing table that holds the IP address and virtual coordinate zone of each of its immediate neighbors in the coordinate space. In a d-dimensional coordinate space, two nodes are neighbors are their coordinate spans overlap along d-1 dimensions and abut along one dimension. This purely local neighbor state is sufficient to route between two arbitrary points in the space. A message in our framework includes the destination coordinates. Using its neighbor coordinate set, a node routes a message towards its destination by simple greedy forwarding to the neighbor with coordinates closer to the destination coordinates. For example, Fig. 2 shows message routing in a framework of 4-dimensional coordinate space.

For a d-dimensional space partitioned into n equal zones, the average routing path length is $(d/4)(n^{1/d})$ hops and individual nodes maintain $2d$ neighbors where n is the number of nodes in the framework. These scaling results mean that for a d-dimensional space, we can grow the number of nodes without increasing per node state while the average path length grows as $O(n^{1/d})$. Note that many different paths

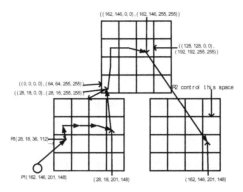

Fig. 2. Routing message in the framework with 4-dimension space

exist between two points in the space and so, even if one or more of a node's neighbors were to crash, a node can automatically route along the next best available path.

When nodes leave our system, we need to ensure that the zones they occupied are taken over by the remaining nodes. The normal procedure for doing this is for a node to explicitly hand over its zone and the associated $(s1, s)$ database to one of its neighbors. If the zone of one of the neighbors can be merged with the departing node's zone to produce a valid single zone. Then this is done. If not, then the zone is handed to the neighbor whose current zone is smallest, and that node will then temporarily handle both zones. Our framework also needs to be robust to node or network failures, where one or more nodes simply become unreachable. This is handled through an immediate takeover algorithm that ensures one of the failed node's neighbors takes over the zone. However in this case the $(s1, s)$ pairs held by the departing node are lost until the state is refreshed by the holders of the data. To prevent stale entries as well as to refresh lost entries, nodes that insert $(s1, s)$ pairs into our system periodically refresh these entries. For example consider the topology in Fig. 3. Node A use LSI to get service vector then it combine service vector and service address to form pair $(s1, s)$. It map service vector to point P which is owned by node G. Then pair $(s1, s)$ is transmitted to node E and E transmits it to G. In this way, the information about service is registered in correspond node G and A register $(s1, s)$ periodically to prevent the information about $(s1, s)$ in G is stale.

Under normal conditions a node sends periodic update messages to each of its neighbors giving its zone coordinates and a list of its neighbors and their zone coordinates. The prolonged absence of an update message from a neighbor signals its failure. Once a node has decided that its neighbor has died it initiates the takeover mechanism and starts a takeover timer running. Each neighbor of the failed node will do this independently, with the timer initialized in proportion to the volume of the node's own zone. When the timer expires, a node sends a TAKEOVER message conveying its own zone volume to all of the failed node's neighbors. On receipt of

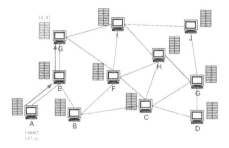

Fig. 3. The process of refreshing service register

a TAKEOVER message, a node cancels its own timer if the zone volume in the message is smaller that its own zone volume, or it replies with its own TAKEOVER message. In this way, a neighboring node is efficiently chosen that is still alive and has a small zone volume. Additional metrics such as load or the quality of connectivity can also be taken into account, but in the interests of simplicity we won't discuss these further here. Under certain failure scenarios involving the simultaneous failure of multiple adjacent nodes, it is possible that a node detects a failure, but less than half of the failed node's neighbors are still reachable. If the node takes over another zone under these circumstances, it is possible for our framework state to become inconsistent. In such cases, prior to triggering the repair mechanism, the node performs an expanding ring search for any nodes residing beyond the failure region and hence it eventually rebuilds sufficient neighbor state to initiate a takeover safely.

4.3 Service Layer

The service layer is used to specify access to computational resources, storage resources, and networks etc., in a unified way. The granularity of a service can vary, and a service can be hosted on a single machine, or it may be distributed. In our framework we adopt WSRF as our service layer. So in our system Grid service is web service and the semantic overlay network layer transform description of web service to semantic vector using LSI. The WSRF is defined by five normative specifications those are WS-ResourceLifetime, WS-ResourceProperties, WS-RenewableReferences, WS-ServiceGroup, WS-BaseFaults.

5 Conclusions and Future Work

We propose a new Grid framework that discovery services through the flat, fully decentralized overlay network in this paper. Most of Grid service discoveries are based on simple keyword matching, ignoring advanced relevance between queries and descriptions. The service discovery in this paper is based on Grid description and queries semantics vectors generated by Latent Semantic Indexing (LSI). The semantic discovery process in our framework relies on Grid service description, containing high-level abstract descriptions of service requirements and behavior. This framework uses WSRF as its base architecture and regards each Grid node as a register node to publish service that enables it has better scalability. Comparing with other Grid services discovery techniques those are based on simple keyword matching, our framework has better accuracy for it considers the advanced relevance among Grid descriptions.

However, there are still some problems to be explored. How can we use hierarchical architecture to improve query efficiency? We will explore this issue in the future.

Acknowledgements. This paper is supported by 973 project (No.2002CB312002) of China, and grand project of the Science and Technology Commission of Shanghai Municipality (No. 03dz15027 and No. 03dz15028).

References

1. S. C. Deerwester, S. T. Dumais, T. K. Landauer, G. W. Furnas, and R. A. Harshman. Indexing by Latent Semantic Analysis. *Journal of the American Society of Information Science*, 41(6):391–407, 1990
2. I. Foster and C. Kesselman, editors. *The Grid: Blueprint for a Future Computing Infrastructure*. 1999
3. Ian Foster, Carl Kesselman, Jeffrey M. Nick, Steven Tuecke, "The Physiology of the Grid:An Open Grid Services Architecture for Distributed Systems Integration". Downloadable as: http://www.globus.org/research/papers/ogsa.pdf, 2002
4. Prashant Chandra, Yang-Hua Chu, Allan Fisher, Jun Gao, Corey Kosak, T.S. Eugene Ng, Peter Steenkiste, Eduardo Takahashi, and Hui Zhang, "Darwin: Customisable Resource Management for Value-Added Network Services," IEEE Network, Number 1, Volume 15, January 2001
5. Arnod, O. Sullivand, Scheier, Waldo, and Wollrath. *The Jini Specification*. Sun Microsystems, 1999
6. XML Protocol Activity. http://www.w3.org/2000/xp, 2000
7. Web Services Description Language (WSDL). http://www.w3.org/TR/wsdl, 2001
8. Universal Description, Discovery and Integration of Business of the Web. www.uddi.org, 2001
9. Foster, I., Kesselman, C., Nick, J.M. and Tuecke, S. "The Physiology of the Grid", Computer,35(6), 2002
10. M. Berry, Z. Drmac, and E. Jessup. Matrices, Vector Spaces, and Information Retrieval. *SIAM Review*, 41(2):335–362, 1999
11. S. Ratnasamy, P. Francis, M. Handley, R. Karp, and S. Shenker. A scalable -addressable network. In *ACM SIGCOMM'01*, August 2001
12. K. Czajkowski, D.Ferguson and I. Foster etc. The WS-Resource Framework. In GGF10, March 2004

Toward a Formal Common Information Model Ontology

Stephen Quirolgico[1], Pedro Assis[2], Andrea Westerinen[3], Michael Baskey[4], and
Ellen Stokes[5]

[1] National Institute of Standards and Technology, Gaithersburg MD 20899, USA
[2] Instituto Politécnico do Porto, Dept. of Electrical Engineering, 4200-072 Porto, Portugal
[3] Cisco Systems, San Jose CA 95134, USA
[4] IBM, Poughkeepsie NY 12601, USA
[5] IBM, Austin TX 78758, USA

Abstract. Self-managing systems will be highly dependent upon information acquired from disparate applications, devices, components and subsystems. To be effectively managed, such information will need to conform to a common model. One standard that provides a common model for describing disparate computer and network information is the Common Information Model (CIM). Although CIM defines the models necessary for inferring properties about distributed systems, its specification as a semi-formal ontology limits its ability to support important requirements of a self-managing distributed system including knowledge interoperability and aggregation, as well as reasoning. To support these requirements, there is a need to model, represent and share CIM as a formal ontology. In this paper, we propose a framework for constructing a CIM ontology based upon previous research that identified mappings from Unified Modeling Language (UML) constructs to ontology language constructs. We extend and apply these mappings to a UML representation of the CIM Schema in order to derive a semantically valid and consistent formal CIM ontology.

1 Introduction

The increasing complexity of modern distributed systems has recently led to large-scale research initiatives in self-managing distributed systems; that is, distributed systems capable of configuring, optimizing, healing and protecting themselves [1]. A self-managing distributed system will, in general, be dependent upon reasoning mechanisms for inferring properties about its (distributed) operational domain. Such reasoning mechanisms will, in turn, be highly dependent upon information acquired from nodes within the distributed system. For example, a self-managing distributed system tasked with optimizing network performance between multiple nodes may need to reason over information (e.g., processor speed, memory capacity, packet loss, network configurations and other instrumentation) acquired from its nodes' CPUs, operating systems, network applications and network devices.

In order to effectively manage information generated by disparate applications, devices, components and subsystems from multiple nodes in a self-managing distributed system, such information must conform to a common model [2]. One standard that is expected to provide such a model is the Common Information Model (CIM) [3]. CIM is a comprehensive set of object-oriented models that specify concepts about a computing

C. Bussler et al. (Eds.): WISE 2004 Workshops, LNCS 3307, pp. 11–21, 2004.
© Springer-Verlag Berlin Heidelberg 2004

or network environment; it comprises a *core* model that defines a basic classification of elements and associations for a managed environment (e.g., logical and physical elements, capabilities, settings and profiles) as well as *common* models that define concepts that are common to particular management areas (e.g., applications, systems, devices and policies). The core and common models together are referred to as the *CIM Schema* [4].

Although the CIM Schema defines the models necessary for inferring properties about distributed systems, its specification as a *semi-formal* ontology [5,6,7,8] limits its ability to support important requirements of a self-managing distributed system including knowledge interoperability, knowledge aggregation and reasoning. These limitations are due, in part, to the constraints imposed by the languages (e.g., XML and XML Schema) used to model, represent and share semi-formal ontologies. With respect to knowledge interoperability, for example, such languages do not (1) provide globally-understood constructs for expressing semantics nor (2) impose a common interpretation of the meta-data contained within the model [9]. Thus, semi-formal ontologies encoded by these languages can only be used by those systems that have a complete and *a priori* understanding of the semantics surrounding the ontology. In an open self-managing distributed system environment, however, knowledge from a network node will need to interoperate among possibly several heterogeneous nodes. With respect to knowledge aggregation, XML-encoded ontologies cannot be arbitrarily combined with other ontologies in a flexible manner [9]. In a self-managing distributed system, however, knowledge about network nodes will need to be aggregated with other knowledge (e.g., domain knowledge). With respect to reasoning, XML-encoded ontologies do not embody the constructs for facilitating parsing, logical deduction or semantic interpretation. However, in a self-managing distributed system, reasoning over knowledge from network nodes will be necessary to infer the operational state of the distributed system.

In order to facilitate the interoperability and aggregation of, as well as the reasoning over, CIM-based knowledge in self-managing distributed systems, there is a need to model, represent and share CIM as a *formal* ontology; that is, an ontology that defines the semantics of its vocabulary by a complete and sound axiomatization [5,6, 7,8]. One language that can be used to construct a formal CIM ontology is the Resource Description Framework (RDF) [10]. RDF is an assertional language that defines (domain-agnostic) semantic constructs for expressing propositions using precise formal vocabularies. In RDF, meta-data is defined using the vocabulary description language RDF Schema (RDFS) [11] that defines not how instances will be expressed (as is the case, for example, with XML Schema), but rather, provides a vocabulary for describing certain features of the data. This vocabulary can be reused in any setting allowing applications to infer properties about RDF/S-specified knowledge without having a prior understanding of the semantics surrounding that knowledge [12]. By using an RDF/S-based CIM ontology, the semantics of CIM-based instances can be partially deduced by systems that have no prior knowledge of the CIM Schema thereby fulfilling the interoperability requirement of a self-managing distributed system. In addition, different vocabularies can be arbitrarily combined to form new knowledge. This feature of RDF/S could allow, for example, knowledge from a CIM ontology to be more easily combined with knowledge from a specific domain ontology (e.g., grid systems) thereby fulfilling the aggregation requirement of a self-managing distributed system. RDF/S also allows for the expression of logical propositions from meta-data descriptions. These propositions can be arbitrarily combined to form a set of (semantically) connected propositions that, in turn, can directly serve as knowledge in a form required for reasoning thereby fulfilling the reasoning requirement of a self-managing distributed system.

In this paper, we aim toward the construction of a formal CIM ontology by proposing a framework based upon previous research that identified mappings from Unified Modeling Language (UML) [13] constructs to ontology language constructs. Here, we extend and apply these mappings to a UML representation of the CIM Schema in order to facilitate the derivation of a semantically valid and consistent CIM ontology. Although our approach provides a first step for constructing a consistent and semantically valid CIM ontology, we identify some issues that must be resolved before a complete, valid and consistent CIM ontology can be derived. We begin by describing the the mapping of CIM UML to CIM RDF/S and also describe limitations associated with these mappings. Next, we describe how the limitations of mapping CIM UML to CIM RDF/S can be overcome by mapping CIM UML to the more powerful Web Ontology Language (OWL). Finally, we identify issues that must be resolved before a complete, valid and consistent CIM ontology can be derived.

2   Constructing a CIM RDF/S Ontology

The construction of an ontology for describing the CIM Schema requires the mapping of CIM concepts to ontology language constructs. When mapping between CIM concepts to ontology language constructs, it is important to determine whether the mapping can preserve the semantics of the original CIM model. This is determined largely by whether the modeling languages used are *semantically equivalent*; that is, given two modeling languages L_1 and L_2, there is a one-to-one correspondence between the semantics of constructs in L_1 and the semantics of constructs in L_2 [14]. In an effort to construct a formal CIM ontology that preserves the semantics of the CIM Schema, we leverage previous research [15,16] that identified (one-way) mappings from UML constructs to RDF/S constructs by applying these mappings to a UML representation of the CIM Schema. By using these mappings, we not only increase the (semantic) validity of the resulting ontology but also ensure the consistency of mappings from CIM UML constructs including classes, attributes and relationships to CIM RDF/S ontology constructs including classes and properties. Table 1 shows an overview of some CIM concepts and their mappings to UML and RDF/S constructs. Note that mappings from a CIM concept to a specific construct in the target language should reflect a full (or at least an approximate) semantic correspondence. In some cases, a CIM concept is mapped to a set of constructs in the target language that fully (or approximately) reflects the semantics of the CIM concept. In other cases, there may be no constructs in the target language that semantically correspond to the CIM concept.

2.1   Mapping CIM Schema Classes and Properties

In the CIM Schema, concepts related to computing and network environments are represented primarily by UML classes. For example, the notion of a (hardware, software

Table 1. CIM Concepts and Related Mappings.

CIM Concept	UML	RDF/S	OWL
Named Element	✓	✓	✓
Class	✓	✓	✓
Property	✓	✧	✧
Method	✓	✧	✧
Generalization	✓	✓	✓
Association/Aggregation	✧	✧	✧
Cardinality	✓	✗	✓
Qualifiers (multiple)	✓✧✗	✓✧✗	✓✧✗
Datatypes	✓	✓	✓

✓ Maps to a specific construct (full/approx. semantic correspondence)

✧ Maps to a set of constructs (full/approx. semantic correspondence)

✗ No defined mapping (no semantic correspondence)

or service-oriented) `Product` is defined as a UML class as shown in Figure 1. Here, we represent a CIM Schema concept as a `rdfs:Class` class that corresponds to a generic notion of a type or category. To represent a CIM Schema concept as an `rdfs:Class` in an RDF/S statement, we use the `rdf:type` property that defines the resource (e.g., a `Product`) as a member of a particular class (e.g., `rdfs:Class`). In addition, we use the namespace prefix `cim:` to refer to the CIM Schema vocabulary defined by an XML namespace declaration such as `xmlns:cim="http://www.dmtf.org/CIMSchema28#"`. For example, we can represent the class `cim:Product` by the triple as shown in Figure 2 (line 5). In addition, we represent a CIM Schema property or method (defined as a UML attribute or operation, respectively) as an `rdf:Property` class. For example, we can represent the attribute `cim:Product.Vendor` by the triple shown in Figure 2 (line 6).

In RDF/S, each `rdf:Property` can be associated with a domain that specifies the class(es) on whose members a property can be used and a range that specifies the class(es) or datatype(s) to which the values of the property are restricted. For example, the property `cim:Product.Vendor` may be used by any instance of `cim:Product` and the value of `cim:Product.Vendor` must be a member of `xsd:string` as shown in Figure 2 (lines 7-8). Note that a mapping of CIM to RDF/S necessitates the mapping of UML datatypes to datatypes used by RDF/S. In UML, attributes may conform to a variety of intrinsic datatypes (e.g., integers, booleans and string datatypes). These datatypes can be mapped directly to those used by RDF/S as defined in the `xsd:` (XML Schema datatype) namespace [17]. For example, a boolean datatype in UML may be mapped to the `xsd:boolean` datatype in RDF/S.

2.2   Mapping CIM Schema Relationships

The structure of the CIM Schema defines a number of relationships between CIM classes. In Figure 1, for example, there exists a generalization relationship between `cim:Product` and `cim:ManagedElement`. In RDF/S, the UML generaliza-

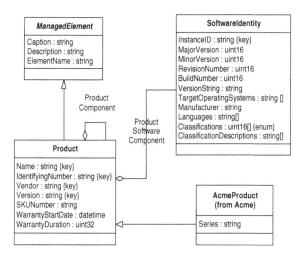

Fig. 1. CIM UML Classes.

tion relationship can be mapped directly to the `rdfs:subClassOf` property. For example, we may represent a generalization relationship between `cim:Product` and `cim:ManagedElement` by the triple shown in Figure 2 (line 9).

In addition to generalization, the CIM Schema also defines other relationships including association and aggregation relationships.[1] In UML, such relationships are represented by association classes. For example, the `cim:ProductSoftwareComponent` association class represents the "ProductSoftwareComponent" aggregation in Figure 1. Since a UML association class is a subclass of a UML class, we may represent `cim:ProductSoftwareComponent` as an `rdfs:Class` as shown in Figure 2 (line 15). Association classes in the CIM Schema include references that define the set of classes that may be linked by the association or aggregation relationship. Each reference is an `rdf:Property` that is represented by the term `cim:REF`. For example, `cim:ProductSoftwareComponent` contains the `cim:REF` `cim.ProductSoftwareComponent.GroupComponent` that is used by instances of `cim:ProductSoftwareComponent` to define the range of classes (i.e., `cim:Product`) that can be associated with one or more `cim:SoftwareIdentity` classes. Similarly, the `cim:REF` `cim.ProductSoftwareComponent.PartComponent` is used by instances of `cim:ProductSoftwareComponent` to define the range of classes (i.e., `cim:SoftwareIdentity`) that can be used to describe a `cim:Product`. These reference definitions are shown in Figure 2 (lines 16-21).

With respect to associations and aggregations, UML roles can also be represented in RDF/S as an `rdf:Property`. To represent UML roles in the CIM ontology, we augment the CIM Schema vocabularies by defining role names using the convention "<*vocabulary*> : *has*<*RoleName*>". For example, a `cim:Product` may have the role `cim:hasSoftwareComponent` with respect to `cim:SoftwareIdentity`. Conversely,

---

[1] Note that an aggregation relationship is a specialization of an association relationship.

```
1    // ManagedElement class
2    cim:ManagedElement rdf:type rdfs:Class .
3
4    // Product class
5    cim:Product rdf:type rdfs:Class .
6    cim:Product.Vendor rdf:type rdf:Property .
7    cim:Product.Vendor rdfs:domain cim:Product .
8    cim:Product.Vendor rdfs:range xsd:string .
9    cim:Product rdfs:subClassOf cim:ManagedElement .
10
11   // SoftwareIdentity class
12   cim:SoftwareIdentity rdf:type rdfs:Class
13
14   // ProductSoftwareComponent (association class)
15   cim:ProductSoftwareComponent rdf:type rdfs:Class .
16   cim:ProductSoftwareComponent.GroupComponent rdf:type cim:REF .
17   cim:ProductSoftwareComponent.GroupComponent rdf:domain cim:ProductSoftwareComponent .
18   cim:ProductSoftwareComponent.GroupComponent rdf:range cim:Product .
19   cim:ProductSoftwareComponent.PartComponent rdf:type cim:REF .
20   cim:ProductSoftwareComponent.PartComponent rdf:domain cim:ProductSoftwareComponent .
21   cim:ProductSoftwareComponent.PartComponent rdf:range cim:SoftwareIdentity .
22
23   // roles
24   cim:hasSoftwareComponent rdf:type rdf:Property .
25   cim:hasSoftwareComponent rdf:domain cim:Product .
26   cim:hasSoftwareComponent rdf:range cim:SoftwareIdentity .
27   cim:isSoftwareComponentOf rdf:type rdf:Property .
28   cim:isSoftwareComponentOf rdf:domain cim:SoftwareIdentity .
29   cim:isSoftwareComponentOf rdf:range cim:Product .
30
31   // AcmeProduct class
32   acme:AcmeProduct rdf:type rdfs:Class .
33   acme:AcmeProduct rdfs:subClassOf cim:Product .
```

Fig. 2. CIM RDF/S Statements.

cim:SoftwareIdentity may have the role cim:isSoftwareComponentOf with respect to cim:Product. These examples are shown in Figure 2 (lines 24-29).

The CIM Schema may also be extended by vendors to suit their particular needs. These vendor-specified extensions to the CIM Schema are referred to as *extension schemas*. Extension schemas extend the CIM Schema by defining classes that inherit from CIM Schema classes. In Figure 1, for example, the vendor-defined class AcmeProduct inherits from the CIM class Product. Because an RDF/S ontology may comprise multiple vocabularies, relationships between concepts from different vocabularies can be defined. This feature of RDF/S allows for the construction of an ontology that defines relationships between concepts in the CIM Schema and concepts defined in a vendor-specified extension schema. For example, we may express the generalization relationship between acme:AcmeProduct and cim:Product as shown in Figure 2 (lines 32-33).

3   Constructing a CIM OWL Ontology

Although RDF/S may be used to express *some* types of knowledge, it deliberately lacks sufficient constructs to adequately express all types of knowledge [15,18]. As shown in Table 1, for example, RDF/S does not provide constructs for expressing cardinality restrictions such as those used for describing association or aggregation relationships between CIM classes. In addition, RDF/S cannot adequately express some CIM *qualifiers* that are used to define constraints on CIM properties. For example, RDF/S cannot directly represent the semantics of the CIM 'key' qualifier which is used to indicate that the value of a CIM property must be unique for all instances of a particular class. Such qualifiers are currently denoted in CIM UML as shown in Figure 1.

The limited expressivity of RDF/S motivated the development of the (semantically-richer) DAML+OIL (DARPA Agent Markup Language and Ontology Inference Layer) ontology markup language [19] which, in turn, formed the basis of the Web Ontology Language (OWL) [20]. OWL is an RDF/S-based language that can explicitly represent the meaning of terms in vocabularies and the relationships between those terms. OWL enhances the expressivity of RDF/S (and DAML+OIL) by adding more vocabulary for describing properties and classes including relations between classes (e.g. disjointness), cardinality, equality, richer typing of properties, characteristics of properties (e.g. symmetry) and enumerated classes. To map the CIM Schema to OWL[2], we extend previous work that identified mappings from UML constructs to DAML+OIL constructs [14,21] as well as preliminary work that identified mappings from UML constructs to OWL constructs [22]. An overview of the mappings from CIM concepts to OWL constructs are shown in Table 1.

One concept that is required for expressing the CIM Schema, but not included in RDF/S, is the notion of cardinality. In OWL, cardinality is stated on a property with respect to a class. For example, `cim:Product` has a minimum and maximum cardinality of one on the `rdf:Property cim:hasSoftwareComponent`. This cardinality restriction can be expressed by the triples shown in Figure 2 (lines 2-4).

Another important CIM concept that cannot be adequately expressed using RDF/S is the concept of uniqueness. In OWL, the `owl:FunctionalProperty` restriction may be used to define mutually distinct properties. With respect to CIM, this is important for ensuring that (1) class names (including association names) are unique within the schema, (2) method names are unique within the domain class and (3) reference names are unique within the scope of the defining association. For example, `owl:FunctionalProperty` may be used to realize the CIM 'key' qualifier on the attribute `cim:Product.Name` as shown in Figure 2 (line 7).

Yet another limitation of RDF/S is its inability to express local range restrictions associated with a particular property for a particular class. Here, if an instance of a class is related by a property to a second object, then the second object can be inferred to be an instance of the local range restriction class. Local range restrictions on a property can be represented using the `owl:allValuesFrom` restriction. For example, `cim:Product` may have `rdf:Property cim:hasSoftwareComponent` restricted to have `owl:allValuesFrom cim:SoftwareIdentity`. This means that if an instance of `cim:Product` is related by the `rdf:Property cim:hasSoftwareComponent` to the instance "Printer Driver", then from this a reasoner can deduce that "Printer Driver" is an instance of the class `cim:SoftwareIdentity`. This example is shown in Figure 2 (lines 10-12).

---

[2] In this paper, we consider only OWL DL.

```
1    // cardinality
2    _:SWIdentityRole rdf:type owl:Restriction .
3    _:SWIdentityRole owl:onProperty cim:Product.hasSoftwareComponent .
4    _:SWIdentityRole owl:cardinality "1"^^xsd:nonNegativeInteger .
5
6    // uniqueness constraints
7    cim:Product.Name rdf:type owl:FunctionalProperty .
8
9    // local range restrictions
10   _:SWIdentityRole rdf:type owl:Restriction .
11   _:SWIdentityRole owl:onProperty cim:Product.hasSoftwareComponent .
12   _:SWIdentityRole owl:allValuesFrom cim:SoftwareIdentity .
13
14   // transitivity
15   _:ProductCompRole rdf:type owl:Restriction .
16   _:ProductCompRole owl:onProperty cim:Product.hasProductComponent .
17   _:ProductCompRole rdf:type owl:TransitiveProperty .
18
19   // inverse
20   cim:hasSoftwareComponent owl:inverseOf cim:isSoftwareComponentOf .
21
22   // property equivalence
23   cim:Product.Vendor owl:equivalentProperty cim:SoftwareIdentity.Manufacturer .
24
25   // imports
26   # owl:imports rdf:resource="http://www.dmtf.org/CIMSchema28" .
```

Fig. 3. CIM OWL Statements.

OWL can also be used to enhance the semantics surrounding relationships between CIM classes. For example, the owl:TransitiveProperty property may be used to express a chain of cim:ProductComponent associations on a cim:Product as shown in Figure 2 (lines 15-17). In addition, the owl:inverseOf property may be used to state the inverse of a relationship. For example, an instance of cim:Product may have a cim:hasSoftwareComponent role with respect to one or more instances of cim:SoftwareIdentity. If cim:isSoftwareComponentOf is the inverse of cim:hasSoftwareComponent, and there exists a cim:Product with property cim:hasSWFeature and property value cim:SoftwareFeature, then a reasoner can deduce that cim:SoftwareIdentity cim:isSoftwareComponentOf cim:Product where cim:isSoftwareComponentOf is the owl:inverseOf cim:hasSoftwareComponent as shown in Figure 2 (line 20).

An important advantage of using OWL to define a CIM ontology is that OWL provides constructs for defining equivalence between classes and properties. In OWL, class and property equivalence is represented using the owl:equivalentClass and owl:equivalentProperty axioms. For example, the property cim:Product.Vendor may be synonymous with cim:SoftwareIdentity.Manufacturer in those environments where all products from a specific company are developed in-house (and thus, the name of the vendor is the same as the manufacturer). This equivalence relationship is shown in Figure 2 (line 23). The OWL equivalence axioms may also be used to facilitate interoperability between, and the merging of, ontologies by describing equivalence relationships between classes and properties defined in CIM and those defined, for example, in the IEEE Standard Upper Ontology (SUO) [23]. In addition, the owl:imports construct may be used to reference another OWL ontology containing definitions whose semantics are considered to be part of the meaning of the importing ontology. This ontology-importing feature can be used to combine a CIM ontology with other ontologies. For example, an ontology that describes military systems may import the CIM ontology to describe the management of its computer and network systems by using the OWL statement as shown in Figure 2 (line 26).

4   Current Limitations

Although the proposed framework provides a first step toward the construction of a formal CIM ontology, a number of issues must first be resolved before such an ontology can be considered consistent, semantically valid, and complete. One issue concerns the mapping of some CIM concepts to UML constructs. Currently, while many CIM concepts can be mapped directly to UML constructs (e.g., CIM Class), some CIM concepts (e.g., some CIM qualifiers) cannot; thus, such concepts must be added to the ontology in an ad-hoc fashion leading to a possibly inconsistent or invalid ontology.

Another related issue concerns CIM concepts (particularly, CIM qualifiers) that have no mappings to either UML constructs or OWL constructs. For example, the notion of a CIM default value does not have a corresponding UML construct nor a corresponding OWL construct. In cases where no direct mapping from CIM concepts to specific terms in the RDF/S or OWL vocabulary can be derived, we define such concepts within the `cim:` vocabulary (e.g., we define `cim:default` as an `rdf:Property` that is used to represent the notion of a default value).

Another issue concerns the inability of OWL to fully express some UML constructs [14,21,22]. For example, OWL provides no constructs for adequately representing a UML abstract class. Thus, some CIM concepts (e.g., `ManagedElement` that is represented by a UML abstract class) cannot be mapped directly to RDF/S or OWL constructs and must be manually included in the `cim:` vocabulary.

Finally, both RDF/S and OWL can only partially express some CIM Schema semantics. For example, CIM methods can be defined as an `rdf:Property`, but cannot be mapped to OWL construct(s) that more closely match the notion of a UML operation.

5   Related Work

The idea of using CIM for facilitating self-managing systems has been previously described by Bantz [24] who proposed the use of CIM information to facilitate decision making in autonomic computing, and by Ganek [2] who proposed the use of CIM to facilitate interoperability between heterogeneous autonomic computing elements.

In addition, the idea of using CIM ontologies for describing management knowledge has been previously proposed. For example, López de Vergara et. al [25] proposed an algorithm for mapping CIM, as well as other information models, into a common DAML+OIL ontology. Also, Lavinal et. al [26] proposed the construction of a CIM ontology using OKBC while Tangmunarunkit [27] proposed the use of an RDF/S-based CIM ontology for grid computing. Finally, Lanfranchi et. al [28] defined a mapping of CIM to the description logic DLR.

The work presented in this paper, however, is distinguished from these previous efforts in that this work leverages and extends research that identified mappings from UML constructs to ontology language constructs in order to achieve semantically valid and consistent mappings from CIM UML to a formal CIM ontology. Previous research in mapping UML to RDF/S and DAML+OIL included works by Chang [15] who described mappings from UML to RDF/S and Cranefield [16] who described an automatic mapping from UML to RDF/S using XMI. In addition, Backlawski *et. al* [14], Falkoych *et. al* [21] and Kogut *et. al* [29] described mappings from UML to DAML+OIL constructs while AT&T [22] described a preliminary analysis of mapping UML to OWL Full.

6   Conclusion

This paper proposed a framework for constructing a formal CIM ontology based upon previously-identified mappings from UML constructs to RDF/S and OWL constructs. We began by presenting details about the mapping of CIM classes, properties and relationships to RDF/S constructs as well as defined a vocabulary for representing concepts associated with the CIM Schema. Given the limitations of RDF/S for expressing the semantics of CIM concepts, we described the mapping of these concepts to the RDF/S-based ontology language OWL. Although OWL provides enhanced expressivity over RDF/S, there exists some CIM concepts that cannot be directly mapped to OWL constructs. In such cases, we proposed the definition of these concepts within the context of the `cim:` vocabulary.

Currently, the specifications for CIM, UML, and OWL are fluid; thus, future research in this area will consider how changes to these specifications affect the derivation of a CIM ontology. Future versions of CIM, for example, are expected to reflect possibly significant changes to the CIM Schema as well as its representation in the forthcoming UML 2.0 (e.g., the use of UML roles for representing CIM qualifiers). Such changes might facilitate the derivation of a more complete CIM ontology by providing a more complete mapping between CIM concepts and UML constructs (and thus, a more direct mapping of CIM concepts, such as qualifiers, to RDF/S and OWL). In addition, research continues on mapping UML constructs to OWL constructs that will directly impact the derivation of a CIM ontology. It is expected that the framework proposed in this paper could be easily extended to support these anticipated changes.

References

1. Kephart, J., Chess, D.: The vision of autonomic computing. IEEE Computer **36** (2003)
2. Ganek, A., Corbi, T.: The dawning of the autonomic computing era. IBM Systems Journal **42** (2003)
3. Distributed Management Task Force: Common information model (CIM) specification version 2.2 (1999)
4. Distributed Management Task Force: CIM schema: Version 2.7 (2003)
5. Fox, M.S., Gruninger, M.: Enterprise modeling. AI Magazine **19** (1998)
6. Gruber, T.: It is what it does: The pragmatics of ontology for knowledge sharing. In: Proceedings of the International CIDOC CRM Symposium, Washington DC (2003)

7. López de Vergara, J., Villagrá, V., Asensio, J., Berrocal, J.: Ontologies: Giving semantics to network management models. IEEE Network **17** (2003)
8. Spyns, P., Meersman, R., Jarrar, M.: Data modelling and ontology engineering. ACM SIG-MOD Record **31** (2002)
9. Decker, S., Melnik, S., Van Harmelen, F., Fensel, D., Klein, M., Broekstra, J., Erdman, M., Horrocks, I.: The semantic web: The roles of XML and RDF. IEEE Internet Computing (2002)
10. World Wide Web Consortium: Resource description framework (RDF) model and syntax specification (1999)
11. World Wide Web Consortium: RDF vocabulary description language 1.0: RDF schema (2003)
12. Nilsson, M., Palmer, M., Naeve, A.: Semantic web meta-data for e-learning – some architectural guidelines. In: Proceedings of the Eleventh International World Wide Web Conference, Honolulu, Hawaii (2002)
13. Object Management Group: Unified modeling language (UML) version 1.5 (2003)
14. Baclawski, K., Kokar, M.K., Kogut, P.A., Hart, L., Smith, J., Holmes III, W.S., Letkowski, J., Aronson, M.L.: Extending UML to support ontology engineering for the semantic web. Lecture Notes in Computer Science **2185** (2001)
15. Chang, W.W.: A discussion of the relationship between RDF-schema and UML, W3C Note (1998)
16. Cranefield, S.: Networked knowledge representation and exchange using UML and RDF. Journal of Digital Information **1** (2001)
17. World Wide Web Consortium: XML schema part 2: Datatypes (2001)
18. Antoniou, G., van Harmelen, F.: Web ontology language: OWL. In Staab, S., Studer, R., eds.: Handbook on Ontologies in Information Systems, Springer-Verlag (2003)
19. van Harmelen, F., Petel-Schneider, P.F., Horrocks, I.: Reference description of the DAML+OIL ontology markup language (2001)
20. World Wide Web Consortium: OWL web ontology language semantics and abstract syntax (2003)
21. Falkovych, K., Sabou, M., Stuckenschmidt, H.: UML for the semantic web: Transformation-based approaches. In Omelayenko, B., Klein, M., eds.: Knowledge Transformation for the Semantic Web, IOS Press (2003)
22. AT&T: OWL Full and UML 2.0 compared. Whitepaper (2004)
23. Niles, I., Pease, A.: Towards a standard upper ontology. In: Proceedings of the International Conference on Formal Ontology in Information Systems, Ogunquit, Maine (2001)
24. Bantz, D.F., Bisdikian, C., Challener, D., Karidis, J.P., Mastrianni, S., Mohindra, A., Shea, D.G., Vanover, M.: Autonomic personal computing. IBM Systems Journal **42** (2003)
25. López de Vergara, J., Villagrá, V., Berrocal, J.: An ontology-based method to merge and map management information models. In: Proceedings of the HP Openview University Association Tenth Plenary Workshop, Geneva, Switzerland (2003)
26. Lavinal, E., Desprats, T., Raynaud, Y.: A conceptual framework for building CIM-based ontologies. In: Proceedings of the Eighth IFIP/IEEE International Symposium on Integrated Network Management (IM 2003), Colorado Springs, Colorado (2003)
27. Tangmunarunkit, H., Decker, S., Kesselman, C.: Ontology-based resource matching in the grid – the grid meets the semantic web. In: Proceedings of 2nd International Semantic Web Conference (ISWC2003), Sanibel Island, Florida (2003)
28. Lanfranchi, G., Della Peruta, P., Perrone, A., Calvanese, D.: Toward a new landscape of systems management in an autonomic computing environment. IBM Systems Journal **41** (2003)
29. Kogut, P., Cranefield, S., Hart, L., Dutra, M., Baclawski, K., Kokar, M., Smith, J.: UML for ontology development. Knowledge Engineering Review Journal Special Issue on Ontologies in Agent Systems **17** (2002)

On Using Conceptual Modeling for Ontologies[*]

S. Spaccapietra[1], C. Parent[2], C. Vangenot[1], and N. Cullot[3]

[1] Database Laboratory, EPFL, 1015 Lausanne, Switzerland
{stefano.spaccapietra,christelle.vangenot}@epfl.ch
[2] HEC-INFORGE, University of Lausanne, 1015 Lausanne, Switzerland
christine.parent@unil.ch
[3]LE2I Laboratory, University of Burgundy, 21000 Dijon, France
nadine.cullot@u-bourgogne.fr

Abstract. Are database concepts and techniques suitable for ontology design and management? The question has been on the floor for some time already. It gets a new emphasis today, thanks to the focus on ontologies and ontology services due to the spread of web services as a new paradigm for information management. This paper analyzes some of the arguments that are relevant to the debate, in particular the question whether conceptual data models would adequately support the design and use of ontologies. It concludes suggesting a hybrid approach, combining databases and logic-based services.

1 Introduction

Nowadays, all major economic players have decentralized organizational structures, with multiple autonomous units acting in parallel. New information systems have to handle a variety of information sources, from proprietary ones to those available in web services worldwide. Their complexity is best controlled using a network of coordinated web services capable of grasping relevant information wherever it may be and exchanging information with all potential partners. Data semantics is at the heart of such multi-agent systems. Interacting agents in an open environment do not necessarily share a common understanding of the world at hand, as used to be the case in traditional enterprise information systems. For instance, in a single enterprise environment, the concept of "employee" has a unique definition shared by every application within the enterprise. In a multi-agent system, the interpretation of the "employee" concept may vary based on whether or not specific types of personnel (e.g., students in their summer jobs, trainees, visitors) have also to be considered as employees. Another example is obviously provided by contextual information, such as whether a sentence about trees refers to the vegetal or to the mathematical structure. This is also a form of semantic disambiguation.

---

[*] This work is supported, in the framework of the EPFL Center for Global Computing, by the Swiss National Funding Agency OFES as part of the European projects KnowledgeWeb (FP6-507482) and DIP (FP6-507483). It is also supported by the MICS NCCR funded by FNRS in Switzerland, under grant number 5005-67322.

C. Bussler et al. (Eds.): WISE 2004 Workshops, LNCS 3307, pp. 22–33, 2004.

Lack of common background calls for explicit guidance in understanding the exact meaning of the data. XML-like formatting does not help much in this. Ontologies increasingly appear as the solution to the problem. They are the most sophisticated form of semantics repository. From a database perspective, they may be intuitively understood as the most recent form of data dictionaries, i.e. a knowledge repository whose purpose is to explain how concepts and terms relevant to a given domain should be understood. Although ontology as a science comes from philosophy, ontologies as computerized support for semantics have mainly been developed by the artificial intelligence community. This community has focused on developing reasoning mechanisms that would alleviate the task of enriching an ontology by addition of new concepts. Typically, an ontological reasoner is expected to be able to check the consistency of new concepts with already known ones and to determine their most accurate placement within the (most often hierarchical) structure of the ontology.

With ontologies becoming a necessary component of modern, interoperable information systems, we are likely to see a proliferation of ontologies and a massive growth in size and complexity of the set of concepts described in an ontology. We foresee that their role will evolve from a repository of terms that denote concepts (whose most well-known example is Wordnet) to a repository for complex information, where the description of a concept includes a formal description of a prototypical data structure (a design pattern) showing all the components of a concept, the intra-relationships between these components, and the inter-relationships between the concept and the other concepts in the ontology. These richer ontologies will have to be easily understandable, and processable, by humans and by computerized agents in search of semantics. Briefly stated, we expect significantly increasing similarity between ontologies and current database schemas.

This raises the question whether database technology could be reused to provide services for ontology design and management. The purpose of this paper is to develop some arguments for such a discussion. The arguments we present here focus on structural aspects, as we are interested in showing the benefits of using conceptual data models for modeling ontologies. Other arguments (e.g., discussion of defined versus derived objects, axioms, schema and instance querying, constraints) are also surveyed. For a more detailed analysis of the latter the reader is referred to [3]. Our idea is that database techniques could nicely complement logic-based techniques (using formalisms such as description logics or F-Logic) and a common framework could be built that would exploit the technique that best fits the task on hand.

The next section introduces an example that we use in Section 3 (after briefly recalling the concepts of the underlying conceptual data model) to illustrate how a conceptualization can be formulated using a conceptual data modeling formalism. Section 4 discusses respective merits of using data modeling versus description logic formalism. Section 5 concludes suggesting to combine both formalisms into a hybrid system. We assume the reader is familiar with the features supported by ontological formalisms (e.g., description logics).

2   A Motivating Example

The example we show hereinafter has been first introduced by Boris Motik as part of deliverable D1.1 of DIP, an European project aiming at developing semantic web services. Let INT be a company that wants to provide a web service consisting in an integrated tourism portal offering hotel information. INT does not itself own hotel data. Instead, it simply integrates web services by various providers. Each provider classifies its hotel data in a proprietary structure. Let us assume that there are two providers of such information, TUI and Thomas Cook, TC for short. Fig. 1 presents the conceptualization that TUI uses to describe his offers. The drawing uses a simple notation, based on an underlying binary data model, the kind of model many ontology tools adhere to. Oval nodes (e.g. Hotel) denote conceptual entities. Nodes without a surrounding oval (e.g. name) denote properties of the corresponding entities. Labeled arcs between oval nodes denote a relationship between the conceptual entities. Non-labeled arcs link a conceptual entity to its properties.

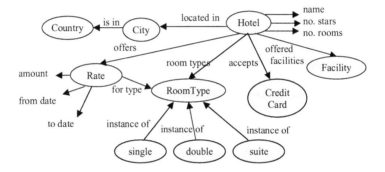

Fig. 1. Conceptualization of TUI

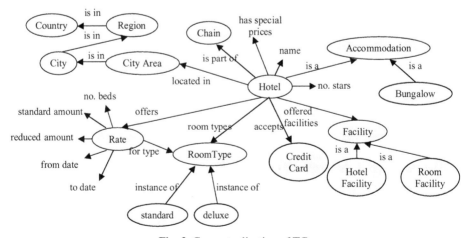

Fig. 2. Conceptualization of TC

TC uses a different conceptualization of his business domain (cf. Fig. 2). For example, geographical information is more fine-grained, as it represents the country, region, and the area within the city where a certain hotel is situated. Room types are split according to a different criterion. The rate structure is also different.

To create its portal, INT needs to bridge the semantic differences between the information coming from TUI and from TC. First, INT must decide upon its own conceptualization of the domain. It may either accept one of the existing conceptualizations, or choose from existing domain standards, or develop its own proprietary conceptualization. After choosing the conceptualization formalism and creating its own conceptualization, INT has to describe how data in each source relates to its own conceptualization. Conceptualization formalisms offer different primitives for performing this task. Ontological work focuses mainly on logic-based conceptualization formalisms, because their inference capabilities are commonly seen as a key to solving this type of problem. For example, dependencies between the conceptualization of INT and those of the sources can be expressed as logical axioms, which, when executed, can be used to actually perform data integration. On the other hand, conceptual modeling approaches most frequently use data manipulation languages to express the mapping between a global integrated schema (here, the INT conceptualization) and its corresponding source schemas. Alternatives for the description of these mappings are well documented in the literature.

3 Conceptual Modeling for Ontologies

As ontologies grow in size and in practical relevance, it is legitimate to question whether database techniques could provide interesting support for ontology management. On the one hand, database systems are known to offer scalable and efficient management of huge amounts of structured data, which is what ontologies may become in the near future. On the other hand, conceptual modeling approaches (that have specifically been designed to support a semantically rich description of structured data sets) could, at least to some extent, handle the description of the conceptualization that is the subject of an ontology. Exploring this idea is definitely worth a discussion. Arguments in favor of "highly intuitive" ontology models, with a "frame-like look and feel" or "database schema" alike, have already been developed in e.g. [8], [5] and [7]. Specific proposals include [6] and [3]. Mappings from conceptual models to description logics have been proposed in e.g. [2] and [1].

The following brief description of conceptual modeling expressiveness is based on work on extended entity-relationship (EER) models, which are most frequently seen as offering the richest semantic expressiveness. In EER models and alike, data structures are basically graphs of object types interconnected by relationship types. Both object and relationship types may be characterized by associated properties (attributes and methods). Attributes may be atomic (as in relational tables) or composed of other attributes, thus allowing the definition of multilevel property trees for object and relationship types. It is then possible, for instance, to represent a real world entity as a single object in the database. Attribute cardinalities state whether an attribute is optional or mandatory, and monovalued or multivalued (list, set, or bag). Relationship types connect object types via roles. A relationship type may be defined with 2 (for binary relationships) to n roles. When two or more roles connect to the same object type, the relationship type is said to be cyclic. Relationship types may be adorned with specific semantics, of which the most well known is aggregation semantics (expressing that an object is a component of another object).

Object and relationship instances bear a system-defined, unique identity. Object types and relationship types may be organized into generalization/specialization lattices using is-a links. Inheritance, refinement, redefinition and overloading mechanisms apply as proposed in traditional object-oriented data models. Some advanced conceptual models, however, depart from object-oriented rules by adopting a multi-instantiation paradigm, i.e. allowing the same real world entity to be simultaneously represented by several instances in different classes that are not in a sub-type/super-type relationship. Allowing multi-instantiation is necessary from the modeling point of view, in particular to be able to properly describe situations such as, for instance, a real world object being at the same time a hotel and a restaurant (assuming Hotel and Restaurant are two object types) without forcing the definition of a so-called intersection class, Hotel&Restaurant, sub-class of both Hotel and Restaurant. Another facility from some conceptual model is classification dynamicity, i.e. the possibility for an instance to move to another class (e.g., a guesthouse becoming a hotel, a student becoming a faculty).

Good conceptual models come with formal definitions, rules to translate conceptual specifications into logical level specifications, and implementations in several marketed CASE tools and in research prototypes.

3.1 Conceptual Design for the Example Databases

The TUI conceptualization from Fig. 1 can be easily reformulated in an EER formalism by using the following very simple (but not very intelligent) rules:

- Ignore links labeled "instanceOf" and their source ellipsis (EER schemas do not describe instances),
- Each ellipsis translates into an object type,
- Each link between ellipses translates into a binary relationship named after the label associated to the link,
- Each label not in an ellipsis translates into a property (an attribute) of the object type it is linked to.
  Fig. 3 shows the diagram for this EER schema.

However, such a schema definition, although syntactically correct, does not fully use the power of conceptual models to organize the TUI conceptualization. Basically, it does not use the facility to define complex attributes, which allows elaborating a description of a real world entity as a single object type. Using this facility (for e.g., rates), and assuming TUI wants to keep a catalogue of cities and countries, the conceptual schema for the TUI conceptualization reduces to the one illustrated in Fig. 4, with Fig. 5 showing the attributes of Hotel (indenting is used to visualize attribute composition). The figures show cardinality constraints (on roles of relationship types

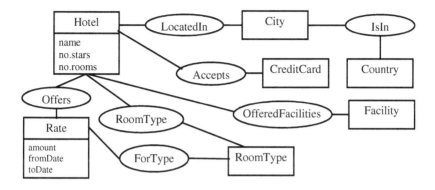

Fig. 3. Straight reformulation of the TUI conceptualization (Fig. 1) using EER formalism

attributes), as these are traditionally included in an EER schema definition. In Fig. 4 we have assumed that a country includes many cities and a city has many hotels, while a hotel may only be located in one city (but some hotels are in no city) and a city is located in only one country. Fig. 5 assumes that a hotel may have many facilities, may accept several credit cards, and offers many rates (at least one), a TUI rate possibly holding for different types of rooms (e.g. a hotel having the same rate for single and double rooms).

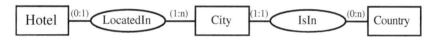

Fig. 4. An EER diagram for a proper conceptual schema of the TUI conceptualization

Hotel
name (1:1)
no.stars (1:1)
no.rooms (1:1)
facilities (0:n)
creditCards (0:n)
rates (1:n)
amount(1:1)
fromDate(1:1)
toDate (1:1)
roomTypes (1:n)

Hotel
name (1:1)
no.stars (1:1)
creditCards (0:n)
roomFacilities (0:n)
hotelFacilities (0:n)
rates (1:n)
no.beds (1:1)
standardAmount(1:1)
reducedAmount(1:1)
fromDate(1:1)
toDate (1:1)
roomType (1:1)

Fig. 5. Hotel attributes in the TUI (left) and TC (right) conceptualizations

The same reasoning scheme may be applied to produce an EER schema for the TC conceptualization shown in Fig. 2. The structural difference is that the is-a links to Accomodation in the TC structure will be mapped onto is-a links (rather than relationship types) in the EER design. A possible schema diagram for the TC conceptualization is shown in Fig. 6. TC Hotel attributes are shown Fig. 5.

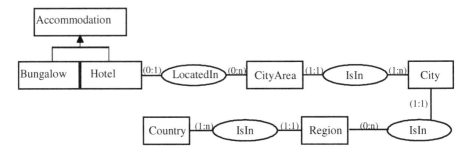

Fig. 6. A possible EER design for the TC conceptualization

3.2 Integration

Bridging the semantic differences between the TUI and TC descriptions requires a precise identification of how things modeled in one description correspond to things modeled in the other description. Such mapping knowledge is expressed as interschema corresponding assertions, which we show below in the format suggested in [10] for the TUI and TC Hotel object types as described in Fig. 5. For instance, assuming the hotel concept has the same semantics in TUI and TC, and assuming both providers may have offers for the same hotel, an assertion may be:

TUI.Hotel ∩ TC.Hotel
WCI   TUI.Hotel.name ≡ TC.Hotel.name
WCA TUI.Hotel.creditCards ≡ TC.Hotel.creditCards
WCA TUI.Hotel.facilities ⊇ TC.Hotel.(roomFacilities ∪ hotelFacilities)
WCA TUI.Hotel.rates.amount   TC.Hotel.rates.(standardAmount ∪ reducedAmount)

The first line asserts that the Hotel object types in TUI and TC describe overlapping sets of real world entities, i.e. the same hotel may be instantiated in both TUI and TC. Beyond overlapping, other possible choices are equality, inclusion and disjointedness.

The second line (WCI stands for With Corresponding Identifiers) states that two instances in TUI.Hotel and TC.Hotel represent the same real world hotel if the value for the name attribute is the same in the two instances. This provides knowledge about the mapping between instances of TUI and TC. This mapping enables gathering all information about a real world thing that is available in two interrelated sources. The following lines, introduced by the WCA (With Corresponding Attributes) acronym, define corresponding attributes for the related types, i.e. attributes that at least partially represent the same real world property, irrespectively of how it is coded in the representation. The first WCA line states that for corresponding instances the creditCards attributes hold identical information in both TUI and TC. The second WCA line states that facilities in TUI include the facilities that in TC are split into roomFacilities and hotelFacilities. The third WCA line states that although the two rates attributes hold the same semantics (i.e., they denote the cost for a room), the set of values in TUI and TC are different (TUI and TC record different rates even for the same hotel). Hence, to retrieve all the rates offered by a given hotel, both TUI and TC have to be searched and the results have to be merged.

Similar assertions hold for relationships types. An example is:

$$TUI.LocatedIN \equiv TC.LocatedIn.IsIn$$

which states that the TUI relationship, LocatedIn, is equivalent to the composition of the two TC relationships, LocatedIn and IsIn. Both provide the same path between Hotel and City.

From these assertions, the INT conceptualization may be built almost automatically by an integration tool. "almost" refers here to the fact that many alternative INT views may be elaborated from the same set of assertions, depending on designers' preferences (e.g., one designer may prefer a more concise schema while another designer may prefer a more exhaustive schema). The integration tool generates also the mappings that relate the INT view to both sources, TUI and TC. These mappings are used by the query execution tool that translates the user queries expressed on the INT view into queries for the sources.

Logic-based approaches follow a simpler, manual integration strategy. The definition of the INT view is directly done by the users. They have to define each concept and role of the INT view, through a logic formula on the TUI and TC concepts and roles, as in the following examples.

$$INT:Hotel \equiv TUI:Hotel \cup TC:Hotel$$

$$INT:CreditCard \equiv TUI:CreditCard \cup TC:CreditCard$$

$$INT:accepts(Hotel, CreditCard) \supseteq TUI:accepts(Hotel, CreditCard)$$

The inference engine will automatically check if the INT description is consistent with the TUI and TC descriptions, thus showing a clear advantage for DL over DB technology. It will also automatically infer the answers to queries on the INT view from the definitions of the INT view. However, should automatic, rather than manual, integration be the goal, a corresponding DL-based integration tool remains to be specified.

4 Discussion

This section briefly surveys advantages and disadvantages of using a conceptual modeling and database approach, versus using a (description) logic approach, for the description and management of ontologies.

4.1 Data Modeling

EER conceptual models support direct modeling of rich data structures, leading to representations that are close to how humans perceive things in the real world. EER synthetic schemas are easily apprehended. Instead, most description logics rely on simple binary data structures. This leads to an explosion in the number of concepts that are needed, similar but worse than what happens in relational databases. A one-page EER schema is likely to require several pages of description logics (DL) axioms to describe the same representation. In addition, having only binary structures blurs the distinction between what describes composite things (e.g., entities and links) and what merely describes a property. The reader of a DL description has to perform a reverse engineering process to reconstruct something that resembles her/his perception of the real world that is described. EER conciseness is definitely an advantage for humans. It is also an advantage for computer agents. Agents would also have an easier task in exploring a conceptual schema showing a clear distinction between objects and complex properties than in exploring a long list of DL axioms. Finally, to visualize an ontology structure, EER diagrams are likely to be easier to capture at a glance than the DL diagrams supported by recent DL editors.

In terms of supporting description of defined or derived concepts, the advantage currently goes to DLs. DLs allow users to define new concepts by a logical formula as complex as needed. The inference mechanisms automatically check the consistency of the definitions, deduce where the new concepts are placed in the generalization hierarchy, and infer their instances. Some conceptual models support a few derived concepts (e.g., derived object types, derived classes, derived attributes), whose instances and values can be automatically inferred. But they do not support concepts that designers would define by a logical formula without knowing where they will fit in the generalization hierarchy or even knowing the generalization hierarchy. Moreover, a derived construct in a schema has different properties than a non-derived construct (e.g., it cannot be instantiated), while defined concepts in DLs are treated as base concepts. DLs also allow users to state axioms of type inclusion, equivalence, and disjointedness involving complex terms. As DLs work with the open world assumption (OWA), all the assertions (definitions of concepts and axioms) are used by the logic reasoners for inferring new knowledge.

On the other hand, DBMS, which work with the closed world assumption (CWA), enforce integrity constraints that avoid inappropriate data to enter the database, where inappropriate means data that is not consistent with the current state of the database, assuming this state is the whole universe of discourse. Conceptual models have a number of predefined integrity constraints (e.g., cardinality constraints, key constraints) that are easily described. However, to support a declarative formulation of general integrity constraints, they have to resort to an associated logic language (usually the FOL). On the other hand, in DLs it is very difficult to assert a constraint on the known part of the world [4].

4.2 Data Manipulation

Instance creation is unconstrained in DL. Instances may be created without being attached to a concept. The creation of a new instance may not conform to the rules described by the axioms. In fact, the creation of an instance leads to one of three cases: 1) the instance fully conforms to all existing assertions; 2) the instance contradicts existing assertions, in which case the user is warned about the contradiction; and 3) the instance neither fully conforms nor contradicts existing assertions, in which case the DL reasoner infers that there is some missing knowledge that, if known, would make the new instance conforming to the axioms. Indeed, description logic systems naturally adhere to the OWA, which assumes that present data is just the explicitly known subset of the valid data, and more valid data may be inferred by reasoning. For instance, if axioms state that every hotel has a name, the creation of a new hotel is accepted even if no name is attached to the new hotel.

On the contrary, databases follow the CWA, stating that only information that is present in the database (or derivable by explicitly defined derivation rules) is valid. If a fact is not in the database, the fact is considered false. As a consequence, the creation of new instances has to obey all integrity constraints that apply to the instance. For instance, if the schema prescribes that every hotel instance must hold a value for the hotel name, the creation of a new hotel without specifying its name is not accepted.

It is uneasy to evaluate which approach is better. In fact, each one is best suited for the purpose it has been designed for. DL and its OWA fit well within an environment where the ontology is incrementally defined, which corresponds to a situation such that at each stage the current ontology only holds part of the world of interest, hence there are many more specifications that are relevant but not yet entered into the ontology. They also fit well with the idea that ontologies evolve as a result of collaborative design, where many independent partners can contribute new specifications to the ontology. The OWA also allows DLs to naturally support incomplete information at the instance level. Inference mechanisms handle case reasoning.

The database approach only offers a partial solution for managing incomplete information, the NULL value, which has no clear semantics and is uneasy to handle. On the other hand, the database approach and its CWA fit well in normative environments, where the ontology has to interact with an information system which assumes that the data it uses comes in a given format and is consistent with the application rules that have been stated in the ontology. In database management, satisfiability issues can be discarded and decidability issues do not arise. Consequently, database systems simply do not need sophisticated reasoners to infer additional information.

Another difference between DLs and databases is that databases rely on the unique name assumption, which assumes that each instance has its own identity, different from all others. In most DLs, unless explicitly stated by the user, nothing prohibits two instances to be the same one. The logic reasoner may infer that two instances, for example h1 and h2, describing two hotels are, in fact, the same one.

In terms of querying the ontology and its instances, databases and description logics offer complementary functionality for instance querying. Database systems usually provide powerful assertional query languages, complemented with efficient query optimization tools. Description logic systems support a set of simple functions for accessing instances that were directly inserted into the Abox (instance set) or are inferred by the reasoning engine. Simply stated, the difference is that databases have been purposely designed to store, manage, and query huge volumes of data instances, while DL approaches have typically been targeted at sophisticated reasoning over a relatively small volume of instances. Similarly, database systems can easily handle value domains (the embedded ones as well as user-defined domains) while description logics experience quite a difficulty in fully handling concrete domains (each concrete domain calls for a careful extension of the reasoning capabilities).

4.3 Beyond Data Structures

Part of the semantics of the real world comes from where things are located in space and time. Traditional modeling approaches (in DL as in conceptual modeling approaches) ignore these components, assuming that the real world of interest is now and here. On the contrary, there are a huge number of applications where spatio-temporal information is essential. Considering our hotel example, spatial information could be used to convey the actual geographical location of hotels, cities and countries. This would enable queries such as "find hotels within 10 miles of a given city". Similarly, room rates are a typical example of information that is valid only within a given time period. In the current description, this is captured using the attributes fromDate and toDate. However, this is a poor solution in the sense that only the user is aware of the temporal semantics of these attributes. From the system viewpoint, these are two "normal" attributes, with a Date domain. No temporal reasoning and no temporal operators (in the sense developed by research in temporal databases) will be deployed by the system on such data.

There has been quite an investment in the DL community to develop temporal extensions of DL languages. There have been only few efforts to similarly develop spatial extensions. Spatio-temporal DLs still are a research item for the future.

The picture is comparatively better in conceptual modeling, where several proposals for spatio-temporal conceptual models exist today, and there is a pretty good understanding of what are the required functionalities. Proposals exist to cover spatio-temporal phenomena, such as e.g. mobile objects and trajectories [9][11], and multi-representation (to support context-dependent information) [12]. Moreover, Geographic Information Systems routinely and efficiently implement all the logical level constructs needed for the description and management of geographic data, including the two views of space: the discrete (or object-based) view and the continuous (or field-based) view.

5 Conclusion

Conceptual modeling and the database approach provide better readability/ understandability of the content of an ontology, and more efficient management for large ontologies and associated knowledge bases. DL approaches provide better reasoning capabilities and new knowledge inference from explicitly defined knowledge. We therefore suggest that, rather than extending either formalism to try to cover all desirable functionality, a hybrid system, where the database component and the logic component would cooperate, each one performing the tasks for which it is best suited, might be the most promising solution for semantically rich information management, in particular semantic web information services. It seems obvious to us that, for instance, ontology description services should rely on conceptual data models, while ontological consistency services and incomplete information handling should be performed using description logics reasoners.

References

1. A. Borgida, R.J. Brachman: Conceptual Modelling with Description Logics. In Description Logic Handbook, F. Baader, D. Calvanese, D. McGuinness, D. Nardi, D., P. Patel-Schneider (Eds.), Cambridge University Press, 349–372, 2002
2. D. Calvanese, M. Lenzerini, D. Nardi: Description logics for conceptual data modeling, in Logics for Databases and Information Systems, J. Chomicki and G. Saake (Eds.), Kluwer Academic Publisher, 1998, 229-264
3. N. Cullot, C. Parent, S. Spaccapietra, C. Vangenot: Ontologies: A contribution to the DL/DB debate, in Proceedings of the VLDB Workshop on Semantic Web and Databases, Berlin, September 2003
4. F.M. Donini, M. Lenzerini, D. Nardi, W. Nutt, A. Schaerf: An epistemic operator for description logics, Artificial Intelligence 100, 1998, 225-274
5. D. Fensel, J. Hendler, H. Liebermann, W. Wahlster: Spinning the semantic web, The MIT Press, Cambridge, Massachusetts (2003)
6. M. Jarrar. J. Demey, R. Meersman: On Using Conceptual Data Modeling for Ontology Engineering, in Journal of Data Semantics 1, K. Aberer, S. March, S. Spaccapietra (Eds.), LNCS 2800, Springer, 2003
7. M. Klein, J. Broekstra, D. Fensel, F. van Harmelen, I. Horrocks: Ontologies and schema languages on the Web. In Spinning the Semantic Web, D. Fensel & al. (Eds.), The MIT Press, Cambridge, Massachusetts (2003)
8. R. Meersman: Ontologies and Databases: More than a Fleeting Resemblance. In: OES/SEO Workshop Rome, 2001
9. C. Parent, S. Spaccapietra, E. Zimanyi: Spatio-Temporal Conceptual Models: Data Structures + Space + Time, 7th ACM Symposium on Advances in Geographic Information Systems, ACM GIS'99, November 5th-6th, 1999
10. C. Parent, S. Spaccapietra: Database Integration: the key to data interoperability, in Object-Oriented Data Modeling, M. Papazoglou & al. (Eds.), MIT Press, 2000
11. S. Ram, R.T. Snodgrass, V. Khatri, Y. Hwang, DISTIL: A Design Support Environment for Conceptual Modeling of Spatio-temporal Requirements. In Proceedings of the 20th International Conference on Conceptual Modeling, ER 2001, Yokohama, Japan, LNCS 2224, Springer-Verlag, 2001, 70-83
12. C. Vangenot, C. Parent, S. Spaccapietra: Modeling and Manipulating Multiple Representations of Spatial Data, International Conference on Spatial Data Handling, Ottawa, Canada, July 9-11, 2002

MetaData Pro: Ontology-Based Metadata Processing for Web Resources

Ting Wang[1], Ji Wang[2], Yang Yu, Rui Shen, Jinhong Liu, and Huowang Chen

National Laboratory for Parallel and Distributed Processing,
Changsha, Hunan, P.R.China 410073
[1] wonderwang70@hotmail.com, [2] jiwang@mail.edu.cn

Abstract. Metadata is the foundation of Semantic Web. The MetaData Pro project seeks to build a metadata processing platform for web resource. The system architecture has three key components-- Metadata Extraction, Ontology Management, and Metadata Retrieval. The system can automatically extract metadata about web resource: if the web resource itself contains metadata, extracts them; otherwise, automatically generates the metadata for the resource according to Dublin Core by applying automatic keyword extraction and text summarization techniques. To manage the metadata, MetaData Pro integrates Protégé to create domain ontology, makes use of HowNet to help ontology construction, and provides an ontology-based metadata retrieval.

1 Introduction

Semantic Web has complex hierarchy based on XML and RDF, in which metadata plays an important role. Metadata, the data about other data, most commonly refer to the descriptive information about Web resources in the web-age term. The web resource metadata can serve a variety of purposes, such as identifying a resource that meets a particular information need, evaluating resources suitability for use, intelligent browsing, Agent based web service, and so on. Metadata can provide the unstructured data with structures or semi-structures.

Currently many metadata languages have been developed for indexing web information resources with knowledge representations (logical statements) and storing them in web documents [1], for example, the Dublin Core[2], the PRISM[3], XMP[4], IMS Metadata[5], V-Card[6] and so on. The metadata in the web is tremendous and grows quickly. Some of them are contained in web resources such as in html, PDF, JEPG files, and some stand alone as presented in XML files. So it is important to manage them efficiently, which includes extracting and collecting them from various web resources, storing them in uniform representation, and identifying them for particular use.

The MetaData Pro is a platform developed for processing metadata in web resources. Its significant feature is to link the metadata extraction, Natural Language Processing (NLP) and ontology together to achieve continuous metadata information processing. The extraction tool searches online documents and extracts metadata contained in them, or automatically generates the metadata for the resource according to Dublin Core by applying automatic keyword extraction and text summarization

C. Bussler et al. (Eds.): WISE 2004 Workshops, LNCS 3307, pp. 34–45, 2004.

techniques. It stores various metadata in RDF [7] and provides the uniform accessing methods. To manage the metadata, MetaData Pro integrates Protégé to created domain ontology and enhanced the metadata retrieval with ontology-based term expansion mechanism. To facilitate the ontology creation, we build a tool to extract ontology from HowNet -- a Chinese-English bilingual knowledge dictionary [8].

In the rest of this paper, we will first give an overview on the architecture of MetaData Pro. After that, we will present its three key components -- Metadata Extraction, Ontology Management, and Metadata Retrieval. Finally, we will summarize the work and give the way ahead.

2 Architecture of MetaData Pro

MetaData Pro's architecture (see Fig. 1) comprises three key components: Semantic Metadata Extracting, Ontology Management, and Metadata Retrieval. At first, the web resources (including various file types: html, xml, PDF, JEPG...etc) are collected by a spider. The Semantic Metadata Extraction tool gleans metadata from the obtained resources and passes the information to the Metadata Base (MB) and stores the data in the RDF triple model. The Ontology Management tool provides ontology editing by using Protégé [9]. The ontologies outputted by Protégé are stored in the Knowledge Base (KB) in RDF model also. The Metadata Retrieval tool accepts user requests expressed in ontology vocabulary which is converted to a RDF query using a calculating engine on the Knowledge Base and retrieval the satisfied metadata in MB. All the tools are integrated into Protégé as plugins.

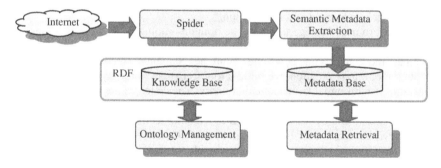

Fig. 1. Architecture of MetaData Pro

2.1 Metadata Representation

Although MetaData Pro is aimed to manage various widely used metadata such as Dublin Core, PRSIM and XMP, it in fact can extract more metadata other than these types. All the metadata satisfying one of the following conditions can be extracted automatically by MetaData Pro:

- The metadata is contained in html files and expressed as "<META>"tags.
- The metadata is contained in html files and expressed as embedded RDF content.
- The metadata is contained in xml files using RDF/XML.

- The metadata is contained in files (PDF, JEPG,…, etc) satisfying XMP standard.

In fact, Metadata Pro is sensitive to the expressing way of metadata rather than the metadata vocabulary itself. For a kind of metadata other than the above three types, if it is contained in web resources in the ways listed above, it can be fully processed by MetaData Pro. Moreover, even the expressing way changed, we can add a new extractor to capture it conveniently.

Metadata can be expressed fairly differently in various resources. A unified representation form is needed. RDF provides a framework for metadata. All the extracted metadata can be converted to RDF model and stored in database.

In MetaData Pro, both the metadata and knowledge (ontologies) are all expressed in RDF model. The storing of RDF data has two solutions: one is the RDF specified database, such as Guha's RDFDB [10]; the other is to store RDF in relational database. To achieve more scalability, we choose the later way to store both the MB and KB RDF data. To manipulate these RDF data, we apply Jena [11] to provide query language--RDQL, a query language for RDF.

2.2   Modules

The Semantic Metadata Extraction searches online documents and extracts metadata from Web resources in two ways: if the web resource contains metadata, it extracts them directly; if doesn't, it will automatically generate the metadata for the resource according to Dublin Core. When generates metadata, some are obtained with the help of HTTP and html parsing, such as Identifier, Format, Date and Title; some is obtained by applying automatic keyword extraction and text summarization techniques, such as Subject and Description.

MetaData Pro uses Protégé to create the domain ontologies. Protégé is a graphical tool for ontology editing and knowledge acquisition that we can adapt to enable conceptual modeling with new and evolving Semantic Web languages[9]. To facilitate the ontology creation, we build a tool to extract ontology from HowNet -- a Chinese-English bilingual knowledge dictionary. The concepts are converted from the lexicon entry and related according to its semantic definition and the sememe hierarchy. The ontologies are stored in KB in RDF model also.

To retrieve metadata, user requests can be expressed in the query language, which is defined as a logical expression augmented with ontology vocabulary and operators. The query expression will be converted to a RDF query using a naive calculating engine on the KB. The calculating engine provides an ontology-based term expansion mechanism. At last Jena will do the RDF query and return the satisfied metadata.

3   Metadata Extraction

Currently more and more metadata are now contained in the web resources to index web information resources with structured or semi-structured representations. There are many tools can help people to add metadata while creating web resources, for example, Adobe has integrated the XMP framework into Adobe Photoshop, Acrobat, FrameMaker, GoLive, InCopy, InDesign, Illustrator, and LiveMotion. So the resources produced by these tools, such as HTML, XML, PDF, JEPG files and so on, will contain metadata to describe the resources itself. For the metadata contained in these web resources, MetaData Pro can extract them according to their corresponding expression methods.

However, as Semantic Web is still on its way, there are great amount of available web resources not annotated with metadata, so these resources will not be managed in the Semantic Web frame. There is a strong need to develop tools to automatically generate metadata for these resources. With the help of these tools, most of the web resources without annotated metadata can be shifted to Semantic Web frame, as well as the generated metadata will give the resources more structured descriptive information. Of course, these tools must be designed according to certain metadata standard. In MetaData Pro, Dublin Core is taken as the annotated standard for the generated metadata.

3.1 Extract Metadata from Web Resources

The metadata standards define the vocabulary used to describe the metadata, but its expression way may vary from file types to types. For each expression way, there should be a corresponding extractor.

- For the metadata contained in html files, if the metadata is expressed as "<META>" tags, the extractor will produce the RDF triple statements by adding the URL of the web document as the Subject and convert the Name-Content pairs contained in <META> tag to the Predicate and Object of RDF triple.
- For the metadata contained in html files, if the metadata is expressed as embedded RDF content, the extractor also produces the RDF triple statements by converting the value of rdf:about attribute to the Subject, and other attribute-value pairs to the Predicates and Objects of RDF triple.
- If the metadata is contained in xml files using RDF/XML, the extractor treats this case just as the above one.
- If the metadata is contained in web resource files, such as PDF, JEPG and so on, satisfying XMP standard, the extractor will first scan the document to locate the metadata according to the XML Packet format defined by XMP, and then convert the RDF/XML metadata to RDF triple statements.

All the extracted metadata is converted to RDF triple statements and stored in the MB through Jena.

3.2 Automatically Generate Metadata for Web Pages

As Semantic Web is still on its way, there is a strong need to develop tools to generate metadata for the annotated web resources. Metadata Pro provides the feature to generate metadata for the web pages (HTML, XML) not annotated with metadata, taking Dublin Core as the annotated standard for the generated metadata. Thus these resources can be shifted forward to Semantic Web frame.

Dublin Core is widely used as the vocabulary to describe the information about web resources. It defines a metadata element set consisted of 15 elements, some of which can be generated according to HTTP header, some can be got by HTML parsing, and some can be obtained by applying NLP techniques such as automatic keyword extraction and text summarization. Table 1 shows the generated metadata element and how its value is generated.

Table 1. Generated metadata element and its value generating method

Element	Value generating method
Identifier	Using the URL of the page.
Format	Get from the content type in HTTP header.
Date	Set to the created or last modified date of the page, got from HTTP header.
Title	Set to the text extracted from the <title> tag in the html page.
Subject	Set to the text extracted from the page by keyword extraction.
Description	Set to the text extracted from the page by text summarization.
Creator	Set to "Metadata Pro" indicating it is generated by the software.

3.3   Automatic Keyword Extraction and Text Summarization

According to the specification of Dublin Core, the Subject element is used to describe the subject and keywords. Typically, a subject will be expressed as keywords, key phrases or classification codes that describe a topic of the resource. The Description element may include but is not limited to: an abstract, table of contents, reference to a graphical representation of content or a free-text account of the content. Metadata Pro applies the NLP techniques to generate the values of the Subject and Description: using automatic keyword extraction to get the keywords from the document and using text summarization to get the summary of the document.

In Metadata Pro, automatic keyword extraction and text summarization are closely related. The former is the foundation of the later, as shown in Fig. 2.

Fig. 2. The workflow of automatic keyword extraction and text summarization

The simplest way to extracting the keywords from a text is based on finding the most frequent words in the text. The basic intuition underlying this approach is that the most important concepts in the texts are likely to be referred to repeatedly, or, at least, more frequently than minor concepts [12]. Although this basic intuition is sensible, it is too simple to achieve our goal. In Metadata Pro, what we should do is to extract keywords from the html page, which is marked with tags. Many tags have certain semantic meaning which can give us the information about the structure of document. Moreover, the location of each word in the text also brings different implication for its contributes to the text [13].

To improve the extraction and summarization, five factors have been considered:

- Word Processing: Metadata Pro is aimed to process web pages in both English and Chinese, so the word processing is a little trouble. For English pages, stemming is requested when break the text into words, while for Chinese, the sentences should be segmented into words because there is no blank between the words as English do. Segmenting is an important technology for Chinese text processing.
- Stop words: the words appear in most document frequently should not be the candidates, that is to say the stop words should be filtered out.
- Frequency: the most frequent words in the text tend to be the keywords candidates; the sentences containing most keywords candidates tend to be in the summary.
- Location: the location of each word in the html document should be given different weight. For example, the text appear in TITLE tag and sub title tags (H1~H6) will certainly convey more important meaning of the document than general text. Also sentences in different position play different roles in the meaning expression. It is reported that about 85% topic sentences appear at the begin of the paragraph as well as about 7% topic sentences is the last one of the paragraph. Here we consider the following locations: title, sub title, begin of paragraph, end of paragraph, middle of paragraph, first paragraph, last paragraph and so on, each of these locations is associated with a weight w_l (where l indicates different location).
- Length of the document: we can set the number of keywords to, for example 5 or 10(5 is default in the system), but it is improper to fix the number of sentences in summary, because the lengths of web pages vary greatly. It is more rational to set the ratios of the summary compare to the total document. The ratio is user-defined, which is set as 10% in default.

Now we can give the keyword extraction and text summarization methods. Metadata Pro first parses the html files, scans the text to recognize the word. For English text, it stems each word; for Chinese text, it segments the string into words using Longest-Match method [14]. Then the stop words should be filtered out. Then we can calculate the weight for each word as follow: for each word i, its weight is

$$WordWeight_i = \sum_l w_l * N_{li} \tag{1}$$

where w_l is the associated word weight of the location l, N_{li} is the occurrence frequency of word i in the location l in the total document. So $WordWeight_i$ is the weight of word i to the document. The words with top 5 weights are taken as the keywords of the document.

After calculating the weight for each word in the document, we can produce the summary as follows: for each sentence i in the document, calculate its weight as,

$$SentWeight_i = \sum_j WordWeight_j + s_l \tag{2}$$

where $WordWeight_j$ is the weight of word j in the sentence calculated as formula (1), s_l is the associated weight of the sentence's location l, So $SentWeight_i$ is the weight of sentence i to the document. The sentences with top N weights are taken as the summary of the document, where N = the ratio of summary * (the number of sentences in the document). The selected sentences are arranged according to their original order of their occurrence in the document. Of course, the reduplicate sentences must be deleted.

4 Ontology Management

4.1 Using Protégé-2000

Protégé [9] is an extensible, platform-independent environment for creating and editing ontologies and knowledge bases. It is a tool which allows the user to construct the domain ontology, customize data entry forms and enter data. It is also a platform which can be extended with graphical widgets for tables, diagrams, animation components to access other knowledge-based systems embedded applications. Protégé can also be a library which multiple applications can share to access and display knowledge bases.

Metadata Pro fully takes these advantages of Protégé by applying it in two ways:

• Using it as a visual tool to construct domain ontology.
• Taking it as an integrated platform for metadata extraction and retrieval tools.

4.2 Extract Ontology from HowNet

Knowledge acquisition is always the bottleneck of AI applications. Before the Semantic Web becomes practical and useful, there is a critical barrier we must breakthrough -- large-scale ontology construction. Two main approaches can aid this work [15]. The first one facilitates manual ontology engineering by providing natural language processing tools, including editors, consistency checkers, mediators to support shared decisions, and ontology import tools, such as Protégé. The second approach relies on machine learning and automated language-processing techniques to extract concepts and ontological relations from structured and unstructured data or text such as OntoLearn. The later approach causes more and more research interest. There are many machine readable structured resources, for example, various lexicons or dictionaries, such as WordNet which used in many works related to ontology [15]. Metadata Pro makes use of HowNet, a Chinese-English bilingual knowledge dictionary to help ontology construction.

HowNet is an on-line common-sense knowledge base unveiling inter-conceptual relations and inter-attribute relations of concepts as connoting in lexicons of the Chinese and their English equivalents [8]. It has been widely used to support semantic analysis [16]. As a knowledge base, the knowledge structured by HowNet is a graph rather than a tree. It is devoted to demonstrate the general and specific properties of concepts. In HowNet, every concept is an entry, comprising four items which are all made up of two portions joined by the "=" sign. The left hand side of the "=" sign is the data field, while the right hand side is the data value. The items are arranged as:

W_X= word / phrase form
G_X = word / phrase syntactic class
E_X = example of usage
DEF = concept definition

Now the dictionary provide both Chinese and English knowledge, so here X can be either Chinese(C for short) or English (E for short). For example, Fig. 3 shows the entries for the concept *doctor*, *hospital*, *invalid* and *patient*:

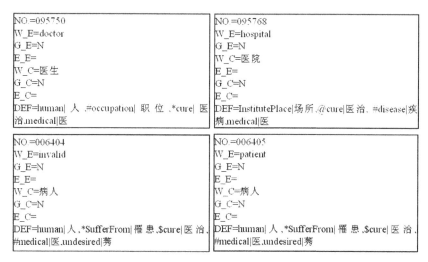

Fig. 3. Entries for the concept *doctor, hospital , invalid* and *patient* in HowNet

The entries numbered as 006404 and 006405 has the same DEF, both of them express the same concept which can be express in Chinese as word "病人" and "patient" or "invalid" in English. In both languages, its syntactic classes are all N which means noun. The most important part of every concept entry is DEF, which should include at least one feature expressed in sememe (the basic semantic unit in HowNet) and the first item in the DEF is the main feature. DEF also can express the relations between the concepts by specifying event role information. As shown in the example, expression "#medical|医 " means the concept is co-relation to the concepts whose DEF contain the "medical|医 " feature. Here, symbol *, $, @ and # are relation marks. The relations represented by them are shown in Table 2.

Table 2. Relations represented by the marks

Symbol	Relation
*	*agent-event*
$	*patient-event*
#	*concepts co-relation.*
@	*location-event*

The sememe system in HowNet is organized in Hypernym-Hyponym hierarchy. Fig. 4 gives a brief view of it. Together with the event role relationship expressed in DEF, there will be 16 relations between the concepts in HowNet, such as Hypernym-Hyponym, synonym, antonym, part-whole, agent-event, instrument-event and so on. So the concepts in the dictionary are connected as a network by those relations (this is why the dictionary is called HowNet). It should be note that, the relations between the concepts are not directly at concept level but established on sememe system. So if we want to extract ontology from the dictionary, we must infer from the DEF, using the sememe features and relation marks defined in it.

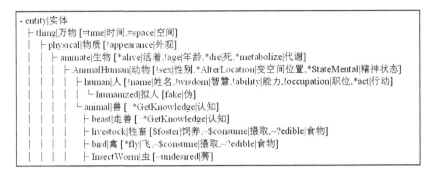

Fig. 4. A brief view of sememe hierarchy

To extract ontologies, there are two tasks:

- Extract concepts. In HowNet, different entries can represent the same concept, these entries has the same DEF, for example, the entries of invalid and patient in Fig. 3. We must first group the entries into concepts by the DEF.

- Extract the relations between concepts. The Hypernym-Hyponym relation is implied by main features of concepts. For example, the DEF of concept *tiger* is "beast|走兽", and the concept *mammal* is defined as "AnimalHuman|动物", from the sememe hierarch shown in Fig. 4, we can create a Hypernym-Hyponym relation between the *mammal* and *tiger*. The event role relationships expressed in DEF can also bring relations between concepts. As a more complex example, the concepts and their relations extracted from the entries shown in Fig. 3 are:

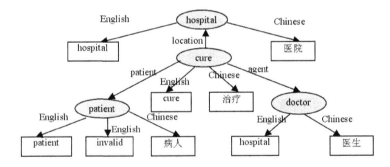

Fig. 5. The concepts and relations extracted from Fig. 3

In Fig. 5, the nodes (drawn as ovals) represent concepts and arcs represent named properties or predicate or relations. Nodes that represent string literals will be drawn as rectangles. The word in ovals nodes is just a label of the concept, while the words expressing the concept in English and Chinese are set as the value of corresponding properties (such as the *English* and *Chinese* relations).

The extracted ontologies are stored in KB in RDF model. The ontologies in KB can be used to express the metadata query, which is defined as a logical expression augmented with ontology vocabulary and operators.

5 Metadata Retrieval

5.1 Concept-Based Retrieval

Current information retrieval tools mostly are based on keyword search, which is unsatisfied because of its low precision and recall. However, if we consider the query words as concepts rather than literals, then we can retrieve relevant documents even if they do not contain the specific words used in the query. Recently concept-based information retrieval tools have been developed in both academic and industrial research environments, even some of them offer search facilities for the web [17].

In Metadata Pro, metadata itself is a retrieval object, for example, the value of the RDF statement is often been queried. In fact the metadata retrieval is quite like general text information retrieval for the metadata itself is text.

For concept-based information representation and retrieval, the key issue is how to represent the concepts. Most works treat concepts as thesaurus, some also use co-occurrences of words to present concept related words [17]. We think all these methods are reasonable but they need and could be used synthetically rather than individually. Ontology may be the integrated bed to represent the knowledge. As shown in Fig. 5, the words representing the same concept can be described as the properties of the concept. Moreover all different relations of words can be represented in the ontology by the means of concept-properties model. So in Metadata Pro, we implement concept-based retrieval by using ontology to express the user query request. A query language is designed based on the common logical expression augmented with ontology vocabulary and operators.

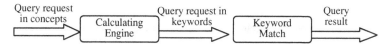

Fig. 6. The workflow of metadata query

5.2 Query Language

In Metadata Pro, the metadata retrieval tool consists of a query language and a calculating engine. With the query language, query request will be represented in the concepts or relations described in KB. This request will be converted to the final search request – Boolean expression on keywords, by the calculating engine using ontologies from KB. At last, the keyword match is run on metadata, and the related data will be fetched out (Fig. 6).

Because all the metadata is stored in RDF triples, the retrieval request can specify both the Predicate and Object, that is to say, user can specify both the Predicates to indicate the search scope and the criteria which the Object value should match:

Predicate = <Predicate List>
Object = <Criterion-expression>

where <Predicate List> specifies the Predicate set, and <Criterion-expression> is defined as:

<Criterion-expression > ::= < Item > | <Criterion-expression > or <Item >

\<Item> ::= \< Factor> | \<Item > and \<Factor >

\<Factor> ::= \<Criterion-expression>)|\<Ontology-factor>| not \<Criterion-expression >

\<Ontology-factor> ::= \<Concept> | literal | relation (\<Ontology- factor >)

\<Concept> ::= class | instance

The bone of the query language is based on the common logical expression, but the basic \<Factor> has been augmented with ontology vocabulary and operators. The \<Factor> can be concepts, literals (keywords) and relations.

When the query request in concept is converted to query request in keywords, the ontology vocabulary and operators in the query will be interpreted as below:

- First, calculating the *relation(\<Ontology-factor>)* sub expression, it will be interpreted as the classes or instances which have the relation with the concept represented by *\<Ontology-factor>*. Repeat the step until all the relations have been calculated. Now ontology vocabulary in the query is just classes, instances or literals (keywords).
- Secondly, all the classes and instances in the query will be replaced by the labels of the class and instance.
- Till now, the query is converted to common Boolean expression on literals (keywords), which can be processed by Jena's RDQL to retrieval RDF data.

Taking the ontology in Fig. 5 as example, if the query request is to find the metadata whose object value matches the class *patient*, the request can be refined and described in the query language as follow:

Predicate = *

Object = English ({ patient }) or Chinese ({ patient })

where { patient } means the concept patient, and the query means to search all the predicate types and find the triples whose Object contains words "patient" or "invalid" or "病人". This example demonstrates that with the query language, both thesaurus based and cross language search can be implemented on the ontology representation. Of course, more complex criterion expressions can be constructed, even related concepts retrieval can be implemented by using the relations between the concepts to specify the user query.

6   Conclusion

Metadata plays an important role in Semantic Web. The MetaData Pro is a platform for the processing of web resource metadata. It provides metadata extraction, ontology management, and metadata retrieval. The MetaData Pro project links the metadata extraction, NLP and ontology together to achieve continuous metadata information processing. The system has been implemented on the base of Protégé-2000. Protégé-2000 itself is used to construct ontologies. Both KB and MB are stored in RDF triples in relational database. A bridge has been developed to link the Protégé-2000 and RDF database by applying Jena. Both the metadata extraction and retrieval modules have been integrated into Protégé as its plugin tables.

We will develop more powerful and sophisticated technology. This problem can also lead to an important work--information structuralization. Metadata is normally understood to mean structured data about various resources that can be used to help support a wide range of operations, so it can be undertaken the responsibility to structure web information. We plan to further investigate and develop tools to improve the structural extent of web information by converting them into high quality metadata.

Acknowledgement. This research is supported in part by the National Natural Science Foundation and the National High Technology Research and Development Program (2002AA116070) of China.

References

1.   James Mayfield and Tim Finin: Information retrieval on the Semantic Web: Integrating inference and retrieval. SIGIR Workshop on the Semantic Web, Toronto, 1 Aug. (2003)
2.   Dublin Core Metadata Element Set 1.1: Reference Description,
     http://dublincore.org/documents/dces/
3.   PRISM Specification, http://xml.coverpages.org/prismv1b.pdf
4.   ADOBE XMP.
     http://partners.adobe.com/asn/developer/xmp/pdf/MetadataFramework.pdf.
5.   IMS Learning Resource Meta-data Specification.
     http://www.imsglobal.org/metadata/index.cfm
6.   vCard: The Electronic Business Card, http://www.imc.org/pdi/vcard-21.txt.
7.   Resource Description Framework Model and Syntax Specification,
     http://www.w3.org/TR/REC-rdf-syntax
8.   HowNet. http://www.keenage.com/
9.   Natalya F. Noy, Michael Sintek, Stefan Decker, Monica Crubézy, Ray W. Fergerson, and Mark A. Musen. Creating Semantic Web Contents with Protégé-2000. IEEE Intelligent Systems, March/April (2001)
10. R.V.Guha. rdfDB : An RDF Database. http://www.guha.com/rdfdb/
11. Jena 2 - A Semantic Web Framework. http://www.hpl.hp.com/semweb/jena.htm
12. Paolo Tonella, Filippo Ricca, Emanuele Pianta and Christian Girardi. Using Keyword Extraction for Web Site Clustering. Proc. of WSE 2003, 5th International Workshop on Web Site Evolution, Amsterdam, The Netherlands, September 22 (2003)
13. H.P.Edmundson. New Methods in Automatic Extracting. Journal of the ACM, Vol. 16(2) (1969)
14. Kaiying Liu. Chinese Text Segmenting and Tagging. Beijing, the Commercial Press (2000)
15. Roberto Navigli and Paola Velardi. Ontology Learning and Its Application to Automated Terminology Translation. IEEE Intelligent Systems, January/February (2003)
16. Xuan Qi, Ting Wang and Huowang Chen. Research on the Automatic Semantic Tagging Method. Journal of Chinese Information Processing, Vol.15, No.3 (2001) 9-15
17. H-M. Haav and J. F. Nilsson. Appr.ches to Concept Based Exploration of Information Resources. In: W. Abramowicz and J. Zurada (eds.): Knowledge Discovery for Business Information Systems. Kluwer Academic Publishers (2001) 89-109

Service-Oriented Semantic Peer-to-Peer Systems

Peter Haase, Sudhir Agarwal, and York Sure

Institute AIFB
University of Karlsruhe, Germany
{haase, agarwal, sure}@aifb.uni-karlsruhe.de

Abstract. In Peer-to-Peer data sharing systems, peers typically play equal roles and have equal capabilities. From the service perspective, peers provide a single service. For this reason, there is no need to explicitly model services. We argue, that for knowledge sharing systems, we need an effective combination of the capabilities of the peers both in terms of the services as well as the content they provide. In this paper we present an approach for modeling peers with content and service capability descriptions that allows a decentralized discovery and selection of peers. We show instantiations for various kinds of bibliographic services that are realized in the Bibster system, a semantics-based Peer-to-Peer system for sharing bibliographic metadata.

1 Introduction

Technology for knowledge sharing nowadays benefits from a number of recent research topics such as Semantic Web, Web Services and Peer-To-Peer. We aim at the convergence of these technologies for effective support of knowledge sharing in a distributed manner. Before presenting the outline for the remainder of this paper we motivate potential benefits of combining these three core technologies.

Peer-to-Peer networks allow peers (nodes) in the network to directly exploit resources available at other nodes without intervention of a central server. Nodes may join and leave the network in an ad-hoc manner. The advantages of Peer-to-Peer architectures over centralized approaches have been well advertised, and to some extent realized in existing applications: no centralized server (thus avoiding a bottleneck for both computational performance and information update), robustness against failure of any single component, scalability both in data-volumes and the number of connected parties. However, besides being the solution to many problems, the large degree of distribution of Peer-to-Peer systems is also the cause of a number of new problems: The lack of a single coherent schema for organizing information sources across the Peer-to-Peer network hampers the discovery of resources and formulation of requests. Further, request routing and network topology (which peers to connect to, and which peers to send/forward queries to) are significant problems.

The research community has recently turned to the use of **Semantic Web** technologies in Peer-to-Peer networks to alleviate these problems. "The Semantic Web is an extension of the current web in which information is given well-defined meaning, better enabling computers and people to work in cooperation" (*cf.* [1]). The key enabler for the Semantic Web is the need of many communities to put machine-understandable

C. Bussler et al. (Eds.): WISE 2004 Workshops, LNCS 3307, pp. 46–57, 2004.
© Springer-Verlag Berlin Heidelberg 2004

data on the Web which can be shared and processed by automated tools as well as by people. Machines should not just be able to display data, but rather be able to use it for automation, integration and reuse across various applications.

The combination of **Semantic Web and Peer-to-Peer** technologies, *i.e.* the use of semantic descriptions of datasources stored by peers and indeed of semantic descriptions of peers themselves, is claimed to help in formulating queries in such a way that they can be understood by other peers, in merging the answers received from different peers, and in directing queries across the network. In particular, the use of ontologies and of Semantic Web technologies in general has been identified as promising for Peer-to-Peer systems [2], [3], [4] and first approaches exist on how to engineer ontologies in such dynamic environments [5].

However, so far both Semantic Web and Peer-to-Peer technologies were aiming for static information, in contrast to dynamic services. On the other hand, **Web Services** can be seen as a new programming paradigm for distributed systems. They include a bundle of technologies such as descriptions of interfaces, properties of implementations of these interfaces, descriptions of data exchange formats and data exchange quality aspects, registry of components, composition of components and security aspects during exchange of components. In a nutshell, web services are software objects which can be assembled by using standard protocols to perform functions or execute business processes. **Semantic Web Services** are expected to allow automatic Web Service discovery, invocation, composition and interoperability, as well as execution monitoring.

In this work we are aiming at **Semantic Peer-to-Peer Services**. The potential of the convergence of Peer-to-Peer, Web Service and Semantic Web technology is widely accepted and has for example been outlined in [6]. Yet, so far there has been little systematic effort in examining the intersection between Peer-to-Peer, Semantic Web and Web Services. Among the challenges are the discovery of services and other resources in a decentralized manner, the selection of peers to send request to, and efficient and scalable routing of requests. In our work we focus on service discovery and selection based on semantic descriptions of peers and their services.

We present a novel approach for modeling peer services, integrating semantic descriptions of the peers in terms of their content and the services they provide (Section 2). We instantiate the model for a set of bibliographic peer services. In Section 3 we demonstrate how the discovery and matching is realized based on the semantic descriptions of peers and their services. In Section 4 we present the architecture of Bibster, a semantics-based Peer-to-Peer system, which has been extended for the explicit support of peer services. We present related work in Section 5 and conclude with a summary and outlook on future work in Section 6.

2   Peer Service Modeling

For the modeling of peer services, we follow a layered approach, as shown in Figure 1: The model is based on the OWL-S model (top layer), which we extend with peer service specific aspects (medium layer). Concrete peer services for a certain domain (bottom layer) are modeled as extensions to the peer service layer. These three layers of service modeling will be described in the following.

2.1   Semantic Service Descriptions with OWL-S

We will first review the core modeling primitives of OWL-S. OWL-S consists of three main parts, namely, *Service Profile*, *Process Model* and *Grounding*. Further, each service is provided by a resource, which can be any type of actor. In the following, we give a short introduction to each part and refer to [7] for details.

- *Service Profile:* The service profile describes, what a service does. The capability of a service is represented as transformation from the inputs and the preconditions of the Web service to the set of outputs produced and any side effects that result from the execution of the service. Implicitly, service profiles specify the intended purpose of the service, because they specify only the functionalities that the Web service is willing to provide publicly. Service profiles are used for populating service registries, for automated service discovery, and service selection. From a service profile one can derive service advertisements and service requests.
- *Process Model:* The OWL-S Process Model provides a more detailed view of the Web service than the profile by showing a (partial) view of the workflow of the provider. The process model allows the requester to verify whether the interaction with the provider leads to the results that were declared in the profile. The process model is used for planning, composition and monitoring the execution of services.
- *Grounding:* The role of OWL-S grounding is to separate the abstract information exchange described by the process model from the implementation details, message format and so on. The OWL-S grounding is responsible for mapping atomic processes into WSDL operations in such a way that the execution of one atomic process corresponds to the invocation of an operation on the server side. In addition, the grounding provides a way to translate the messages exchanged into OWL-S classes and instances that can be referred to by the process model.

2.2   Peer Service Extensions

In our peer service model, the peers are the resources that provide peer services (c.f. Figure 1). In our work, we focus on the peer service discovery and selection process. Therefore, the most relevant part of the peer service description is the peer service profile, as the discovery and selection process will be based on it. The peer service profile extends the service profile of OWL-S[1].

Another important extension is the explicit modeling of expertise of the peers. An expertise description is an abstract, semantic description of the local knowledge base of a peer based on the shared ontology. This shared ontology can for example be a topic hierarchy of a particular domain. In this case, the expertise description would contain references to topics that the peer is knowledgeable about. While the expertise describes the content available on the peer, the peer services describe an operational dimension. These dimensions are orthogonal: Different peers might provide the same operations, but have distinct expertise. Analogously, peers might have the same expertise, but provide different services.

---

[1] The definition of peer service process models with the goal of service composition is beyond the scope of this paper (see future work). For the service grounding we rely on the mechanisms provide by the WSDL grounding of OWL-S.

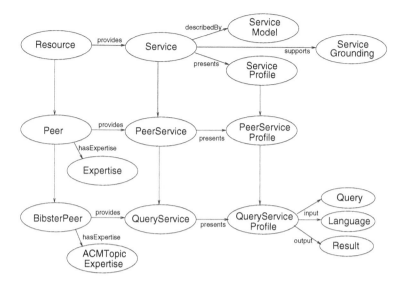

Fig. 1. Peer Service Ontology

2.3   Bibliographic Peer Services

We will now explain how peer services are modeled in our particular application scenario of a bibliographic Peer-to-Peer systems: Bibster [8] is a semantics-based Peer-to-Peer system for exchanging bibliographic data among researchers. As a typical Peer-to-Peer data-sharing systems, the Bibster system initially only provided one type of service: processing search request. However, for our bibliographic Peer-to-Peer system many more types of services are conceivable, some of them have already been realized in the Bibster system:

- *Query Service:* The query service is the service that is prominent in all Peer-to-Peer data sharing systems, although it may not explicitly modeled as a services. A query service returns a set of relevant results that match a query specification provided in some query language.
- *Retrieval Service:* Based on the results of the query service, which in our system only provides metadata, it is possible to realize a service that retrieves the corresponding full texts.
- *Classification Service:* This classification service may be based on the metadata, which potentially includes an abstract, or on the full text of the publication.
- *Recommendation Service:* The availability of a peer profile (incl. expertise model, etc.) allows to define services that proactively recommend bibliographic metadata based on these profiles. [9] presents a set of recommendation services based on content and usage information.
- *Transformation Service:* There are many different standards for the representation of bibliographic metadata. This requires services that are able to transform instances between these various representations.

In the following, we will explain one of these services – the *QueryService* – in detail.

Example 1 (Service Profile). The functional description of the peer service is described by its peer service profile in terms of the inputs required and the outputs produced. The function of the *QueryService* is to evaluate a given query – specified in a particular query language – against a knowledge base, and to return the corresponding query results, as shown in the following OWL-S fragment:

```
<PeerServiceProfile rdf:ID="Profile_Query_Service">
    <profile:input>
      <profile:ParameterDescription rdf:ID="Query">
        <profile:restrictedTo rdf:resource="&xsd;#string"/>
      </profile:ParameterDescription>
    </profile:input>

    <profile:input>
      <profile:ParameterDescription rdf:ID="Language">
        <profile:restrictedTo rdf:resource="RDFQueryLanguage"/>
      </profile:ParameterDescription>
    </profile:input>

    <profile:output>
      <profile:ParameterDescription rdf:ID="Result">
        <profile:restrictedTo rdf:resource="RDFQueryResult"/>
      </profile:ParameterDescription>
    </profile:output>
</PeerServiceProfile>
```

The query is represented in the profile as input parameter of type String. The query language, represented by the input parameter Language, is restricted to be of type RDFQueryLanguage, for which there may be various specific more specific types. For example, the Sesame RDF store used in the Bibster system supports SeRQL and RDQL:

```
<rdfs:Class rdf:ID="SeRQLQueryLanguage">
  <rdfs:subClassOf rdf:resource="RDFQueryLanguage"/>
</rdfs:Class>

<rdfs:Class rdf:ID=''RDQLQueryLanguage">
  <rdfs:subClassOf rdf:resource="RDFQueryLanguage"/>
</rdfs:Class>
```

Analogously, the query result has to be of type RDFQueryResult, for which there may be more specific representations. For example, Sesame allows to return query results either as an RDF graph or as tuples:

```
<rdfs:Class rdf:ID="GraphQueryResult">
  <rdfs:subClassOf rdf:resource="RDFQueryResult"/>
</rdfs:Class>

<rdfs:Class rdf:ID="TupleQueryResult">
  <rdfs:subClassOf rdf:resource="RDFQueryResult"/>
</rdfs:Class>
```

For the satisfying execution of these requests, it is not sufficient that the peers provide a requested service. For example, a peer may very well be able to execute a query, but if it does not have the appropriate expertise, it may simply return an empty result set. Analogously, the recommendation service may return (subjectively) irrelevant recommendations, if the expertise does not match that of the service provider.

We therefore also provide a model for expertise. For the bibliographic domain, we use a topic hierarchy – the ACM classification scheme[2] – as the basis of our expertise

---

[2] http://www.acm.org/class/1998/

model. It describes specific categories of literature for the Computer Science domain, covering 1287 topics. The expertise of a peer is thus described by a set of ACM topics, for which a peer provides classified instances.

Example 2 (Peer Profile). The following fragment shows the profile a peer whose expertise is on the ACM topics *Information Systems* and *Artificial Intelligence*.

```
<Peer rdf:ID="jxta:uuid-59616261646162614A78746150325033CD144F82DED74E">
  <hasExpertise>
    <ACMTopicExpertise>
      <isAbout rdf:resource="&acm;#ACMTopic/Information_Systems"/>
      <isAbout rdf:resource="&acm;#ACMTopic/Computing_Methodologies/
       Artificial_Intelligence"/>
    </ACMTopicExpertise>
  </hasExpertise>
</Peer>
```

3   Peer Service Discovery and Matching

A transaction in a typical web service scenario involves three parties: The requester, the provider, and an infrastructure components such as registries for the discovery and matchmaking between providers and requesters.

In Peer-to-Peer applications however, peers typically have equal roles, such that each peer can act as both provider and requester. Furthermore, in completely decentralized Peer-to-Peer systems, there may be no infrastructure component such as a centralized registry for the matchmaking between capability descriptions and requests. In this section, we will present a completely decentralized approach for the discovery and matching between providers and requesters. This approach does not only consider service capabilities in terms of the service profiles for the selection, but also involves the profile of the peers in terms of their expertise.

For the peer service discovery and matching we extend our model of expertise-based peer selection presented in [10]. In this model, peers use a shared ontology to advertise semantic descriptions of their expertise in the Peer-to-Peer network. In the following we will present the model with its extensions for service matching.

3.1   Advertisements

Advertisements are used to promote semantic descriptions of peer (according to the peer service model presented in the previous section) in the network. An advertisement thus associates a peer with an expertise and a service capability description. Every peer maintains its own local registry of advertisements. Peers decide autonomously, without central control, whom to promote advertisements to and which advertisements to accept. This decision can for example be based on the semantic similarity between expertise descriptions.

3.2   Matching and Peer Selection

During the process of peer selection, the specification of a request is matched against the available capability descriptions known from the advertisements stored in the local registry of the peer. The matching is performed in two steps: In a first step – service profile matching – a set of peers is selected that are able to perform the requested service based on their advertised service profiles. In a second step – expertise-based matching – the potential peers are then ranked based on how well their expertise matches the subject of the request. The peer selection algorithm returns a ranked set of peers, where the rank value is equal to the similarity value provided by a similarity function. Therefore, peers that have an expertise more similar to that of the subject of the request will have a higher rank. From this set of ranked peers one can, for example, select the best n peers, or all peers whose rank value is above a certain threshold.

Service Profile Matching. The matching process at the service profile level recognizes a match between the advertisement and the request, when the advertised service could be used in place of the requested service [11]. Operationally, this is correct when the outputs of the advertisement are equivalent or more general than the outputs of the request and when the inputs of the request are equivalent or more general than the inputs of the advertisement. The matcher differentiates among *exact match*, *plugIn match* and *subsumed match*.

Suppose, in_{Ad} and in_{Req} represent the inputs of the advertisement and request respectively, and out_{Ad} and out_{Req} represent their outputs. The matchmaker recognizes an exact output match when $out_{Ad} = out_{Req}$ and an exact input match when $in_{Ad} = in_{Req}$. A plugIn match is recognized, when $out_{Ad} \sqsupseteq out_{Req}$ or $in_{Req} \sqsupseteq in_{Ad}$. A subsumed match is recognized when $out_{Req} \sqsupseteq out_{Ad}$ or $in_{Ad} \sqsupseteq in_{Req}$.

The three types of matching are scored as in the order: exact match $>$ plugIn match $>$ subsumed match $>$ fail. Further, the matchmaker prefers output matches over input matches, since a requester in general has better idea of what he expects from the service than what the service needs from him.

Example 3 (Service Profile Matching). Consider the following service profile, which is the specification of a request for a service that is able to take a query provides as String in SeRQL (SeRQLQueryLanguage) as input and returns the result as an RDF graph (GraphQueryResult):

```
<PeerServiceProfile rdf:ID="Profile_Query_Service_Request">
    <profile:input>
      <profile:ParameterDescription rdf:ID="Language">
        <profile:restrictedTo rdf:resource="SeRQLQueryLanguage"/>
      </profile:ParameterDescription>
    </profile:input>
    <profile:input>
      <profile:ParameterDescription rdf:ID="Query">
        <profile:restrictedTo rdf:resource="&xsd;#string"/>
      </profile:ParameterDescription>
    </profile:input>
    <profile:output>
      <profile:ParameterDescription rdf:ID="Result">
        <profile:restrictedTo rdf:resource="GraphQueryResult"/>
      </profile:ParameterDescription>
    </profile:output>
</PeerServiceProfile>
```

When matching this service request against the capability description from Example 1, we see that the input parameter Query matches exactly. The input parameter Language in the request is less general than in the advertisement. Hence, the matcher will detect an input subsumed match. The output parameter `Result` in the request is also less general than in the advertisement. Hence, the matcher will detect an output plugIn match. Consequently, the capability description would qualify to process the request.

Expertise-Based Matching. After we have in the first step filtered out the set of peers that are able to process a service request, in the second we try to select those peers that are likely to provide satisfying responses. The expertise-based matching builds on the idea that only those peers should be selected whose expertise is close to that of the requested service. It employs a similarity function to match subjects against expertise descriptions. A *subject* is an abstract description of a given service request expressed in terms of the expertise ontology, e.g. the ACM topic hierarchy in the bibliographic domain. The subject specifies the required expertise to process a request. For example, for a query request, the subject is extracted from the query string.

The *similarity function* $Sim : S \times E \mapsto [0, 1]$ yields the semantic similarity between a subject $s \in S$ and an expertise description $e \in E$. An increasing value indicates increasing similarity. If the value is 0, s and e are not similar at all, if the value is 1, they match exactly.

For a topic hierarchy the similarity function Sim_{Topics} can based on the idea that topics which are close according to their positions in the topic hierarchy are more similar than topics that have a larger distance. [12] have compared different similarity measures and have shown that for measuring the similarity between concepts in a hierarchical structured semantic network, like the ACM topic hierarchy, the following similarity measure yields the best results:

$$
sim_{Topic}(t_1, t_2) = \begin{cases} e^{-\alpha l} \cdot \dfrac{e^{\beta h} - e^{-\beta h}}{e^{\beta h} + e^{-\beta h}} & \text{if } t_1 \neq t_2, \\ 1 & \text{otherwise} \end{cases}
$$

Here l is the length of the shortest path between topic t_1 and t_2 in the graph spanned by the *SubTopic* relation. h is the level in the tree of the direct common subsumer from t_1 and t_2. $\alpha \geq 0$ and $\beta \geq 0$ are parameters scaling the contribution of shortest path length l and depth h, respectively. Based on their benchmark data set, the optimal values are: $\alpha = 0.2$, $\beta = 0.6$.

Example 4 (Expertise Matching). Consider the following SeRQL query, which asks for articles by Codd about the topic of *Database Management*:

```
construct {s} prop {val}
from
    {s} <rdf:type> {<swrc:Article>};
        prop {val};
        <swrc:isAbout> {<acm:ACMTopic/Information_Systems/Database_Management>};
        <swrc:author> {x}  <swrc:lastName> {"Codd"}
using namespace
    swrc = <!http://www.semanticweb.org/ontologies/swrc-onto-2001-12-11.daml#>,
    acm = <!http://daml.umbc.edu/ontologies/classification#>
```

The extracted subject of this query according to the ACM topic hierarchy is *Database Management*, i.e. an expert on that topic would likely be able to answer the query. The

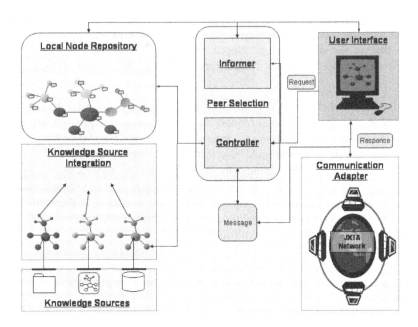

Fig. 2. Bibster System Architecture

peer selection tries to match this topic against the available expertise descriptions, and might for example find that the closest match according to the similarity function is the expert on the ACM topic *Information Systems* from Example 2. The query request would be forwarded to this peer, which would then return the corresponding query result. Furthermore, the peer might be linked to more peers who are experts on the requested topic and might decide to forward the request accordingly. The requests can thus be routed along the gradient of increasing similarity between the requested subject and expertise of the peers.

4   Peer Services in the Bibster Architecture

In this section we describe how the peer service model presented in the previous sections has been incorporated into the Bibster system architecture. Bibster[3] [2] is an application of the use of semantics in Peer-to-Peer systems, which is aimed at researchers that share bibliographic metadata. Figure 2 shows a high-level design of the architecture of a single node in the Peer-to-Peer system. We now present the individual components which reflect the service-oriented aspects.

The *Knowledge Sources* in the Bibster system are the sources of bibliographic metadata, such as BibTeX files stored locally in the file system of the user. The *Knowledge Source Integrator* is responsible for the extraction and integration of internal and external

---

[3] http://bibster.semanticweb.org/

knowledge sources into the Local Node Repository. This includes extracting expertise descriptions from these knowledge sources, which are advertised as part of the peer profile. The *Local Node Repository* provides the following functionality: (1) It serves as storage for and provide views on the available knowledge, (2) it supports operations on the available knowledge, such as query formulation and processing, and (3) it acts as a local registry for peer service advertisements as the basis for peer service selection. In the Bibster system, the Local Node Repository is based on the RDF-S Repository Sesame [13]. Sesame supports various query languages, among them SeRQL, RQL and RDQL, to formulate semantic queries against the Local Node Repository.

The task of the *Informer* is to proactively advertise the available knowledge of a peer and the corresponding services in the Peer-to-Peer network and to discover peers with knowledge and provided services that may be relevant for processing the user's requests. This is realized by sending advertisements about the expertise and service capabilities of a peer. In the Bibster system, the expertise descriptions contain a set of topics that the peer is an expert in and service descriptions as described in 2. Peers may accept – i.e. remember – these advertisements, thus creating a semantic link to the other peer. The *Controller* is the coordinating component controlling the process of handling and distributing service request. It receives requests generated from the user interface or from other peers. The controller initiates the processing of the requests locally and may decide to distribute it further according to the specification of the service request, according to the model of peer selection presented in the previous section. The *User Interface* user interface allows the user to easily create service requests, e.g. to formulate queries. The *Communication Adapter* is responsible for the network communication between peers. It serves as a transport layer for other parts of the system, for sending and forwarding service requests, such as queries. In the specific implementation of the Bibster system we use JXTA as the communication platform. Services are invoked using regular SOAP requests and responses which are encapsulated in JXTA messages.

5   Related Work

Various research projects address the use of semantics in Peer-to-Peer systems and have implemented running prototypes: For example, Edutella (*cf. eg.* [14]) is a Peer-to-Peer system based on the JXTA platform for the exchange of learning material. P-Grid [15] is a structured, yet fully-decentralized Peer-to-Peer system based on a virtual distributed search tree. It aims at providing load-balancing and fault-tolerance, assuming that peers fail frequently and are online with low probability. However, as these systems focus on sharing data, none of these systems explicitly address the explicit modeling of services. On the other hand, the idea of capability based matching has been long known and applied in the agent community[16]. Capability based matching has recently also been applied for matching of Web Services, e.g. [17], [11]. However, none of these approaches have considered specifics of Peer-to-Peer systems.

With respect to services on the bibliographic domain, the Open Archive Initiative (OAI) is an attempt to achieve technical interoperability among distributed archives. Its core protocol, the OAI Protocol for Metadata Harvesting (OAI-PMH), based on HTTP, XML and the Dublic Core metadata scheme. The OAI-PMH assumes a separation between data and service providers: A Data Provider maintains one or more repositories (web servers) that support the OAI-PMH as a means of exposing metadata. A Service Provider issues OAI-PMH requests to data providers and uses the metadata as a basis for building value-added services. The OAI-PMH makes no attempt for semantic descriptions of the capabilities of service providers in terms of services and content. In this sense, the semantic descriptions proposed in our paper can be seen as complementary to the OAI-PMH efforts.

[18] extends the idea of open archives with Peer-to-Peer concepts. There, data providers, i.e. research institutes, form a Peer-to-Peer network which supports distributed search over all the connected metadata repositories. In this architecture, there is no separation between data and service providers. This scenario is similar to our bibliographic Peer-to-Peer scenario, however, their system has not been implemented up to this point.

6 Conclusion

The combination of semantics-based Peer-to-Peer systems with semantic services holds great potential. In this paper we have presented a model for describing peers with their content and services in an integrated manner. Key benefits of our approach include (i) the decentralized discovery of resources in the Peer-to-Peer network based on semantic descriptions and (ii) efficient and scalable peer selection (also based on semantic descriptions). The peer service extensions to Bibster have partially been implemented at the time of writing.

There are many directions for future work: So far we have only considered simple, *i.e.* atomic, services. However, in a heteregeneous Peer-to-Peer systems, where peers provide varying capabilities, it will be interesting to explore how complex requests can be processed that require multiple to peers to fulfill a goal. For this composition of peer services we will need extensions of the service process model to capture the specifics of executing complex composite services in a Peer-to-Peer environment. Some work in the direction of process-based integration of information sources has been done in [19].

Acknowledgments. Research reported in this paper has been partially financed by the EU in the projects IST-2001-34103 SWAP (http://swap.semanticweb.org) and IST-2003-506826 SEKT (http://sekt.semanticweb.org) and by the Federal Ministry of Education and Research (BMBF) in the project Internetoekonomie-SESAM.

References

1. Berners-Lee, T., Hendler, J., Lassila, O.: The semantic web. Scientific American **2001** (2001)
2. Haase, P., et al.: Bibster - a semantics-based bibliographic peer-to-peer system. In: Proc. of the 3rd Int. Semantic Web Conference, Hiroshima, Japan, 2004. (2004)
3. Castano, A., Ferrara, S., Montanelli, S., Pagani, E., Rossi, G.: Ontology-addressable contents in p2p networks. In: Proceedings of the WWW'03 Workshop on Semantics in Peer-to-Peer and Grid Computing. (2003)
4. Nejdl, W., Wolf, B., Qu, C., Decker, S., Sintek, M., Naeve, A., Nilsson, M., Palmér, M., Risch, T.: Edutella: A P2P networking infrastructure based on rdf. In: Proceedings to the Eleventh International World Wide Web Conference. (2002)

5. Pinto, H., Tempich, C., S., Sure, Y.: DILIGENT: Towards a fine-grained methodology for DIstributed, Loosely-controlled and evolvInG Engingeering of oNTologies. In: Proceedings of the 16th European Conference on Artificial Intelligence (ECAI 2004), August 22nd - 27th, 2004, Valencia, Spain. (2004)
6. Maedche, A., Staab, S.: Services on the move - towards p2p-enabled semantic web services. In: Procs. 10th Int. Conf. On Information Technology and Travel and Tourism, ENTER, 2003. (2003)
7. Sycara, K., Paolucci, M., Ankolekar, A., Srinivasan, N.: Automated discovery, interaction and composition of semantic web services. Journal of Web Semantics **1** (2003) 27–46
8. Broekstra, J., Ehrig, M., Haase, P., Harmelen, F., Menken, M., Mika, P., Schnizler, B., Siebes, R.: Bibster - a semantics-based bibliographic peer-to-peer system. In: Proceedings of the WWW'04 Workshop on Semantics in Peer-to-Peer and Grid Computing. (2004)
9. Haase, P., Ehrig, M., Hotho, A., Schnizler, B.: Personalized information access in a bibliographic peer-to-peer system. In: Proceedings of the AAAI Workshop on Semantic Web Personalization, 2004. (2004)
10. Haase, P., Siebes, R., van Harmelen, F.: Peer selection in peer-to-peer networks with semantic topologies. In: International Conference on Semantics of a Networked World: Semantics for Grid Databases, 2004, Paris. (2004)
11. Paolucci, M., anf T. R. Payne, T.K., Sycara, K.: Semantic matching of web services capabilities. In: ISWC2002: Ist International Semantic Web Conference, Sardinia, Italy. Lecture Notes in Computer Science, Springer (2002)
12. Li, Y., Bandar, Z.A., McLean, D.: An approach for measuring semantic similarity between words using multiple information sources. Transactions on Knowledge and Data Engineering **15** (2003) 871–882
13. Broekstra, J., Kampman, A., van Harmelen, F.: Sesame: An architecture for storing and querying rdf data and schema information (2001)
14. Nejdl, W., et al.: Super-peer-based routing and clustering strategies for rdf-based peer-to-peer networks. In: Proceedings of the Twelfth International World Wide Web Conference (WWW 2003), Budapest, Hungary (2003)
15. Aberer, K., Mauroux, P.C., Datta, A., Despotovic, Z., Hauswirth, M., Punceva, M., Schmidt, R.: P-Grid: a self-organizing structured p2p system. ACM SIGMOD Record **32** (2003) 29–33
16. Sycara, K., Decker, K., Williamson, M.: Middle-agents for the internet. In: Proceedings of IJCAI-97. (1997)
17. Li, L., Horrocks, I.: A software framework for matchmaking based on semantic web technology. In: Proceedings of the Twelfth International World Wide Web Conference (WWW 2003), ACM (2003) 331–339
18. Ahlborn, B., Nejdl, W., Siberski, W.: OAI-P2P: A peer-to-peer network for open archives. In: Workshop on Distributed Computing Architectures for Digital Libraries - ICPP2002. (2002)
19. Agarwal, S., Haase, P.: Process-based integration of heterogeneous information sources. In: Proceedings of the GI-Workshop Semantische Technologien fuer Informationsportale, Ulm, Germany, 2004. To appear. (2004)

Towards Cross-Domain Security Properties Supported by Ontologies

York Sure[1] and Jochen Haller[2]

[1] Institute AIFB, University of Karlsruhe
76128 Karlsruhe, Germany
sure@aifb.uni-karlsruhe.de
[2] SAP Research
Vincenz-Priessnitz-Str. 1, 76131 Karlsruhe, Germany
jochen.haller@sap.com

Abstract. Security is considered as a major driver for the success of E-Business, especially in a business-to-business environment. Current research activities in this area are conducted in European Union funded research projects, such as TrustCoM putting an emphasis on the collaborative aspects of business processes across administrative and trust domains. With respect to the tendency of business partners to set up their own security islands, e.g. based on isolated Public Key Infrastructures (PKIs), this development introduces a contradiction for collaborative business process. Clearly expressed process related security requirements across domains can not be met by domain specific security infrastructures. This contribution explores the possibility to bridge the identified gap using semantic relationships contributed by ontologies.

1 Introduction

1.1 Motivation

Current research in European Union funded research projects is focussing on electronic business (e-business) in a business-to-business (B2B) setting. B2B is perceived in terms of collaborating organizations, so called virtual organizations (VOs) being dynamically-evolving virtual business entities. In a virtual organization different member entities, such as companies, individuals or government departments, form a construct where the participating entities pool resources, information and knowledge in order to achieve common objectives. These objectives cannot be met by one or a subset of members alone. It is envisioned that such VOs are self-managed spanning different administrative domains enabling the on-demand creation of networks of collaborative business processes. In B2B scenarios, security is clearly stated as a major requirement for the success and acceptance of business processes being enacted across multiple administrative domains [1]. A company participating in a VO still considers its business processes as assets which must not be exposed to the outside world in an uncontrolled manner. The outside world is hereby seen as everything outside the company's administrative domain, e.g. the company intranet. Research in the area of secure business process enactment in

C. Bussler et al. (Eds.): WISE 2004 Workshops, LNCS 3307, pp. 58–69, 2004.

VOs is for instance conducted in the TrustCoM[1] project. Security infrastructures as well as the security mechanisms have to meet VO security requirements across the multiple administrative domains spanned by the business processes. Such infrastructures are currently unavailable since security infrastructures are systematically deployed in a domain specific fashion. Security infrastructures, even on multiple layers ranging from network to application layer, were not meant to interact or collaborate across domains. Popular examples are e.g. firewalls on the network layer, protecting per definition everything outside a pre-set domain [2], considering everything outside as "evil" or Public Key Infrastructures (PKIs) [3], already offering configuration mechanisms for interaction and trust across domains. But in the case of PKIs, these are typically deployed only to be used in one domain being unaware of other PKIs, specifically unaware of what is certified and how the certification is conducted. Especially larger enterprises are frequently running an own PKI which is only used company internally. "Introducing" a PKI to another, a process commonly called cross-certification, requires a certain amount of administrative effort, meaning in terms of VOs a hindrance in the required dynamic, on demand security support for collaborative business processes.

In summary, security infrastructures are currently rather isolated, administrative islands of security domains. Since already running domain specific security infrastructures were in most cases expensive to deploy, this contribution explores an approach to connect such existing set-ups rather than entirely replacing running systems. The approach taken is to provide an additional semantic layer on top of existing security infrastructures, particularly using the concept of ontologies for describing declaratively the security properties, thus enabling an automatic approach for cross-domain certification.

1.2 Outline

Section 2 introduces the basic concepts and technologies of currently existing domain specific security set-ups. Further on in Section 3 a concrete example, namely a Virtual Organization in the setting of an aerospace collaborative engineering, is described to illustrate the practical relevance. Section 4 introduces the notion of ontology and presents how ontologies can be used to declaratively describe security properties. The paper concludes with related work in Section 5 and an overall conclusion in Section 6.

2 Current Domain Specific Security Set-Ups

Entities participating in a virtual organization (VO) are in first instance pursuing their own objectives, particularly their business interest. A participating entity therefore manages its own IT infrastructure, including security related systems, in its own administrative domain. When coming together in a VO context, they start a collaboration in order to achieve a common goal. Section 3 will provide a tangible example of this arrangement. This is also the start of an effort to inter-connect heterogeneous IT systems owned by different entities and most importantly managed and administered following domain

---

[1] http://www.eu-trustcom.com

specific policies. An approach published in [4] similar to the one described in this contribution, focussing on harmonizing policies across domains, supports the adopted solution. The described heterogeneity is one of the gravest hindrances in achieving proactive
and automated secure collaboration across domains. Before introducing the envisioned
solution by adding a semantic layer spanning domain specific security set-ups, a target example for later solution validation is prepared. Public key infrastructures (PKI)
are popular security infrastructures offering mainly authentication, digital signature and
asymmetric encryption for users in domains where their authority is respected. PKIs are
typically run in a specific domain providing services only for this domain, obtruding
themselves as dedicated examples since the provided services are essential for stated
secure collaboration.

A PKI is a representative example in current times for the frequently mentioned term
"domain specific security set-up". PKI is an abbreviation for Public Key Infrastructure.
The term already mentions the foundation of a PKI quite often lying in asymmetric or
public key cryptography. But public key cryptography is not essential, a PKI is rather a
infrastructure based on a trusted third party (TTP) vouching and certifying for identities
of principals, e.g. employees in a company, by binding public keys to principals. A PKI
consists in simplified terms of the following components:

- a root of trust, the topmost certification authority (CA)
- a sequence of CAs inheriting trust from the root along a certification path
- certificates being the formal expression of trust assigned to a principal containing
  evidence of the issuing CA
- principals, the entities to whom certificates are assigned to

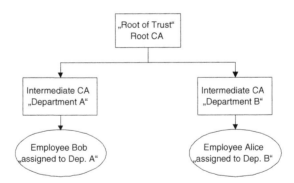

Fig. 1. simplified PKI structure

A CAs duty, the issuing of certificates is also based on public key cryptography. A CA
owns a private/public key pair. Certification involves digital signature using the private
key. The public key being embedded in a digital certificate, is attached as evidence for
later signature verification to issued certificates. Since the root of trust has to be protected

as the component of utmost criticality, direct issuing of certificates to principals is the task of one or more CAs inheriting trust from the root. Inheriting is also based on digital certificates issued to them from the root. An inheriting CA's certificate also contains certificate information from the sequence of issuing CAs leading to the formation of a so-called certification path or chain. This high-level description of a PKI is not very detailed, nor exhaustive, but sufficient for the understanding of the following sections. More detailed information can be acquired at [5].

It was already mentioned that PKIs are frequently deployed by larger companies, mainly for authentication purposes. Such an installation then encompasses several complex computer systems assigned to different company intranet network segments and being tied into other integral IT parts such as corporate directories, e.g. based on LDAP. Directories are used to store the user's certificates containing the public key among other properties. The isolated management of PKIs does not necessarily imply that a PKI has to be unaware of another. Mechanisms like cross-certification exists where an CA C in a PKI P is able to sign a CA D's certificate being part of another PKI structure O. Cross-certification may be bi- or unidirectional, but the cross-certifying CA C is expressing a certain trust in the PKI hierarchy O. In reality, this mechanism is rarely used on a operational level among companies, since it is tedious to manage, involving a lot of careful negotiation on an inter-domain level and enforcing their outcome on an IT level in authorisations and access control [6].

Having mentioned certificates frequently, it is now time for a closer look on their structure. Certificates bind properties to principals, generally users. A common standard for digital certificates is X.509 [7]. A sample certificate structure in text form would look like the following:

```
* Certificate
      o Version
      o Serial Number
      o Algorithm ID
      o Issuer
      o Validity
             + Not Before
             + Not After

      o Subject
      o Subject Public Key Info
             + Public Key Algorithm
             + Subject Public Key
      o Issuer Unique Identifier
      o Subject Unique Identifier
      o Basic Constraints
      o Extensions
             + ...
* Certificate Signature Algorithm
* Certificate Signature
```

Basically, it contains information about

- the issuing CA
- the certification path
- the time period of validity
- the principal, the subject to whom it was issued
- the certificate's basic constraints enumerating its intended usage, such as authentication, encryption and (digital) signature

3   A B2B Example in a Virtual Organization Set-Up

Virtual Organizations are considered as an important focus in recent European research conducted in the E-Business area. VOs are perceived as a way to model dynamically collaborating and rapidly evolving B2B scenarios. This section intends to commence a real-life example for domain-specific security setup-ups based on a PKI which inherently part of most existing VOs. More concretely, the chosen example is situated in an aerospace collaborative engineering context. Whenever a tender for manufacturing a new plane is announced, one organization or company alone is not able to perform all required tasks. The actors of the VO encompass all organizations dynamically, as fast as possible joining together to meet the tender's requirements. Figure 2 depicts a snapshot of the overall VO context, the actors meeting the immediate first objective of a plane design, other objectives encompass the actual manufacturing and maintenance which are not considered here.

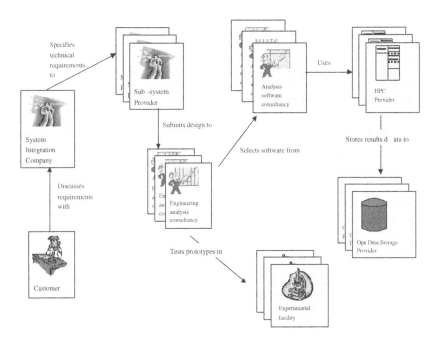

Fig. 2. VO example - collaborative engineering design (Source: TrustCoM project)

All depicted organizations are in general independent organizations and companies having their own agendas and are protecting their assets. For the latter, domain specific security set-ups such as PKIs are in place which have to interact in the dynamically evolving VO context [8]. In the following approach, the example focusses on the interaction of two partners, the Analysis Software Company and the High Performance Computing provider (HPC), in the following called Organizations A and B. All other interaction involving three and more partners can be traced back to this basic example. We assume two employees, Smith working for A and Anderson working for B. A runs a CA A issuing certificates to its employees and B runs CA B.

Design and later manufacturing of planes is imposing a complex set of security requirements since the market competition is high or the tender issuer, e.g. the military already introduces these from the beginning. In the following, two simple security requirements are modeled:

- trust between A and B based on a list of trusted CA certificates
- confidentiality, based on the basic constraint encryption

Trust criteria are hereby rather simplified and static, this contribution doesn't intend to enter the highly speculative and vast arena of defining trust. Each organizations manages a list of CAs it trusts, if A trusts B this is represented by entering the certificate of CA B to A's list. Confidentiality means that information is only accessible to principals to whom it is intended to be accessible. A typical example is the set up of a confidential channel e.g. by the means of asymmetric cryptography using certificates (and corresponding private keys). The intended usage "Encryption" has therefore to be specified in the certificate's basic constraints field. In a real-life but more complex scenario, mechanisms like SSL would be used for confidential channels, using less resource consuming symmetric encryption for bulk data.

In summary, this chapter described a process beginning with trust establishment based on information offered by the respective domain specific PKIs. The process then continues asserting trust to meet e.g. business objectives. How this will be done, by modeling an ontology, will be described in the following chapter. In the end, the business objective is met by finally exploiting trust in conducting collaborative business.

The simplified basic example is now depicted in Figure 3. Typical use case for VOs is to establish a collaborative business process between employees, here coming from the organizations Orga A and Orga B. Both organizations have specified different security properties which not necessarily match to each other. We will show in the following section how to use an ontology to (i) describe both security properties declaratively and (ii) enable the automatic derivation of the fact whether employee Smith from Orga A is allowed to perform a collaborative business process with employee Anderson from Orga B.

4 Ontology for Domain-Specific Security Setups

4.1 Introduction to Ontologies

In recent years ontologies have become a topic of interest in computer science. There are different 'definitions' in the literature of what an ontology should be, the most prominent being published by Tom Gruber [9]: *"An ontology is an explicit specification of a conceptualization. The term is borrowed from philosophy, where an Ontology is a systematic account of Existence. For AI systems, what 'exists' is that which can be represented."*

A conceptualization refers to an abstract model of some phenomenon in the world by identifying the relevant concept of that phenomenon. Explicit means that the types

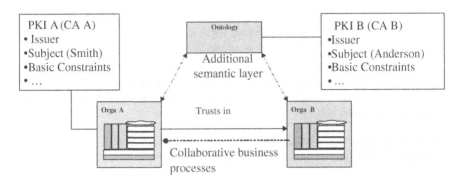

Fig. 3. Adding a semantic layer

of concepts used and the constraints on their use are explicitly defined. This definition is often extended by three additional conditions: *"An ontology is an explicit, formal specification of a shared conceptualization of a domain of interest."* Formal refers to the fact that the ontology should be machine readable (which excludes for instance natural language). Shared reflects the notion that an ontology captures consensual knowledge, that is, it is not private to some individual, but accepted as a group. The reference to a domain of interest indicates that for domain ontologies one is not interested in modelling the whole world, but rather in modelling just the parts which are relevant to the task at hand. Methods and tools already exist to support engineering of ontologies (e.g. [10, 11]).

The informed reader might be aware that within the layered W3C[2] Semantic Web language stack currently the "logic" layer on top of the recommendation OWL [12] is being addressed. Thus, there might be a feasible solution to combine OWL with rules, but this is work to be done in future. Therefore we rely in the following example on F-Logic as representation language (*cf.* [13]), basically due to the fact that we want to model rules as mechanism for declaratively specifying business logic.

We will now introduce subsequently the building blocks of an example security ontology, namely concepts, relations, instances and rules. Such an ontology reflects the domain specific entities and allows for description of security logic supporting business processes in form of rules. Such an ontology enables users to declaratively describe their domain-specific security properties in a machine processable manner leading to improved automation. Thus, by using an inference engine such as Ontobroker [14] these security properties can be applied during runtime on the fly.

4.2   Concepts and Relations

Goal of this and the following subsections is to show the feasibility of formalizing the previously mentioned example scenario (see Figure 3). Please note that we will not describe all concepts and relationships etc., but rather the most relevant ones. Before we

---
[2] http://www.w3c.org/

introduce the most relevant concepts we declare two namespaces, one for XML Schema and one as a default namespace.

```
ontons:xsd="http://www.w3.org/2001/XMLSchema"
ontons="http://x.y.z"
```

Core concept is a `Certificate` according to the X.509 standard (see Section 2) which has certain properties. These properties are modelled on the one hand as relations such as `version` or `serial Number` who have XML Schema datatypes such as `STRING` as range, and on the other hand as relations such as `issuer` who have another concept such as `Certification Authority` as range.

```
#Certificate[#version=>>xsd#STRING;
    #serial_Number=>>xsd#STRING;
    #algorithm_ID=>>xsd#STRING;
    #issuer=>>#Certification_Authority;
    #validity_not_before=>>xsd#STRING;
    #validity_not_after=>>xsd#STRING;
    #subject=>>#Principal;
    #basic_constraints=>>#Basic_Constraints].
```

A `Certification Authority` typically is `managed` by an `Organization`. The concept `Principal` is typically be part of a role hierarchy which we will not elaborate on here. We will show later in the next section what kind of `Basic Constraints` exist.

```
#Certification_Authority[#has_X500_name=>>xsd#STRING;
    #is_managed_by=>>#Organization].

#Principal[#has_X500_name=>>xsd#STRING].

#Basic_Constraints.
```

Each `Organization` typically has a list of `Trusted Root Certificates` which makes explicit in which `Certification Authority` an organization `trusts in`.

```
#Organization[#employs=>>#Employee;
    #manages=>>#Certification_Authority;
    #has_list_of=>>#Trusted_Root_Certificates].

#Trusted_Root_Certificates[#has_X500_name=>>xsd#STRING;
    #trusts_in=>>#Certification_Authority].
```

Central for business activities are `Employees` who `work for` an `Organization` and have the role of a `Principal`. Each time they want to perform a `Task` which has a certain level of `confidentiality` with another partner in the VO (such as a collaborative business task), they will need a `Certificate`.

```
#Employee[#works_for=>>#Organization;
    #has_role=>>#Principal;
    #owns_certificate=>>Certificate;
    #performs=>>#Task].

#Task[#involves=>>Employee;
    #confidentiality=>>xsd#BOOLEAN].
```

4.3   Exemplary Instances

The ontology provides a schema for general purposes which can be reused by different applications. We now instantiate the given ontology e.g. with two organizations Orga A and Orga B, two employees Smith and Anderson who at the same time play the role of being a specific Principal, e.g. Principal A.

```
#Orga_A:#Organization.
#Orga_B:#Organization.

#Smith:#Employee[#works_for->>#Orga_A;
    #has_role->>#Principal_A;
    #performs->>#Business_Task_1].
#Anderson:#Employee[#works_for->>#Orga_B;
    #has_role->>#Principal_B].

#Principal_A:#Principal.
#Principal_B:#Principal.
```

Each employee owns a specific Certificate, both having different basic constraints such as Authentication, Encryption and Signature.

```
#Certificate_A:#Certificate[#subject->>#Principal_A;
    #basic_constraints->>#Authentication;
    #basic_constraints->>#Encryption;
    #basic_constraints->>#Signature].
#Certificate_B:#Certificate[#subject->>#Principal_B;
    #basic_constraints->>#Authentication;
    #basic_constraints->>#Encryption].

#Encryption:#Basic_Constraints.
#Authentication:#Basic_Constraints.
#Signature:#Basic_Constraints.
```

CA A is a specific Certification Authority which is managed by the organization Orga A who has a specific list of Trusted Root Certificates, namely TRC A. Furthermore, Orga A trusts himself and Orga B, but Orga B only trusts himself (and not yet or not in general Orga A).

```
#CA_A:#Certification_Authority[#is_managed_by->>#Orga_A].
#CA_B:#Certification_Authority[#is_managed_by->>#Orga_B].

#Orga_A[#has_list_of->>#TRC_A].

#TRC_A:#Trusted_Root_Certificates[#trusts_in->>#CA_A;
    #trusts_in->>#CA_B].
#TRC_B:#Trusted_Root_Certificates[#trusts_in->>#CA_B].
```

Last, but not least, the employee Anderson is involved in a specific business task, namely Business Task 1.

```
#Business_Task_1:#Task[#involves->>#Anderson].
```

4.4   Rules

To describe business logic declaratively we use so-called rules. Simple rules e.g. allow for a more complete knowledge, e.g. saying that *if "X employs Y" then "Y works for X" and vice versa.*

```
FORALL X,Y
    X[#employs->>Y] <-> Y[#works_for->>X].
```

A more complex rule is the following one which basically says *if "X is a specific employee who has the role of being a specific Principal Y" and "Y is a specific Certificate who has as subject the specific Principal Y" then "the specific employee X owns the specific certificate Y"*. Thus, this rule links different entities playing a role in the security properties, namely employees, principals and certificates.

```
FORALL X,Y,Z
    X[#owns_certificate->>Y]
    <-
    X:#Employee[#has_role->>Z:#Principal] AND
    Y:#Certificate[#subject->>Z].
```

Finally, the following rule allows us to derive the fact whether an employee is able to perform a security-enabled task with another employee coming from a different organization. The rule itself reads similar to the previous one.

```
FORALL X
    X[#confidentiality->>"true"]
    <-
    EXISTS A,B,C,D,F,G,H,I
    A:#Employee[#works_for->>B:#Organization] AND
    A[#owns_certificate->>C:#Certificate] AND
    B[#has_list_of->>D:#Trusted_Root_Certificates] AND
    D[#trusts_in->>F:#Certification_Authority] AND
    F[#is_managed_by->>G:#Organization] AND
    H:#Employee[#works_for->>G] AND
    H[#owns_certificate->>I:#Certificate] AND
    C[#basic_constraints->>#Encryption] AND
    I[#basic_constraints->>#Encryption] AND
    X:#Task[#involves->>A] AND
    X[#involves->>H].
```

To sum up, in a practical setting each organization makes its security properties explicitly available as an ontology. Additional rules make existing knowledge more complete and allow for linking of existing security properties in a previously unforseen manner to support the dynamic environment of VOs.

As an afterthought, the presented work did not elaborate on the topic of deployment yet, who will host the ontology. It would be possible that the ontology is run and maintained, from a security perspective, by a trusted third party or each organisation runs its own instance. The latter would make the administration process regarding updates and corrections more difficult.

5 Related Work

Related work on the semantic layer as well as supporting technologies and mechanisms is conducted on different layers in similar fields, but not quite related to integrating domain specific security set-ups in B2B scenarios. KaOS [4] for instance is looking in the field of policy and domain services and how these may be connected on the semantic layer across domains. In the area of trust management and security, approaches based on a particular domain specific and authoritative PKI called SPKI/SDSI [3] using different forms of mediation are taken [15][16]. This work is still below the semantic layer and would still need a semantic mapping of expressed domain specific security properties. In [17], similar work using properties stored in directory structures, specifically LDAP, was conducted. The work is therefore emphasizing on pure property mapping, but not relying on embedding these on a domain specific security set-up such as a PKI. Research from a trust perspective in VOs and similar concepts, even on logic level, is conducted in [18]. This work is laying a foundation for security and trust requirements towards the semantic layer. On the level of supporting technologies, particularly the (web) service layer, adding semantics to services is a recent research topic [19]. Such development will influence the standardization conducted in the WS-I gremium, being responsible for most security related web service (WS-) standards as will, such as WS-Security, WS-Trust, WS-Federation or WS-(Secure)Conversation. Mentioned standardization can not be considered mature at this stage, not all standards are yet fully specified. On a deeper technological level, protocols like SAML which is standardized in the OASIS body, may be used to provide interoperability of security related statements, such as assertions. The presented semantic solution would be supported on the transport layer by such mechanisms.

6   Conclusion

To conclude, we demonstrated the feasibility of using the semantic layer namely an ontology to span administrative domains. The emphasis was put on domain specific security properties which should be known, understood and employed to meet security requirements which extend a domain horizon and become cross-domain properties. The approach was successfully exercised in a concrete example, a VO context in collaborative engineering. However, the approach was not without hurdles. In the security community especially in trust management, research is conducted up to a service layer – but not further. Solutions requiring property mapping and translation are expected from the semantic layer – and rightfully though. The introduced example validated this expectation. But what is not considered in such expectations is the administrative effort to initialize the required ontology until it is able to perform its duties. This work raised interesting questions for future work, e.g. how easy will it be, to port an ontology "instance" like the one derived here and port it to another setting or how much of the rule set and other concepts can be re-used? How much effort is it in average to link a new organization to an existing VO? We expect further work in this area especially since the upper layers of the Semantic Web pyramid which are to be solved include proof and trust.

Acknowledgments. Research reported in this paper has been partially financed by the EU in the IST projects TrustCoM (IST-2003-01945)[3] and SEKT (IST-2003-506826)[4]. We would like to thank our colleagues for fruitful discussions.

---

[3] http://www.eu-trustcom.com/
[4] http://sekt.semanticweb.org

References

1. Herbert, J.: Introducing security to the small business enterprise. GIAC (2003)
2. Robinson, P., Haller, J.: Revisiting the firewall abolition act. HICCS-36 (2002)
3. SPKI-WorkingGroup: SPKI/SDSI. IETF RFC 2692 and 2693 (1996) available at http://theworld.com/ cme/html/spki.html#1-SPKI/SDSI.
4. Uszok, A., Bradshaw, J., Jeffers, R., Suri, N., Hayes, P., Breedy, M., Bunch, L., Johnson, M., Kulkarni, S., Lott, J.: KAoS policy and domain services: Toward a description-logic approach to policy representation, deconfliction, and enforcement. Workshop on Web Services and Agent-based Engineering (2003)
5. Gutman, P.: Everything you never wanted to know about pki but were forced to find out. (2001) available at http://www.cs.auckland.ac.nz/ pgut001/pubs/pkitutorial.pdf.
6. Turnbull, J.: Cross-certification and pki policy networking. Entrust (2000)
7. Brickley, D., Guha, R.V.: X.509. IETF RFC 2459 (2004) available at http://www.ietf.org/html.charters/pkix-charter.html.
8. Strader, T., Lin, F., Shaw, M.: Information structure for electronic virtual organization management, decision support systems. (1998) 75–94
9. Gruber, T.: Towards principles for the design of ontologies used for knowledge sharing. International Journal of Human-Computer Studies **43** (1995)
10. Sure, Y., Angele, J., Staab, S.: OntoEdit: Multifaceted inferencing for ontology engineering. Journal on Data Semantics **LNCS** (2003) 128–152
11. Pinto, H., Tempich, C., Staab, S., Sure, Y.: DILIGENT: Towards a fine-grained methodology for DIstributed, Loosely-controlled and evolvInG Engineering of oNTologies. In: Proceedings of the 16th European Conference on Artificial Intelligence (ECAI 2004), August 22nd - 27th, 2004, Valencia, Spain. (2004)
12. Smith, M.K., Welty, C., McGuinness, D.: OWL Web Ontology Language Guide (2004) W3C Recommendation 10 February 2004, available at http://www.w3.org/TR/owl-guide/.
13. Kifer, M., Lausen, G., Wu, J.: Logical foundations of object-oriented and frame-based languages. Journal of the ACM **42** (1995) 741–843
14. Decker, S., Erdmann, M., Fensel, D., Studer, R. In: Ontobroker: Ontology Based Access to Distributed and Semi-Structured Information. Kluwer Academic Publisher (1999) 351–369
15. Biskup, J., Karabulut, Y.: A hybrid pki model with an application for secure mediation. 16th Annual IFIP WG 11.3 Working Conference on Data and Application Security (2002) 271–282
16. Karabulut, Y.: Towards a next-generation trust management infrastructure for open computing systems. SPPC: Workshop on Security and Privacy in Pervasive Computing (2004)
17. Ahmedi, L., Marron, P.J., Lausen, G.: Ldap-based ontology for information integration. 9. Fachtagung Datenbanksysteme in Buero, Technik und Wissenschaft (2001)
18. Josang, A.: Logic for uncertain probabilities. International Journal of Uncertainty, Fuzziness and Knowledge-Based Systems (2001) 279–311 Available at: http://security.dstc.edu.au/papers/logunprob.pdf.
19. McIlraith, S.A., Son, T.C., Zeng, H.: Semantic web services. IEEE Intelligent Systems **16** (2001) 46–53

Short Papers

Open Knowledge Exchange for Workforce Development

Peter A. Creticos[1] and Jian Qin[2]

[1]Institute for Work and the Economy, c/o Center for Governmental Studies,
Northern Illinois University,
DeKalb, IL 60115 USA
creticos@workandeconomy.org
[2]School of Information Sciences, 4-187 Center for Science & Technology, Syracuse University,
Syracuse, NY 13244 USA
jqin@syr.edu

Abstract. A knowledge exchange platform, or Open Knowledge Exchange, (OKE) is an effective means for sharing and re-using knowledge among all members under the workforce development umbrella in the United States. The OKE is a necessary step in shaping and pushing forward the evolution of a workforce development system. The authors are the principals for a pilot OKE initiative that includes 1) a workforce ontology that serves as a semantic framework connecting various disciplines, organizations and programs engaged in workforce development; 2) a knowledge base; and 3) user interfaces, and tools and templates for automatic knowledge capture. The OKE, the project will lead to the development of a comprehensive OKE and associated products supporting interoperable workforce information systems.

1 Introduction

Public financing of workforce development in the United States has evolved from a handful initiatives beginning in 1933 into a broad array of services and programs supported by a wide range of policies, practices and points of view and performed by a diverse set of public agencies, educational institutions, not-for-profit intermediaries, private providers and employers. The component functions include employment and training, education, economic development, human resources management, community development, human services, disability services, veterans' services, labor policy and immigrant services. Each is supported by its own theories, policies, practices, performance goals and vocabularies, adding significant complexity to the meaning and management of "workforce development".

Domestic economic realities and global competition require that workforce development be pulled together into a coherent system. These have prompted policy makers and practitioners at all levels to push for greater integration and collaboration across all institutions and programs. By in large, these efforts have floundered. Although the problems appear rooted in conflicts of laws, regulations, mission, and performance management structures, a deeper analysis suggests that the issues are more systemic: different assumptions about the nature of workforce-related problems,

C. Bussler et al. (Eds.): WISE 2004 Workshops, LNCS 3307, pp. 73–81, 2004.
© Springer-Verlag Berlin Heidelberg 2004

different cultures, different logical frameworks and theories, different processes and solutions and different vocabularies.

The advent of the World Wide Web and the apparent ease by which people are able to exchange information on a myriad of topics have contributed to the expectation that knowledge can easily be shared and re-used. Therefore, it is ironic that an abundance of web sites serving practitioners and policy-makers in workforce development have not bridged professional and organizational isolation. More important, neither job seekers nor businesses feel well served by the workforce system. The tendencies towards specialization and targeted strategies and growing fragmentation in funding contribute to the shared belief that available resources are increasingly outpaced by the occurrence of new problems. Although there are other factors, the experiences of other disciplines suggest that a common ontology is may transcend organizational cultures and support the transfer and re-use of knowledge from one organization to another.

Knowledge is socially produced and reproduced: the processes by which it is manipulated (generated, mobilized, applied) are constrained by the social and cultural contexts in which it is embedded [1]. Research shows that knowledge and culture are inextricably linked in organizations. It recognizes the role of organizational culture - a set of tacit assumptions about how the world is and ought to be that a group of people share and that determines their perceptions, thoughts, feelings, and to some extent their overt behavior - as a major barrier to leveraging knowledge [2]. Consequently, the solution for making tacit knowledge held by individuals within an organization explicit and communicable to those in other organizations requires a clear explication of the differences and similarities in value systems, a shared vocabulary, and the selection of appropriate knowledge transfer modes [1]. Even seemingly explicit knowledge such as that contained in a document is linked inextricably to a set of culturally based tacit understandings about the problems and range of appropriate solutions addressed in the document. Consequently, a reader who does not share the same values as the author may dismiss the document as irrelevant or misinterpret the findings and apply them in a way that is inappropriate.

There are difficult challenges in explicating the tacit knowledge in workforce development. Value systems differ by public agency, by community and by intermediary. Vocabularies are comprised of many common terms having subtle, but significant differences in meaning. Methods for transferring knowledge vary by technology, financial resources and organizational culture. However, despite these differences, practitioners and policymakers across a broad range of disciplines identify themselves as members of the workforce development field and consider that field to be a system. There clearly is a sense within the field that much more can be achieved were it not for the enormous difficulties encountered in exchanging and reusing knowledge.

2   The Initiative

We developed a digital knowledge center and early prototype ontology for workforce development beginning early 2001. Development of this early prototype was designed as a proof of concept demonstration and was structured initially on a simple quality management hierarchy. The knowledge center brings together training resources, digital library functions, and peer-to-peer sharing in order to promote knowledge reuse and advancement. Three web portals are in operation currently: one gives special emphasis to promising practices; another covers the gamut of workforce issues with special attention given to the needs of workforce professional; the third is supported by the State of Colorado and serves job seekers and employers as well as workforce professionals. A mission of all three portals is to drive continuous improvement in the workforce development system.

The process of early ontology development involved experts from several communities: workforce administrators and frontline staff from state and local workforce systems and from the Employment and Training Administration at the U.S. Department of Labor (DOL/ETA), metadata and ontology experts from Syracuse University and other academic institutions, system developers from the corporate world, and workforce development researchers from Northern Illinois University and the Institute for Work and the Economy. Significant challenges were encountered while reaching common understandings on many issues and terms. There were debates on the method for constructing the knowledge structure, on the terms used to represent concepts, on the relationships among various concepts, and on implementation of the knowledge structure so as to accommodate browsing, searching, and navigation.

The project team adopted a contextual design approach [3] [4] in which data addressing both the knowledge structure of workforce development and the system to be built upon that knowledge structure were collected through face-to-face meetings, teleconferences, e-mails, virtual team rooms, mockup interfaces and prototypes. The team distributed the draft conceptual model to content experts. It later was iteratively revised and tested. The first version of this ontology-based system was launched in April 2001. It has been serving since as a framework for capturing and meta-tagging knowledge for the three portals.

3 The Open Knowledge Exchange for Workforce Development

After two years' trial, we redesigned the ontology and developed a web-based ontology system (Figure 1). The new version is intended as an Open Knowledge Exchange (OKE) that will integrate and map semantics, including both knowledge structures and vocabularies, used by communities of workforce development practice, which will become the semantic foundation for all workforce development functions.

We established four outcomes for a comprehensive OKE:

- A workforce ontology that contains a hierarchy of concept classes with their properties and relationships;
- A knowledge base that stores the classes, properties, relationships, instances, and rules;
- User interfaces for collaborative ontology management and knowledge exchange applications; and
- Tools for automatic knowledge capture for ontology development and automatic document processing.

Based on this larger view, we constructed a working prototype of the OKE supporting a discrete range of user groups within the workforce development system. The ontology contains seven main classes (see Figure 1), each of which may have subclasses and a set of properties. All except class *Taxonomy* are entities involved in workforce development. Since definitions for class properties are essentially a vocabulary issue, we created the *Taxonomy* class as a vocabulary control to provide preferred terms as well as references to related and synonymous terms.

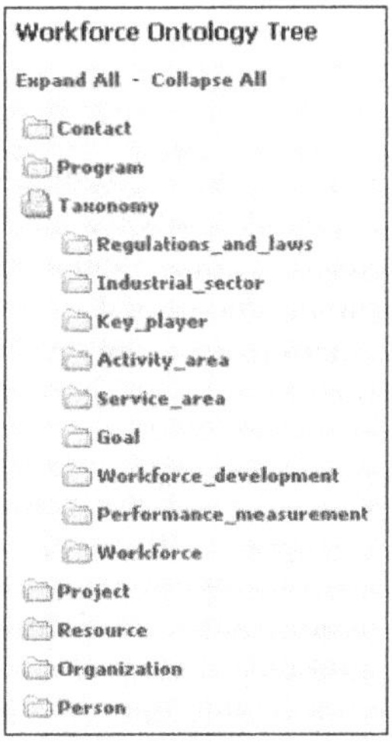

Workforce Ontology Tree

Expand All - Collapse All

📂 Contact
📂 Program
📂 Taxonomy
    📂 Regulations_and_laws
    📂 Industrial_sector
    📂 Key_player
    📂 Activity_area
    📂 Service_area
    📂 Goal
    📂 Workforce_development
    📂 Performance_measurement
    📂 Workforce
📂 Project
📂 Resource
📂 Organization
📂 Person

Fig. 1. The main classes in the OKE ontology

The core element of the OKE is an ontology that is "an explicit specification of … (a) … shared conceptualization" [5] of workforce development and aimed at facilitating communication between people and organizations and interoperability between information systems [1]. Such a specification defines "workforce system" and provides the foundation for its growth and evolution by enabling policymakers and practitioners to learn and build from the accumulated knowledge and experiences of all. It provides detailed, accurate, consistent, sound and meaningful distinctions among concepts and words used within workforce development. Such distinctions are required to support effective communication among constituents of workforce development and decision-making through effective information search and retrieval, knowledge management, and intelligent databases. Specifically, this ontology will support knowledge exchange processes in three areas: knowledge generation, knowledge mobilization and knowledge application [1].

Based on the ontology, we developed two modules for representing and organizing information about promising practices and workforce development resources. Figure 2 (below) is a screenshot from the promising practices module, in which instances are organized by the same structure as that in the ontology and the terms defined in the *Taxonomy* class are used in each record to categorize the data from promising practice instances. The workforce resource module uses the similar structure and representation.

One major advantage of the ontology is that the metadata and even the content can adopt a consistent set of elements as the semantic markup and use a standard vocabulary for the indexing, where the vocabulary is controlled by mapping the preferred terms to related and synonymous terms. As it has been proven in information retrieval research, such a combination of controlled vocabulary and free-text terms allows a higher level of performance in information retrieval [6]. The ontology also provides a uniform interface for the search and browsing functions as shown in the screenshots. This will provide users with a familiar environment as they navigate between modules.

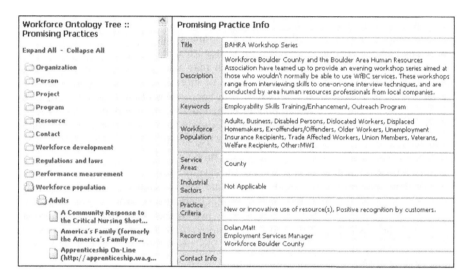

Fig. 2. The Promising Practices module: The left column is the ontology tree and records are displayed under each class; the right column is the record detail, which follows the structure and vocabulary from the ontology

4   Technical Processes in Developing the OKE

Building a comprehensive OKE system is a large-scale research and development activity. We have learned that both a well-planned process and effective data collection methods are required to ensure the validity and usability of the ontology. We also learned that a comprehensive ontology cannot be developed *ad hoc*. The effort must be organized by a strategy that is sensitive to the diversity of the workforce development community. Therefore, the process of building the OKE may be divided into three areas of effort: collection of data and terminologies, knowledge modeling, and development of systems and tools.

The primary sources of terminology used in the development of the preliminary ontology are workforce documents produced or published by government agencies, educational and research institutions, and workforce intermediaries and the recorded vocabularies used in daily communications by workforce practitioners that may not be reflected in formal documents. These recorded vocabularies are captured through internal written communications and expert panels. The main concept classes were based on analyses of these sources. We also created a small number of mappings between the preferred terms for a concept and the free-text terms to test the ontology functionality.

Knowledge modeling is a process of classifying concepts to form a hierarchical structure while categorizing them as either concrete or abstract. We must then define the attributes for concrete concepts and establish a knowledge web encompassing both abstract and concrete.

We use both *bottom-up* and *top-down* approaches in modeling a domain structure. The bottom-up technique is used where many terms already have been collected and pooled. The task is to group these terms into categories. In the top-down approach, we first design a structure based on needs (which may take the form of a pre-defined framework). This structure may consist of two or more levels within a hierarchy and each level may have a number of classes. Both approaches often are used together in different stages of ontology development. Conceptually, the modeling process leads to the determination as to whether the ontology should be organized first into modules or remain as one large structure. However, the use of modules requires the adoption of an over-arching framework for relating each module to the others.

Workforce development is a multi-disciplinary domain, involving knowledge of labor, government, business, social and welfare issues, education, regulations and laws, and public and business administration. Each area deals with specific aspects of workforce development. We are employing two tracks in order to ensure the effectiveness and usability of the ontology system: A *technical* track that combined both the bottom-up and top-down approaches for structuring the knowledge domain and a *communities of practice* track that involves stakeholders in developing the workforce ontology through an iterative process. The communities of practice track draws in the disciplines, perspectives, activists, and policy and decision makers, as well as practitioners and researchers, to obtain as broad as possible input and consensus on the ontology. The pilot OKE focuses on a discrete number of user groups within workforce development. These user groups cross geographic regions and types of providers (public, intermediaries, etc.) and are limited to specific disciplines, mostly established by program area.

The knowledge modeling process generated the following result:

– A **concept tree** *for the workforce development domain:* It consists of a number of important entities involved in the workforce development as shown in Figure 1. A concept class may as many as four levels of subclasses. This concept tree also serves as the taxonomy for categorizing and indexing documents and other recorded experiences, as well as for front-end browsing, searching, and navigation.
– A **knowledge base framework** *derived from the ontology:* It was designed initially for: 1) capturing instances of person, organization, law and regulation, credentialing and certification standards, and 2) capturing workforce practices. We

used a small number of instances to test the appropriateness of the ontology structure. Once the structure is stabilized, a knowledge base will be built as a distributed collaborative tool for knowledge sharing and reuse among workforce development communities. This framework will evolve as it is extended across communities.

– A ***thesaurus*** *mapping relationships among terms*: Keywords having similar semantic meanings and others that are related will be mapped to concept terms (preferred terms). The thesaurus will be useful for indexing and for search and browsing.

The construction of an ontology is the *first* and *necessary* step for an Open Knowledge Exchange, but ***not a sufficient condition.*** Systems and tools are required to implement the structure and to use the products of knowledge modeling. To the extent feasible, implementation will take advantage of existing systems. Tools related to ontology development include a set of Web forms for viewing and searching existing concepts, submit new concepts, and send feedback and comments.

Our foray into ontology development demonstrated that it is an intellectually intensive and time-consuming process requiring close collaboration among experts from different disciplines – both within workforce development and among the areas of workforce development, computer science, library and information science and linguistics. We learned also that while many may want a comprehensive OKE that bridges many disciplines, few will invest either time or effort absent a common context or reference. Consequently, work is organized along communities of practice and therefore modules, requiring the development and extension of an over-arching framework as new modules are added.

Testing and evaluation comprise the last step of the process. A working group of subject matter and technical experts will assess the current and subsequent ontologies in four areas:

– Appropriateness, inclusiveness, and usability of the knowledge structure: These are key in validating the ontology and provide feedback for future development decisions
– Concepts and relationships: The linguistic and semantic aspects of the vocabulary and mapping will be assessed through user queries and focus groups
– Users' opinions on the appropriateness and usefulness of the pilot and tools, and
– The effectiveness of the system as a whole.

The assessment will be achieved through surveys, focus groups, and follow-up interviews. Participants for the surveys and focus groups will be selected using sampling methods. Feedback also will be solicited and obtained in the course of presentations and working conferences and through the project's web site.

5 Extending the Open Knowledge Exchange Throughout Workforce Development

The final stage is to extend the OKE throughout the workforce development system. The primary challenges are scaling, standardization, legacy databases, maintenance and further growth as the workforce system evolves and grows. The effort is labor intensive and is a function of both the number of disciplines it incorporates and the number of members within each discipline. Content developers (e.g., workforce professionals, researchers, etc.), managers, funding institutions and the knowledge management community must adopt and adapt the OKE to their specific needs while supporting its cross-functionality. Tools must be developed and proven that substantially reduce both time and effort in adapting legacy databases to the OKE.

There are three paths for reaching these audiences:

- Communities of practice supporting improvement and expansion of the base OKE. The development of the OKE will be incremental and by community of practice. These groups may work in face-to-face gatherings or virtually. The work of these groups may be recorded and disseminated to the workforce and knowledge management communities through bulletin boards, electronic team rooms, stringed discussion groups, conferences and meetings.
- Users conferences targeted to workforce content developers, content managers, and funding organizations. The primary objectives of these conferences are to introduce the OKE, associated tools and templates, and demonstrate the value and application of the OKE and associated products
- Technical conferences targeted to the knowledge management community. The primary objectives are to promote peer review of the OKE, promote the development of tools and templates to support further development and use of the OKE, and to promote additional research in the use of ontologies in support of workforce development

Over the long term, the OKE must be maintained and grown as workforce development evolves. This presents significant logistical and funding challenges since it will require the open collaboration of a diverse group of professionals and policymakers. Consequently, processes to extend the OKE across the system will be developed concurrently with the OKE itself. This will be accomplished primarily by a committee comprised of content managers from organizations maintaining large collections of electronic content and through system-wide conferences, one coinciding with initial deployment of the OKE. The committee will oversee the development of collection and modeling processes in large-scale applications that economically feasible and appropriate for use in the workforce development setting. It also will address the challenges that result to the external and internal validity of OKE. The project also will rely on other *ad hoc* user groups. These groups are also *de facto* stakeholders supporting dissemination of the ontology through informal networks. Collaboration technologies and open source strategies will be used to distribute work through the workforce community while maintaining high standards for formal inclusion of modifications to the ontology. Finally, the project will proposed distributed strategies for funding long-term development and maintenance of the open knowledge exchange.

References

1. Abou-Zeid, El-Sayed, Towards a Cultural Ontology for Interorganizational Knowledge Processes. Proceedings of the 36th Hawaii International Conference on System Sciences (HICSS'03), Island of Hawaii, Hawaii, 2002.
2. K. Gill, Knowledge Networking in Cross Cultural Settings, 2001, A. Gupta and V. Govindarajan, "Knowledge Management's Social Dimension: Lesson from Nucor Steel," Sloan Management Review, vol. Fall, 2000, pp. 71-80, and A. Lam, "Embedded Firms, Embedded Knowledge: Problems of Collaboration and Knowledge Transfer in Global Cooperative Ventures," Organizational Studies, vol. 18, no. 6, 1997, pp. 973-996 in El-Sayed, Abou-Zeid, Towards a Cultural Ontology for Interorganizational Knowledge Processes. Proceedings of the 36th Hawaii International Conference on System Sciences (HICSS'03), Island of Hawaii, Hawaii, 2002.
3. Beyer, H. R. and Karen Holtzblatt. Apprenticing with the Customer, Communications of the ACM, 38 (5), 1995, 45-52.
4. Beyer, Hugh, and Karen Holtzblatt. Contextual Design: Defining Customer-Centered Systems. San Francisco: Morgan Kaufmann, 1998.
5. T. Gruber, "Towards Principles for the Design of Ontologies Used for Knowledge Sharing, Int. J. Human-Computer Studies, vol. 43, 1995, pp. 907-928 in Abou-Zeid, El-Sayed, Towards a Cultural Ontology for Interorganizational Knowledge Processes. Proceedings of the 36th Hawaii International Conference on System Sciences (HICSS'03), Island of Hawaii, Hawaii, 2002.
6. Rowley, J. The controlled versus natural indexing languages debate revisited - a perspective on information-retrieval practice and research. Journal of Information Science, 20, pp. 108-119, 1994.

ShanghaiGrid Portal: The Current Stage of Building Information Grid Portal[*]

Ying Li[1,2], Minglu Li[1], Jiadi Yu[1], Feng Hong[1], and Lei Cao[1]

[1] Department of Computer Science and Engineering, Shanghai Jiao Tong University,
Shanghai 200030, China
{liying, li-ml, jdyu}@cs.sjtu.edu.cn
[2] Computer Science and Technology School, Soochow University, Suzhou 215006, China
ingli@suda.edu.cn

Abstract. Grid portal gives a center access point to access Grid applications and resources. Currently the existing Grid portals are mainly designed for computational Grids which put focus on how to view files, submit and monitor jobs. That alleviate the complexity of using the Grid application. The ShanghaiGrid is an Information Grid which puts focus on how to provide various services in Grid environment to public rather than to scientists. In ShanghaiGrid portal the portal information service, workflow service and transaction service are very important to achieve the goal of building a web interface for citizens to seamlessly and transparently use the Grid services located in ShanghaiGrid environment. This paper reports our current research and implementation of the ShanghaiGrid portal.

1 Backgrounds

There exist some research and implementations on building the Grid Portal in Grid society, such as GridPort Toolkit(GPDK)[1], Portal Lab[2], DSG Grid portal [3], Legion Grid portal [4],GridSphere[5]. Generally speaking, these Grid portal s are designed to provide Grid users an easy way to view files, submit and monitor jobs , and view accounting information. The architecture of the portal is designed to accommodate multiple diverse grid infrastructures, legacy systems and application-specific interfaces [4]. These portals improve researchers' access to advanced computing resources, and the Grid users are mainly scientists and Grid administrators. Meanwhile, the Grid portals are designed case by case for domain-specific Grid applications.

2 The Characteristics of the ShanghaiGrid Portal

The primary goal of ShanghaiGrid[6] is to develop a set of system software for the Information Grid and establish an infrastructure for the grid-based applications in

---

[*] This paper is supported by 973 project (No.2002CB312002)of China, ChinaGrid Program of MOE of China, and grand project of the Science and Technology Commission of Shanghai Municipality (No. 03dz15026, No. 03dz15027 and No. 03dz15028).

C. Bussler et al. (Eds.): WISE 2004 Workshops, LNCS 3307, pp. 82–86, 2004.

Shanghai which is the largest city in China .The ShanghaiGrid is an Information Grid, which means i) gives users and applications secure access to any information anywhere over any type of network[7] ii) integrates heterogeneous information on the web into a homogenous presentation. The ShanghaiGrid portal is a web based interface to achieve such goals.

In ShanghaiGrid project, the terminology of the Information Grid is a Grid environment that provides information (news, weather reports, ticket service, traffic status, financial information, and so on) to the end users rather than provides computational power, data access, and storage resources which are the key activities in Computational Grid. Based on this, the aim and functionality for Computational Grid Portal and Information Grid Portal (IGP) is not quite same. For example, the Computational Grid Portal helps to alleviate the complexity of task management through customizable and personalized graphical interfaces for the users (mainly scientists), emphasizes the need for end users to have more domain knowledge than on the specific details of grid resource management such as how to create a job, schedule and monitor its running in distributed resources, get the results and so on. In contrast, the IGP helps the end users (mainly the people without much knowledge about computer science) get the information they want such as long-term weather forecast, financial analysis and report that based on long-running, complex financial models, and also some simple services like ticket selling, restaurant booking. The IGP must shield the complexity of using such services, giving the same experiences for users accessing Grid Portal like traditional WWW Portal. At the same time, the services must be enormous to meet various needs of users in IGP especially in ShanghaiGrid portal, so the Services provider plays very important role in IGP and the ability of composing existing Services to form a new one which depends on the technologies of workflow and transaction is strongly needed. Fig.1 shows the relationship between the Information Grid services and Computational Grid Services.

From the different purposes of building Grid portal, we can see that currently, the existing Grid portals are not suitable enough to construct a portal for Information Grid. But the design patterns and ideas used in such portals are very usefully to construct the ShanghaiGrid portal. The basic functions for ShanghaiGrid portal are 1) provide end-users seamless access to any services on ShanghaiGrid, hiding the complexity of using Grid Services, 2)provide a platform for service providers to easy deploy their services or compose existing services. To achieve such goals, the Information discovery, Workflow composition and Transaction support are much more important.

3   The Architecture of ShanghaiGrid Portal

The architecture used in ShanghaiGrid portal meets the general requirement of Grid Portal. The notable difference between this architecture and the current existing architecture are on the information discovery, job management which is designed to meet the requirement of Information Grid Portal. The terminology of Information Service domain (ISD) brows the name of the Service Domain which plays important role in IBM's e-business on demand and service-oriented architecture [9].

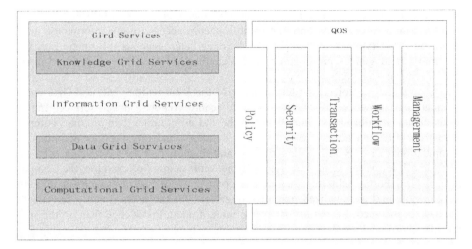

Fig. 1. shows that the Information Grid Services which allow a seamless access to heterogeneous information sources and providing commonly used services are at the top of the Data Grid Services and Computational Grid Services. The Data and Computational Grid Services can be regarded as substructure of Information Grid Services

4 Portal Information Service and Service Discovery

Portal Information Service(PIS) (please distinguish Grid Information Service from the Information Grid Services, the former is a peculiar Grid Service satisfies the requirement of accessing to accurate, up-to-date information on the structure and state of available resources, the later generally refer to Grid Service that hosts in Information Grid to provide users with some information) is one of the key services in every Grid Portal, which usually using the Monitoring and Discovery Service (MDS) provided by the Information Service component of the Globus Toolkit [10].But it is not scalable for thousands of resources. MDS puts focus on the computational resources, network resource, storage resource, not concerns the data resources. Although we can use MDS extensions to address grid-aware application requirements, but it still can not solve problems mentioned above.

In order to solve such problems, we design a distributed, peer to peer architecture for Information Services. We define the Information Service Domain (ISD) as a group of services which has same taxonomy, such as booking services domain, financial services domain. The ISD is an autonomy system based on Grid providing the ability of creates, monitors, recovers and clusters services. Services which are been provided by Service provider will be aggregated into certain ISD, and registers their ports under the comparable portTypes. Each ISD has its own local Service Repository, which currently using UDDI. The UDDI provides a registry for advertising services which are described according to an XML schema defined by the UDDI specification. Clients retrieve advertisements out of the registry based on keyword searching. The information domain agent (IDA) is the interface to communicate portal and ISD, PIS dispatch keywords to every IDA, and the IDA searches the local repository and finds the suitable services.

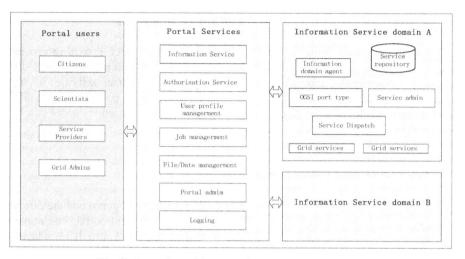

Fig. 2. shows the architecture of the ShanghaiGrid portal

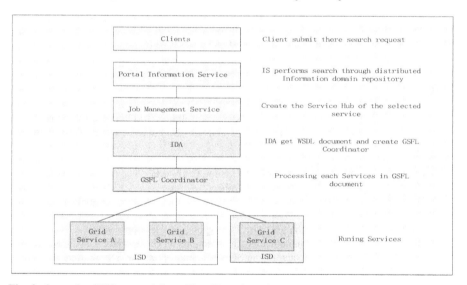

Fig. 3. shows the GSFL control flow. The ISDs where the workflow description located in have responsibility of coordinating the workflow

5 Workflow Support in Information Grid Portal

In real world, Grid Services will be aggregated into more complex services or workflows to offer an even more sophisticated service for either internal use or to offer this encapsulated and augmented service as a new service to the outside world.

We use the Grid Services Flow Language (GSFL) [11] to implement workflow management. The workflow service consists of three parts: GSFL Parser, WSDL generator and GSFL coordinator. The Fig.3 shows the GSFL control flow.

6 Transaction Support in Information Grid Portal

The transactions in the Portal are i) Atomic transactions(AT). AT is used to coordinate activities having short-lived application and executed within limited trust domains. ii) Compensation transaction (CT). CT is used to coordinate activities having long-lived application. In order to improve the concurrency, a compensation model must be applied in CT. The detail implementation of the transaction model can be found in [8].

7 Conclusion and Future Work

In this paper we introduce our notion of building Shanghai Grid portal and the difference between current existing Grid portal   and Information Grid portal. The implementation of Information Service, workflow, transaction support is briefly introduced. Our work is done using commodity technologies including the open-source servlet container Tomcat, Java CoG toolkit, and others. Our next step will be focus on i)web-based service integration environment to compose exiting services ii) enhance the secure issue and policy issue. iii) design a middleware that can provide same interface for Web service, Grid service, and other existing middleware.

References

1. Mary Thomas, The GridPort Toolkit: a System for Building Grid Portal s, 10th HPDC
2. M. Li, Portal Lab: A Web Services Toolkit for Building Semantic Grid Portal s, CCGRID'03
3. http://homer.csm.port.ac.uk/hong
4. Anand Natrajan, Anh Nguyen-Tuong, The Legion Grid Portal .
5. http://www.gridsphere.org/gridsphere/gridsphere
6. Minglu Li, ShanghaiGrid in Action: The First Stage Projects towards Digital City and City Grid, GCC 2003.
7. Melissa Hyatt, The information grid, http://www.ibm.com/developerworks
8. Jiadi Yu, A Framework for Implementing Transactions on Gird Service, CIT04, accepted.
9. Martin Keen, Patterns: Implementing an SOA using an Enterprise Service Bus, IBM Redbook
10. http://www.globus.com
11. S. Krishnan, P. Wagstrom, and G. V. Laszewski. GSFL: A Workflow Framework for Grid Services. Argonne National Laboratory. Aug 2002.

Track2: Advances in Mobile Learning

Learning Communities Support by Mobile Systems Based on Peer-to-Peer Networks*

Felipe G. Leite[1], Milton R. Ramirez[1,2], and Jano M. de Souza[1,2]

[1] COPPE/Sistemas-UFRJ, Rio de Janeiro, RJ, Brasil
{fgl, milton, jano}@cos.ufrj.br
http://www.cos.ufrj.br
[2] Instituto de Matemática-UFRJ, Rio de Janeiro, RJ, Brasil

Abstract. Learning Communities represent a great method to assist in the learning of academic knowledge as well as knowledge experiential. For this reason, we propose, in this work, a new architecture model to support mobile learning communities, based on a PDA approach, thus contributing to the improvement in students' learning. Because of resource limitations in mobile computers, we argue that peer-to-peer – P2P – networks are able to, and suitable for, helping this category of system to minimize these limitations. We explore how well the P2P paradigm can bring new solutions to the issues of mobile data management, data distribution, replication, scalability, robustness and physical failing of a portable system for the individual learner.

1 Introduction

Several works have been written on how the introduction of mobile computers in education may change the current education model and how computers can be used to improve classroom instruction by moving away, from the traditional class, towards augmenting collaborative learning. However, unfortunately, resource limitation and frequent disconnection (planned or not planned) of mobile computers make some of these proposals not applicable. [1], [5] and [13]

In this article we are specially interested in the communities of practice focused on learning, e.g. learning communities, because they are one method both to complement teaching in the traditional classroom and to acquire knowledge experiential. Pawlowski at al. [2] defined a learning community as being an informal group of individuals engaged in a common interest which is, in this case, the improvement of the students' performance. In addition, this group has its events, acts and organizational intelligence shared using the computer networks.

One of the principles of Wenger et al. [3] for cultivating communities of practice is the sharing of knowledge to improve personal knowledge. Another issue toward

---

* This work was partially funded by Brazilian Capes and CNPq agencies.

C. Bussler et al. (Eds.): WISE 2004 Workshops, LNCS 3307, pp. 89–101, 2004.

making a successful community should be intense communication among members. Finally, a community should assist the members to build their personal knowledge.

As ubiquitous is an adjective that defines something which seems to be everywhere or in several places at the same time, there is in an ubiquitous community the possibility for their members to collaborate anytime and anywhere using a mobile computer; therefore, the quantity of collaborations (synchronous and asynchronous) should be higher than in a community based on fixed computers. Mobile computing facilitates the user's life because it is pervasive, so a user can take his knowledge with him wherever he is. In this way, the mobile computers can provide for the members of the community the possibility to build pervasively their personal knowledge and to enable communicate among them.

The users of mobile computers are becoming greatly dependent on mobile computers, and it is reasonable to suppose that, in the near future, the development of mobile systems to manage knowledge would probably cause the user to keep and build his personal knowledge in the mobile computer.

The aim of our work is to research the development of ubiquitous systems to support learning communities. So, in this article we present a proposal of an architecture model of mobile systems to build the personal knowledge of the learning communities' members cooperatively.

The new aspect of the proposed architecture is the use of the P2P model because we believe that this could bring new solutions to the mobile cooperative applications. The new solutions are based on the facilities of the P2P model i.g.: decentralizing community information; robustness to support the frequent and problematic disconnections in a mobile environment; scalability to make bigger the computational power of the mobile community; self organization to support disconnection and computer mobility; and finally, the dynamic behavior of the P2P model, very recommended for use in a mobile community. [16]

The architecture model proposed was based on the following scenario: the students from a class of a specific subject in a graduation course are interested in improve their knowledge, so they arrange a new community of learning. As all the communities should be, this community would be comprised of different levels of participants: some students and the teacher. Everyone will have the responsibility to manage the community, but the teacher will also have three other roles: monitoring the community, guiding the students toward the best way to discover the knowledge and encouraging them to collaborate as much as possible.

Another motivation for this work is to extend the COPPEER project, a cooperative editor of knowledge based on ontology, bringing the knowledge acquired by this group to mobile computing. [9]

This work is organized as follows. In the next section we discuss the previous works, detailing the project KnowMobile. In section 3 we present our proposed model, and, finally, we present a conclusion and future steps of this work.

2 Related Work

There is a certain amount of research in distance education and learning communities supported by mobile computers. These projects have turned into reality because of the great advances in mobile computing research and wireless networking, making these devices powerful and reliable. [4], [5], [6], [20] and [21]

An example of a project focused on distance education using mobile computers is presented by [5], called WILD, proposed in order to assist the student in his learning process when he is far from a school (on a bus, for example). In this project there was no attempt from the researchers to establish a learning community, but, at the end of the project, they were able to observe that mobile computers have sometimes helped users to form occasional groups. But if the mobile computer breaks down, there is not any feature to prevent losing the knowledge stored in that mobile computer. As this project is not aimed to communities of practice, this project does not care about the knowledge built by someone who will leave this occasional group.

The mobile learning community was studied in the KnowMobile project [6], focused on the learning of medical school students. This project has some similarity to the model proposed, but this work did not use P2P networks for data decentralizing, as it will be possible to read in detail in the next section.

The Edutella project [20] is based on P2P networks, aiming at the exchange of learning information. And, to provide a better search service, this project uses the standard RDF with learning objects. According to the Edutella developers, the use of metadata to describe the knowledge is crucial because the learning resources search service is more complex than the search service for music files, for example. As the Edutella project uses the P2P architecture, it provides scalability and learning resource distribution, and all peers have autonomy of association and execution. [19]

There is a project called K-Trek [21], which uses P2P architecture to distribute knowledge over a large geographical area. To reach this objective, this project uses agent technology. Nevertheless, this project is not comprised only by mobile computers, and this project is not focused toward supporting learning communities. The P2P model was chosen by the K-Trek developers. On account of the facilities for distributing knowledge and the K-peer autonomy across the network.

2.1 KnowMobile

In 2000, this project began to be developed by a consortium coordinated by the University of Oslo (school of Medicine). In Norway, a student in the tenth semester should go to a hospital for training classes, so the aim of this project was the improvement of learning specifically for this kind of student.

The main purpose was to develop and evaluate net-based solutions for knowledge access in the distributed and cooperative training of eighteen selected students using their Personal Digital Assistants – PDA. The students, in the opinion of the researchers, should naturally create a learning community.

There were two kinds of information allowed for use in the mobile computer: the knowledge base in the hospital using the wireless connection, or files similar to an e-book, previously downloaded. So, all the knowledge used in this project was centralized on a server, this being computer the project Achilles' heel. Almost all the students preferred the second option, because it was simpler and did not need a wireless connection. Incidentally, a number of users preferred to consult the textbook because they were accustomed to doing so. Certain students felt that they were losing credibility when using the PDA in front of their patients.

After the tests, the researchers perceived that the PDA's were underused because the PDA was both an interesting and confusing new device for the students, so many of the latter had difficulties in using it, mainly to find the information needed. The students concluded that his device it was not reliable on account of its fragility.

There was no data distribution, as all the information was stored in the knowledge base of the hospital, and all the information required by the students was not exchanged between them. Also, there was no supposed learning community because the students preferred others activities than using their PDA's to collaborate when they were out of the hospital, or because they assumed that taking practice actions would be quite difficult when they were in different physical spaces.

A positive conclusion reached by the coordinator of this work concerned the wireless technology, which, for her, was ready to be used in this kind of application, although she perceived that they had to improve their PDA training to prepare the users better in using mobile computers. Regarding the possibility of using P2P technology, probably the students' knowledge exchange could have been higher simply because the knowledge would be not only in the hospital database: it would also be in the students' mobile computers.

3 An Ubiquitous Architecture Model for Learning Communities

Before we establish the definition of Learning Communities to be followed in this work, we should define what our concept is about knowledge, as this is the *object* that to be shared and manipulated in the learning community.

But even before presenting a formal definition of knowledge, two concepts need to be defined: data and information. Data is defined as simple information without any meaning. Information is defined as a set of data processed to be displayed in readable way. So, knowledge is defined as a set of information previously analyzed about its relevance and reliance. Based on constructivism, knowledge is dynamic because it is always changing its definition, and, consequently, simple knowledge could have more than one definition. The model proposed in this article is based on the constructivism, so knowledge will be built following the knowledge already developed by the other members or developed by the user. [17] and [18]

In this work we understand Learning Communities as a group of members which use network-interconnected computers to develop their individual knowledge, about a specific subject, using their personal resources, and in collaboration with the rest of the community members. So, this group will share their knowledge and their computational resources among them. As personal knowledge can be considered an authorial product, mainly in the case of learning communities of knowledge experiential, there could be an amount of personal knowledge that the user did not wish to share, or that maybe the user would share only if there were a counterpart. For example, there could be a learning community about Java (academic knowledge) or about Biological Databases (knowledge experiential).

In the case of learning communities of academic knowledge, it should be noted that the knowledge to be learned by the students is already known by the teacher, and that there are no urgent contents in the community.

To enhance the collaboration in the community, the communication among the members should be as ubiquitous as possible. Communities also have a rhythm, and this is the greatest indicator of their liveliness.

3.1   System Requirements

Based on the literature about learning communities we inferred a list of basic requirements applied to a computational system to support this kind of community practice. A list of basic principles in [3] and [7] should be followed to keep a community of practice alive and successful, independently of the subject of the community, so these principles should also work in a learning community.

a.   All the members must give a small part of their resources (knowledge, memory, etc.) to reach the community's aims together;

b.   To make the members active and helpful, they must have some guarantee that, in a limited period of time after a member receives help, this member will be there assisting; therefore, a person should not be allowed to enter a community, ask for help, receive it and leave the community without giving any collaboration;

c.   All the members in a community must be identified and everyone can consult someone else's record in the community, allowing members to know more about the others members;

d.   The community must have rules and a coordinator to solve the conflicts;

e.   The community subject must be clear to all members and to non-members, thus avoiding non-active members.

List 1: Basic principles of the learning community

The system should permit:

a.   Collaborative development of personal knowledge in a dynamic way: create and edit the user's knowledge; search for the knowledge of other users;

b.   Ubiquitous communication to permit as much collaboration as possible;

c.   Sharing members' resources and services to improve the community production.

d.   Ensure the persistence of the set of personal knowledge of the members, and consequently, community knowledge.

e. Manage the knowledge authorship to privilege the most active participants in the community: deal with the case of private knowledge;

f. Manage the different types of roles in the system: student's role and teacher's role; record of the community member;

g. Scalability because of the great variation of participants, and consequently providing autonomy of association to the participants;

h. Fault tolerant, preventing the community to lose any piece of knowledge because of any catastrophic faults which may happen to the user's computer;

i. Robustness, for the system should continue working even if some members leave the community.

List 2: Mobile System for Learning Community Requirements

3.2   PDA and P2P System Solution

The first requirement of this system is the possibility for the user to build his personal knowledge collaboratively and to keep it safe in his mobile computer. There are two ways to do that: creating a new knowledge from one's own experiences or creating a new one from the knowledge created by the other members. To support these features, the system should have a knowledge editor and a search engine, the latter based on ontology to improve the quality of this service. (item a of list 2)

Our solution to requirement b of list 2, was choosing to use mobile computers to implement an ubiquitous system for we believe that mobile computers are able to provide efficient and functional ubiquitous communication among the members in learning communities.

Despite the variety of mobile computers we have made our choice, based on PDA because currently this kind of mobile computer has more computational power than a cell phone, being more practical than a notebook.

There is a requirement to share resources and services in the learning community, and the P2P architecture allows the peers to share resources and services. In the model proposed, members must share two services: the search service (to discover specific knowledge) and the message service (to exchange messages among them). The members' mobile computers should have a small percentage of the storage capacity to store some community's knowledge even if the owner of the PDA does not use it (the striped area in the Figure 2), aiming at information ubiquity, and consequently making this data easier to be found by the other peers. This rule follows the cooperative paradigm, in which it is necessary to give a small share of resources in order to build a bigger one in the end. (item c of list 2)

Being supported by the mobile computer, the system must provide a safe way to store the personal knowledge of all the members. And, as the community's knowledge is a set of its members' knowledge, the system will consequently provide the persistence of the community's knowledge. (item d of list 2)

The system should manage all the authorship knowledge, as this is an important issue for the political incentive to create knowledge. The architecture will prioritize the user who has the highest amount of knowledge authorship. The author is the only one member of the community authorized to update the definition of his knowledge. And when this occurs, all the users who have any knowledge based on the updated knowledge receive an warning, asking if the user also wants to update his knowledge too. (item e of list 2)

There are two kinds of knowledge in this model, public and private. Public knowledge can be found and copied by everyone. Private knowledge can also be found, but, to be copied, the user should ask for authorization by the author of knowledge. (item e of list 2)

There are two roles of users in this system: the student's role and the teacher's role. The first one has the responsibility of managing the community's environment and build his personal knowledge. The second one, is also able to manage the community, but there are three more responsibilities: guiding the students toward building this personal knowledge, encouraging them to collaborate and monitoring the students' behavior. Another requirement is the storage the record of a member's action in the community, to be stored in the user's mobile computer. (item f of list 2)

This system should be prepared for the dynamism of a mobile computer environment, in which the user enter or leaves frequently. So, there will not be any restrictions to the number of members in this community. Another feature provided by the P2P architecture is the autonomy of association, so that a person could become a member of a learning community easily. (item g of list 2)

In addition, there should be a desktop computer called the "community server", whose aims are to keep safe the current information in the mobile computers and (fault tolerant) store the old and unused information in the past of the community (robustness). (items h, i of list 2)

There are several reasons to use this fixed computer as a server. Firstly, the mobile computers are naturally very exposed to catastrophic faults, like breakage, theft or loss. So, to prevent the community from losing the knowledge stored in a mobile computer when it is broken, the user will be able to backup this knowledge in the community server whenever he wants. This feature makes the proposed architecture fault tolerant. (item h of list 2)

Secondly, when a member leaves the community (a voluntary or planned disconnection), the server computer will be able to store his knowledge before it is used by the other member. (item i of list 2)

Thus, the community server will answer just queries submitted by the members of the community about this specific type of knowledge. Finally, the community server should work as a knowledge repository, for the mobile computers have a number of intrinsic characteristics such as their limited capacity of storage; therefore, it is necessary to store the unused knowledge for the future.

Thus, information exchange between the server community and the mobile computers will be in two directions: the PDA backups their knowledge to be stored in the server community; and the server will send theirs knowledge to the mobile computers when is requested by the mobile computer which aims to restore its knowledge after some problem. This feature provides for a more reliant community.

Should be mentioned that the community server is not essential for community, but its use is strongly recommended because it would make the community fault tolerant, reliant and lightweight because there would not be an overhead of the mobile computer storage capacity. [13] and [15]

The environment for a model of architecture proposed for mobile system support is described in Figure 1, in which great number of mobile computers can be seen, which could be connected to the community server to backup their knowledge or connected among themselves to cooperate. The server community is located in the wired network with other computers which may or may not be other peers in the community.

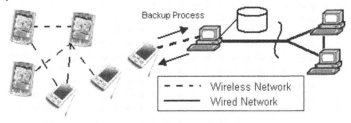

Fig. 1. Environment architecture

Interface	
Community Management	
Editor	Search
Knowledge Store	
Communication	
JXTA	

Fig. 2. Architecture model

In a comparison between the model proposed and the KnowMobile, presented in section 2.1, the main differences are the community server and the use of P2P technology, mainly aiming at better data distribution and data decentralization. Also, the server will m the system more reliable, in case of occasional mobile computers crash, for example.

3.3   The PDA and P2P System Architecture Model

The explanation for each module from Figure 2 is as follows:
- Interface: a simple, lightweight and friendly graphic user interface developed using J2ME and MIDP for Palm OS.
- Community management:

This module will be focused on managing the community and how to make it successful. All the interfaces related with the community participants would be implemented here, such as the authorization or the user profile.

Each user will store in this architecture module his score of knowledge authorship; it should be observed that, when the user submits a query, this score is sent attached because the other peers must know it to decide which query should be processed first. The backup routine will also be implemented in this module, preventing the community from losing any piece of knowledge produced. The routine to store the knowledge of the member who is leaving the community (planned disconnections) will be also implemented in this module.

Some community rules, following of the basic principles cited at the beginning of this section, will be stored. Its purpose is to ascertain the possibility of monitoring the messages, shielding the community from undesirable messages. [3]

- Editor: edit the personal knowledge of the user.

In this module an ontology-based (like proposed in [9]) editor, to build the personal knowledge of the members will be implemented. The P2P and ontology combination seems to works well, as ontology has shown the best choice for structure knowledge and P2P to decentralize it. [11]

Using this editor, the user can build his own knowledge, beginning from zero or from knowledge copied from another member. Then, a user will be able to copy knowledge from other users, edit it in his own mobile computer and store it, building up his personal knowledge. An important observation should be cited: the editor will not be a cooperative editor; it will only allow users to exchange knowledge.

- Search

The search engine will be situated in this module. Knowledge in the community is decentralized, and the JXTA search engine is also decentralized, exposing user services and knowledge for a network of information providers and consumers. This engine defines a common protocol for the exchange of query and response. The search service will be based on semantics of knowledge, not just on the knowledge keywords, because the search service for learning resources is more complex than the search for a music file, for example. [12]

When a member submits a query for some knowledge, the search engine will firstly look into its own index, then look into the peers next to the user, and, finally, if it does not find an answer to the query, it will look into the peers gradually a little father from the user. As written before, this service will prioritize the query submitted by the users who have the higher authorship score.

With the implementation of the two modules above, the system will be able to support the construtivism's paradigm. The Editor module will able the user to develop a new knowledge and the Search module will find others knowledges to base the user's development of a new knowledge.

- Knowledge Store: this module store personal knowledge in the mobile computer. The users must share their all knowledge index, but only public knowledge will be shared. Then, it will be possible for a user to know that specific knowledge exists, but, there are two possibilities if he wants to copy it: he could copy the knowledge because it is public, or he should ask for authorization for the author's private knowledge. As cited before, the storage capacity of a mobile computer is reduced, so, to deal with this problem, the model proposed using a fixed computer for participants to backup some knowledge that they do not use anymore. All the members must contribute with some storage capacity to store some community knowledge even if he does not use it.

- Communication: this module of the architecture will make connections and disconnections with other mobile computers or desktop computers using wireless technology. When a user finds a piece of knowledge, he can copy it in his own mobile computer and edit it, if necessary. The proximity of the members will be important to establish the connection because the nearer they are, the higher the transmission rate is.

- JXTA: this module will enable the architecture to use P2P features, as there is already a project initiated by Sun Microsystems to use this technology for wireless devices.

3.4   PDA and P2P Prototype

We have decided to implement a prototype to analyze how the prototype will work and solutions will be studied in case some critical problems appears in these tests. Furthermore, tests will be done to improve semantic search. Another study to be done in the future will be how this model's performance in networks comprising mobile and fixed computers would be. [14]

The decision for the J2ME programming language choice was its interoperability, solving the diverse types of mobile computers, ranging from simple cell phones to the new mobile computers. But it should be said that, for this language to work properly, the Java Virtual Machine specific for personal digital assistants must be installed in the mobile computer. And implementing wireless connections using J2ME, also requires installing other programs to provide this feature. As it has been decided to use the set of JXTA protocols to implement the P2P solution in this model, it would be correct to choose a language compatible with it, and J2ME is the best choice for it. An important observation is that we intended to use, in this work, only free- and open-source applications and software libraries. [8]

The JXTA project was focused not only on PC-based knowledge, but also oriented to small computers, and this is the reason why the protocols developed have be kept as thin as possible. Mobile computing has some problems to which the P2P architecture bears solutions, such as scalability and robustness. In addition, the JXTA protocols are completely hardware- and language-independent. Another advantage of using JXTA is to follow the recommended patterns to standardize it so as to implement P2P solutions. [10]

As all the mobile computers should have an interface to establish communication in order to exchange knowledge, we decided to initiate implementation using mobile computers built in Wi-Fi technology. We are currently implementing the first prototype in the Tungsten C Palm OS 5.2 simulator. This prototype is already accepted to be used in four undergraduation courses in two Brazilian governmental universities this year.

4   Conclusion and Future Works

After several research works like KnowMobile or WILD, it is possible to state that mobile computing is ready to be used in collaborative applications. The main advantage of the ubiquitous communities is the possible collaboration anytime and anywhere by any member, thus making the community more active. And if this is a learning community, it will improve the members' knowledge.

In this paper we have presented a new architecture model to support ubiquitous learning communities, and, comparing with the other related works in the literature, our proposed model presents ubiquitous communications among the members, the facility to the users to render their personal knowledge collaborative, and a system based on P2P architecture bringing its advantages to our model.

Regarding data distribution, this architecture makes it easier to exchange the knowledge across the P2P networks and prevent the model from being dependent on a single data server or on a central server. Data distribution is essential for the learning community, as each member has his personal knowledge stored in his wireless device. This also makes it possible for a member to contribute wherever and whenever he wants to do so because the members have all their useful knowledge stored in their own mobile computer.

Thus, as the model proposed requires scalability, decentralization, robustness, fault tolerant and self-organization, we decided to implement the it using P2P architecture. Using the P2P approach, this model will probably not have scalability problems because it is based on all mobile computers simultaneously, so the community learning can have any number of participants with whatever needs. Using P2P architecture, this model is also independent of a wired network and thus could work normally without the community server. However, analysis should be performed of who will coordinate the replication of the knowledge produced in the community among the members' mobile computers, and how this will be done.

The semantic search of the knowledge to be carried out should be observed, so that when a user searches for knowledge using a single word, the answer will comprise definitions of this knowledge, not a set of data consisting of information having the keyword in its definition. This decision was based on the success of Edutella's search service.

The main contribution is the increase of computational power in the mobile computing environment using the features provided by the P2P architecture.

Another advantage in the model presented in this work was the architecture reliance, as if something wrong happens with one mobile computer, its knowledge will be safe in the community's server. As the server computer is required just to make the community more reliant, it should be clear that the normal functionality of the community is completely independent from the server community.

Another advantage of JXTA's set of protocols was the transparency of hardware and network technology. Finally, the portability and compatibility with JXTA was important for choosing the J2ME programming language.

We decided not to use mobile agents because it would causes an overhead in the model networks. If the number of participants gets higher, the facilities of mobile agents should be analyzed again.

In our next paper we intend to report the results of future tests that will be done. These tests will check as technical questions (like the behaviour of the wireless network and the mobile computer) and questions about learning (like the behaviour of students and teachers). In a further test, we intend to use an *ad hoc* network to observe how the search engine works and how the knowledge is distributed. This model should be tested without the using of the community server.

References

1. Thomas, S. J., Nishida, T., Laxer, C., et al., "The Impact of Campus-wide Portable Computing on Computer Science Education". In: ITiCSE'98 Working Group on Campus-wide Portable Computing, 1998.
2. Pawlowski, S., Robey, D., Raven, A., "Supporting shared information systems: boundary objects, communities, and brokering", In: ICIS, pp. 329-338, Brisbane, Australia, 2000.
3. Wenger, E., McDermott, R., Snyder, W., "Cultivating communities of Practice: A guide to Managing Knowledge", Harvard Business School Press, March 2002.
4. Barbará, D., "Mobile Computing and Databases – A Survey", IEEE Transactions on knowledge and data engineering, vol. 11, n. 1 (Jan/Feb), pp. 108-117, 1999.
5. Roschelle, J., Pea, R., "A walk on the WILD side: How wireless handhelds may change computer-supported collaborative learning". CSCL-2002, USA, 7-11 January 2002.
6. KnowMobile Project. http://www.intermedia.uio.no/prosjekter/knowmobile, visited on March 19th, 2004.
7. Kollock, O., "Design Principles for Online Communities", The Internet and Society: Harvard Conference Proceedings – O'Reilly & Associates. Cambridge, MA, USA, 1997.
8. JXTA for J2ME (JXME) Project. http://jxme.jxta.org/, visited on May 26th, 2004.
9. Vivacqua, A., Xexéo, G., de Souza J., et al. "Peer-to-peer Collaborative Editing of Ontologies", to appear in CSCWD 2004.
10. Dunne, C. R., "Using Mobile Agents for Network Resource Discovery in Peer-to-peer Networks", ACM SIGecom Exchanges archive, vol. 2, n. 3, pp. 1-9, 2001.
11. Ehrig, M., Tempich, C., Broekstra, J, et al. "SWAP: Ontology-based Knowledge Management with Peer-to-peer Technology", 2a. Konferenz Professionelles Wissens-management, Lucern, April 2-4, 2003.
12. Waterhouse, S., "JXTA Search: Distributed Search for Distributed Networks", Sun Microsystems Inc., 2001.
13. Satyanarayanan, M., "Fundamental Challenges in Mobile Computing", PODC'96, Philadelphia PA, USA, 1996.
14. Palm Software and PDAs – Developers. http://www.palmsource.com/developers, visited on May 4th, 2004.
15. Holliday, J., Agrawal, D. and Abbadi, A. E., "Disconnections Models for Mobile Databases", Wireless Networks 8, pp. 391-402, 2002.

16. Gong, L., Oaks, S., Traversat, B., "JXTA in a Nutshell – A Desktop Quick reference", O'Reilly Press, 1ˢᵗ ed., printed in USA, 2002.
17. Moresi, E. A. D., "Gestão da informação e do conhecimento". In: *Inteligência* Organizacional e Competitiva, Ed. Universidade de Brasília, pp. 111-142, 2001.
18. Satre, G., "Temas transversais em educação – bases para uma formação integral", Ed. Ática, 1997.
19. Nilsson, M., "The Edutella Peer-to-peer Network – Supporting Democratic E-Learning and Communities of Practise", 2001.
20. Nejdl, W., Wolf, B., Qu, C., et al., "Edutella: A Peer-to-peer Networking Infrastructure Based on RDF", WWW2002, May 7-11, 2002, Honolulu, Hawaii, USA.
21. Busetta, P., Bouquet, P., Adami, G., et all, "K-Trek: A Peer-to-peer Approach to Distribute Knowledge in Large Environment", AP2PC 2003, Melbourne, 14-18 July 2003.

A Context-Adaptive Model
for Mobile Learning Applications

Soo-Joong Ghim[1], Yong-Ik Yoon[1], and Ilkyeun Ra[2]

[1] Department of Computer Science, Sookmyung Women's University
Chungpa-Dong 2-Ga, Yongsan-Gu, 140-742, Seoul, Korea
{sjghim, yiyoon}@sookmyung.ac.kr
[2] Department of Computer Science & Engineering, University of Colorado, Denver
Denver, CO 80217, U.S.A.
ikra@carbon.cudenver.edu

Abstract. Emerging technologies, such as multimedia and mobile computing, require a high adaptable middleware platform which provides more flexible services to those applications in heterogeneous computing environments. To support persistent services in distributed wired/wireless environments for advanced learning systems, it is required for applications and middleware to be aware of the frequent and unpredictable changes in users' requirements as well as environmental conditions, and to be able to adapt their behavioural changes. One of the main limitations of current approaches for supporting adaptability is that applications themselves are responsible for triggering and adaptive mechanism when the underling infrastructure notifies them about any changes. In this paper, we present the designing a component-based context-adaptive model for context-aware mobile learning applications to support dynamic adaptation, and demonstrate our being developed mobile agents: adaptation, configuration, and meta agents, that help applications to adapt their computing environments according to rapidly changing contexts such as user-specific preference, application-specific preference, and low-level configurations.

1 Introduction

Weiser described Ubiquitous computing or Pervasive computing is the process of removing the computer out of user awareness and seamlessly integrating it into everyday life [1]. Ubiquitous computing allows application developers to build a large and complex distributed system which can transform physical spaces into computationally active and intelligent environments [2]. The one of core technology for application services in Ubiquitous computing environment is context-awareness.

A context can be defined as any information that represents circumstances being created by the result of any interactions between users, applications, and surrounding environments [13]. Thus, context-awareness research becomes essential in Ubiquitous computing, and is considered as indispensable function for ubiquitous computing applications. To achieve the goal of supporting context-awareness, underlying platforms in Ubiquitous computing should be able to recognize contextual changes so that applications use contexts for evaluating new environments and finding an appropriate action upon the result of evaluation for these changes.

C. Bussler et al. (Eds.): WISE 2004 Workshops, LNCS 3307, pp. 102–113, 2004.
© Springer-Verlag Berlin Heidelberg 2004

Previous many researches in context-awareness have been mainly focusing on location change of users or devices in context-awareness related fields. In ubiquitous computing environment, not only devices or software services can be added to or removed from the system at anytime, but also contexts or preferences of users are changing seamlessly. The users of mobile learning applications tend to access the application under different computing environments from time to time because they are nomadic. The users may interact with heterogeneous system using different devices at different locations over different networks with different quality of service requirements. To facilitate those users' requests, we need a method that cans efficiently aware higher level contexts: user preferences or intended information, and can drive an optimised solution by intelligent decisions. Thus, adaptability is one the most important requirements for Ubiquitous computing systems by frequently occurring of unpredictable changes in different contexts for mobile learning application.

In this paper, we present our on-going work for context-adaptive middleware framework which can support adaptability for mobile learning applications. We describe a component-based context-adaptive model to manage dynamic adaptation in contextual changes. Section 2 introduces our motivations for this research and section 3 explains our conceptual context-adaptive model and component model toward reflective middleware for ubiquitous computing, including mobile learning environments. Section 4 shows how adaptations are triggered by a policy and represents implementations on agents of this framework. Section 5 discusses several related works to this research and section 6 remarks our research results and future works.

2   Motivations

Adaptability is one of the most important requirements for Ubiquitous computing systems because such environments are highly dynamic, characterized by frequent and unpredictable changes in different contexts. Hence, mobile learning applications need to be capable of adapting their behaviors to ensure they continue to offer the best possible level of service to their users. The required levels of adaptation for a system are ranged from the operating system level up to the application level. More generally, adaptation can be applied to a wide range of aspects at different levels of the system. These aspects include the communications aspects as well as several issues such as resources allocated to an activity and the set of external services currently being used. Thus, this adaptation should be driven by awareness of a wide range of issues including communication performance, resource usage, location, cost, and application preference [3]. The extreme emphasis on adaptation at specific level can cause some problems, for example, adaptation at the operating system level can be quite dangerous in terms of affecting integrity and performance. In opposite case, leaving all adaptation to the application level would impose a heavy burden on application programmers. The current approach to providing adaptable services or applications is based upon the classic layered architectural model where adaptation is provided at the various layers (data link, network, transport or application layers) in isolation [4]. Due to the very limited information being shared across protocol layers, adaptation strategies are *uni-dimensional* – i.e. they only consider one parameter at a time – and often are leading to unsatisfactory results [5]. One of the main limitations of current approaches is that applications themselves are responsible for triggering and adaptive mechanism when the underling infrastructure notifies them about any changes [6]. Consequently, to overcome the main limitation, we need a sophisticated approach which can manipulate mixed or customized adaptation in contextual changes.

Even though mobile learning applications can detect changes in their execution environment, they cannot configure the underlying middleware to adapt these changes. It is, therefore, more desirable and effective to manage adaptation at the middleware for providing different adaptive solutions in various situations. In Ubiquitous computing environments for mobile learning applications, middleware architecture itself should be context-aware to manage the communication among objects in a transparent fashion. In addition, the middleware should allow applications to reason about their using different logics and then adapt them to changing contexts.

3   A Context-Adaptive Model

3.1   Definition and Classification of Context

A term called context has different meaning, and it is used extensively. Meaning of a context has been used in many various research fields such as operating systems, programming language, artificial intelligences, and a natural language processing. Moreover, the meaning of context in a user interface design is very different from those areas. It has been agreed on that a context is the key concept in Ubiquitous computing for learning systems, although it is differently understood from and used by other various fields. An ultimate goal of context-awareness is to provide users with information and services persistently and seamlessly without users' interventions whenever changes of user situations or environments are occurred.

In this work, we regard contexts as environmental information which may cause to trigger adaptation mechanisms and as requirements of users or applications. We classify contexts into two levels: high-level and low-level context (figure 1). High-level contexts include preference of users and applications. Preference is the explicit requirements about resources and a quality of service, and resources preference is a use degree of the resources which users or applications request, and quality of service preference can include elements such as resolution, a frame rate, and security. Low-level contexts are subdivided into user configurations and resources configurations. User configurations include user device, location, time, and resource configurations include memory, power, and bandwidth.

Current existing other works have treated the user preference with a video lecture note as a kind of the information that a user wanted like learning information or contents, and to provide services to be suitable for a user through filtering by similarity measurement. However, with taking into consideration of characteristics of

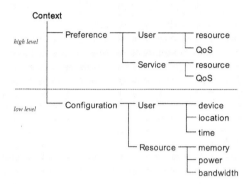

Fig. 1. Classification of context

ubiquitous computing, we define the user preference as 'the explicit requirements for contexts' in order to adapt dynamically delivery of services when context changes are occurred.

3.2 Conceptual Model

3.2.1 Adaptation

We designed a context-adaptive model that defines several elements for context-awareness and adaptation methods. The relationships between elements of the context-adaptive model are shown in the Figure 2.

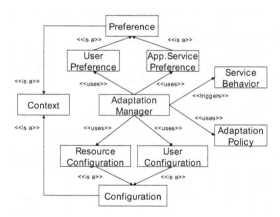

Fig. 2. Adaptation model

Both the user preference and the application preference are considered as the explicit requirements for the usage of resources. We analyze on an associative relationship between these preferences numerically in order to decide on how to provide application services that can maximize satisfaction of user requirements. The configuration information includes user device types, locations, time, resources context of user devices, and adaptation policies which specify association rules between contextual changes of resources and application service behaviours. In our model, the adaptation method reflects preference and configurations, and satisfies user requirements that have user environments to be safe and operational.

3.2.2 Application Service

Our application service model puts a focus with individual behaviours which compose application services, and establish details related to application service offering (figure 3).

An application service is the abstract concept of a task to be performed. The functionality of task is realized by service behaviours. An application service can be expressed with the description about a name and functions. Service behaviour can be composed of operations or methods which are invoked by an agent. In this model, an application consists of application services, adaptation polices and preference for users and services. The adaptation polices in an application are used for the context adaptation.

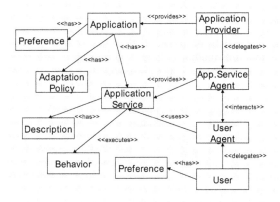

Fig. 3. Application service model

3.3 Adaptation Management

Most existing middleware systems have been designed to develop server applications running on workstations or desktops, and provide suitable functions to applications that have well-known execution patterns and requirements, such as for banking or air ticket reservation. However, mobile learning applications in Ubiquitous computing are unable to use previous execution patterns. Due to the heterogeneity associated with Ubiquitous computing, it is not possible to provide a single static middleware implementation that fits all scenarios [7]. Therefore, the flexibility introduced by a reflective middleware turns out to be an elegant approach to cope with the requirements for Ubiquitous computing [7]. Reflection refers to the capability of a system to reason about and act upon itself [8].

To support reflection actively, a middleware should perform monitoring context sources and should maintain the transparency of adaptation mechanisms by reflecting users' and applications' requirements. Applications running on middleware should be able to dynamically customize middleware behaviors by specifying their necessary context information. We have been motivated these reasons and designed a component-based adaptation management model (figure 4).

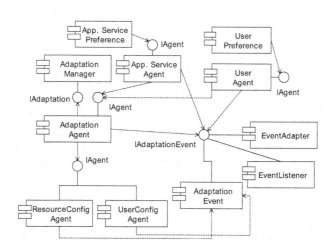

Fig. 4. Component-based architecture for adaptation management

The adaptation management system is composed of the followings:

- AdaptationManager: AdatationManager component performs an adaptation method to decide the most appropriate service delivery for current context using context information, and then triggers the selected service behavior.

- AdaptationAgent: AdaptationAgent is an agency of AdaptationManager. It is responsible for requesting events and delivering required information to AdaptationManager by interacting with ConfigAgent, UserAgent, and AppServiceAgent.

- ConfigAgent: ConfigAgent is responsible for gathering and analyzing configuration information. It offers configuration information to AdaptaionAgent according to AdaptationEvent types, and produces events on configuration changes.

4 Dynamic Context-Adaptation

4.1 Adaptation Policy

Adaptation policy is a set of rules to be used to change application service behaviors with respect to different contexts, and is a key means for the triggered adaptation in this paper. The triggered adaptation does not depend on only the notification mechanism from an underlying system as a voluntary adaptation way of an application about a context. It depends upon the self and dynamic detection for changes in an application behavior according to contextual changes or an application's needs related to controlling an adaptation process.

A mobile learning application consists of several services, and its each service can be provided with one component while multiple behaviors are performed upon context changes. Let's assume that an application called Cyber Classroom is running on a middleware. This application can provide Lecture service and Messaging service. Its each service is carried out a behavior to be exposed to by the current context. For example, if the critical value memory availability of user device is decreased to the below threshold value, Lecture service will be provided with a textOnly method. The Lecture service can be provided a slideShow method if memory availability is increased to the enough level.

To support context-awareness, it is required to process low-level tasks including periodic monitoring and detection of changes. A middleware can conceal the complexity with carrying out this task, and can decrease a burden of application developer. However, applications should inform a middleware about which a service should be adapted, and which a behavior should be triggered for each specific context when applications are being instantiated because it is difficult for a middleware to predict various changes of each context in requirements of an application.

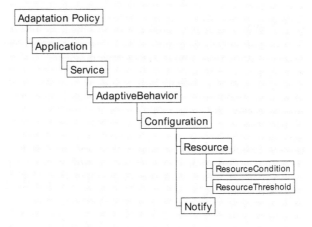

Fig. 5. Adaptation policy hierarchy

As shown in Figure 5, Adaptation policy describes important information for application services, required configuration in offering services, and behaviors to be triggered when certain context changes occur. A middleware would decide which rule is to apply for service delivery in current context using adaptation policy when application service is requested.

4.2 Adaptation Method

A MetaAgent can be considered as a different kind of mobile agent that runs on its own execution environment. The main purpose of meta-agent is to manage and control of adaptation processing. Thus meta-agents are responsible for monitoring the execution of mobile agents and for transferring them to remote hosts. The association between MetaAgents and mobile agents can be performed on the basis of one-to-one or one-to-many relationship. In the former case, one MetaAgent can be created per mobile agent, therefore it allows a MetaAgent to migrate itself which is containing one mobile agent and to keep track of the behavior of that agent on every node where it visits. In the latter case, one meta-agent can manage a group of mobile agents. According to a MetaAgent's own policy for management, the number of mobile agents that one meta-agent can encompass is regulated.

When a mobile agent decides to migrate, its MetaAgent suspends the mobile agent and serializes its state (data state only or data state + execution state) and codes according to the migration strategy. Its MetaAgent establishes a point-to-point channel with the destination meta-agent by a remote communication, which will receive the being migrated mobile agent and de-serialize it. When a mobile agent arrives at its destination, the MetaAgent examines configuration and restarts it from where it was stopped. The MetaAgent continues monitoring the execution of mobile agents and throws an adaptation event to its AdaptationManager when any change occurs by mobile agents. AdaptationAgent keeps tracking of changes in the policy. If the adaptation event is happened, an AdaptationAgent analyses the subtype of that event, and throws an adaptation event to its AdaptationMagner. AdaptationManager interprets it, and validates policy rules, and triggers adaptation mechanism by selection of appropriate service behavior (see figure 6).

The adaptation policies can be specified by the user-specific and application-specific priorities on users' preference to applications, and quality of services, and applications' resource requirements (see figure 7). When any of the contextual changes occurs, the context agent perceives changes, and then the adaptation manager has to decide which adaptation method should be invoked. In the example, an application's non-functional behaviors are separated into several groups according to the application's resource priorities. In order to decide which a behavior is to be invoke, the adaptation agent checks the prioritization of the applications.

4.3 Implementation of Agents

The MetaAgent is responsible for monitoring execution of mobile agents, while the adaptation agent and the context agent are responsible for monitoring changes. The adaptation agent monitors changes of policy and the context agent monitors contextual changes. For the dynamic adaptation, we present MetaAgent,

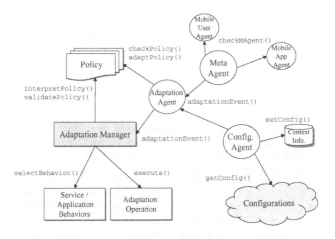

Fig. 6. Adaptation using agents

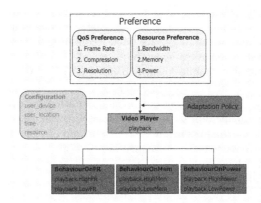

Fig. 7. Adaptation policy and application's behaviors

AdaptationAgent, and ConfigAgent classes to implement our policy-based mechanism, as follows:

Meta-Agent Class
```
class MetaAgent extends UbiAgent implements IAgent{
    . . .
    /* initializes the agent */
    public void initAgent(Obeject[] args)

    /* monitors mobile agents */
    public void checkMAgent(Agent agent){ . . .}

    /* acts on migration event thrown by mobile agents */
    public void migrationEvent(){ . . . }
```

```
/* acts on arrival event thrown by mobile agents */
public void arrivalEvent(){ . . . }

/* acts on adaptation event */
public void adaptationEvent() { . . . }
}
```

Adaptation Agent Class
```
class AdaptationAgent extends UbiAgent implements IAgent {
    . . .
    /* initializes the agent */
    public void initAgent(Object[] args) { . . . }

    /* adapts context */
    public void adaptContext(Context context) { . . . }

    /* monitors adaptation policy */
    public void checkPolicy(Policy policy) { . . . }

    /* adapts adaptation policy */
    public void adaptPolicy(Policy policy) { . . . }

    /* adapts configuration */
    public void adaptConfig(Agent agent) { . . . }

    /* acts on adaptation event */
    public void adaptationEvent() { . . . }
}
```

ConfigAgent Class
```
class ConfigAgent extends UbiAgent implements IAgent {
    . . .
    /* initializes the agent */
    public void initAgent(Object[] args) { . . . }

    /* gets current configuration */
    public void getCofig(Config config) { . . . }

    /* sets changed configuration */
    public void setConfig(Context config) { . . . }

    /* monitors changes in configuration */
    public void checkConfig(Config config) { . . . }
}
```

5 Related Work

Odyssey[8] supports application-aware adaptation based on collaborative model. In Odyssey, an application can decide proper adaptation policy, and its operating system can determine precise resource availability. When applications are notified of resource changes, it is needed to adapt access pattern. However, notification approach can be shown to lead to inefficient solutions because it is lack of support for enabling coordination between the adaptation policies and enable to increase the burden of the application developer.

Gaia [9] offers a more general approach to reactive adaptation to context changes, as it does not focus on one particular service. It converts physical spaces and the ubiquitous computing devices they contain into active spaces. Gaia adapts application requirements to the properties of its associated active space, without the application having to explicitly deal with the particular characteristics of every possible physical space where they can be executed.

OpenORBv2 [10], ReMMoC[11], UIC [7] and LegORB [12]. They all share the idea of exploiting refection and components to achieve dynamic re-configurability of middleware. The ReMMoC project and the Universally Interoperable Core (UIC) aim at overcoming the problems of heterogeneous middleware technology in the mobile environment. They offer developers the ability to specialize the middleware to suit different devices and environments. LegORB exploits reflection and component technology to provide a minimal CORBA implementation for portable devices. OpenORBv2 offers a general approach that achieves both backward compatibility with middleware standards and dynamic and efficient middleware re-configurability.

6   Conclusions and Future Work

The context awareness is the essential technology that middleware must be equipped with in the ubiquitous environment where various computing unit are connected through a various types of network in order to provide continuous service to a user. Therefore, the middleware for mobile learning applications in an ubiquitous computing environment should easily acquire context information from various context sources and should provide service adapted to context changes.

In this paper, we defined a context and described the design of context-adaptive model based on component for mobile learning applications. It can support dynamic adaptation for mobile users and applications using the context(high-level and low-level) information, and we proposed a policy-based adaptation method using mobile agents. The adaptation policies can be specified by the user-specific and application-specific priorities on a user's preference to applications and quality of services, and an application's resource requirements. The implementation of our adaptive middleware framework is currently ongoing, focusing on supporting context-aware mobile applications. In the future work, we intend to develop adaptive middleware services and management mechanism for context information.

Acknowledgement. This research was supported by IRC(Internet Information Retrieval Research Center) in Hankuk Aviation University. IRC is a Kyounggi-Province Regional Research Center designated by Korea Science and Engineering Foundation and Ministry of Science & Technology.

References

1. M. Weiser, The computer for the 21st Century. Scientific American, pp. 94--100, September 1991.
2. A. Ranganathan and R. H. Campbell, A Middleware for Context-Aware Agents in Ubiquitous Computing Environments, In ACM/IFIP/USENIX International Middleware Conference, Rio de Janeiro, Brazil, June 16-20, 2003.
3. G. S. Blair, G. Coulson, A. Anderson, et al., A Principles Approach to Supporting Adaptation in Distributed Mobile Environments. Proceedings of the 5th International Symposium on Software Engineering for Parallel and Distributed Systems (PDSE'2000), Nixon P. & Ritchie I. (eds), Limerick, Ireland, June 10-11, 2000.
4. Z. J. Haas, Designing Methodologies for Adaptive and Multimedia Networks, IEEE Communications Magazine, pp. 106-107, Vol. 39, N.11, November 2001.
5. A. Liotta, A. Yew, C. Bohoris, and G. Pavlou, Supporting Adaptation-aware Services through the Virtual Home Environment, Proceedings of the 9th Workshop of the HP OpenView University Association, June 11-13, 2002.
6. C. Efstratiou, K. Cheverst, N Davices and A. Friday, An Architecture for the Effective Support of Adaptive Context-Aware Applications, Proceedings of the Second International Conference on Mobile Data Management (MDM '2001) , pp. 15-26, January 8 - 10, 2001.
7. M. Román, F. Kon, and R. H. Campbell, Reflective Middleware: From Your Desk to Your Hand, IEEE Distributed Systems Online Journal, Special Issue on Reflective Middleware, Vol. 2 , No. 5, 2001.
8. B. Noble, System Support for Mobile, Adaptive Applications, IEEE Personal Communications, Vol. 7, No. 1, February 2000.
9. M. Roman, C. K. Hess, R. Cerqueira, A. Ranganathan, R. H. Campbell, and K. Nahrstedt. , Gaia: A Middleware Infrastructure to Enable Active Spaces, In IEEE Pervasive Computing, Vol. 1, pp. 74-83, 2002.
10. G. S. Blair, G. Coulson, et. al., The Design and Implementation of OpenORB V2. IEEE Distributed Systems Online Journal, 2(6), 2001.
11. Capra, L., Blair, G. S., Mascolo, C., Emmerich, W., and Grace, P., Exploiting Reflection in Mobile Computing Middleware, ACM Mobile Computing and Communications Review, 6(4), pp. 34-44, 2003.
12. Rom_an, M., Mickunas, D., Kon, F., and Campbell, R. H., LegORB and Ubiquitous CORBA. In IFIP/ACM Middleware 2000 - Workshop on Reflective Middleware, IBM Palisades Executive Conference Center, NY, 2000.
13. A. K. Dey, D. Salber, and G. D. Abowd, A conceptual framework and a toolkit for supporting the rapid prototyping of context-aware applications. Human-Computer Interaction, Vol. 16, 2001.

MobiLearn:
An Open Approach for Structuring Content for Mobile Learning Environments

Maia Zaharieva and Wolfgang Klas

Dept. of Computer Science and Business Informatics
University of Vienna, Austria
{maia.zaharieva,wolfgang.klas}@univie.ac.at

Abstract. Mobile devices are becoming more and more important in the context of e-learning. This requires appropriate models for structuring and delivering content to be used on various devices. Different technical characteristics of devices as well as different needs of learners require specific approaches. In this paper we propose a model for structuring content that allows rendering for different devices like Notebooks, PDAs, and Smartphones as well as presentation of the content in different levels of details according to didactic concepts like case study, definition, example, interaction, motivation, directive. This approach allows adaptation of content (device, granularity of content, content selection based on didactic concepts) at run time to specific needs in a particular learning situation. The approach realized in the joint MobiLearn project of several universities in Austria shows high acceptance by students during an initial pilot application.

1   Introduction

E-learning is going to become a standard element in many educational environments. Approaches and solutions range from very simple FTP-like download-oriented sites to websites providing a high degree of administrative services like student administration and organisation of course material for large student populations. Usually these solutions treat digital learning material as preorchestrated, canned content, very often available as one single piece of material by means of e.g., some slide presentation or PDF-file to be read electronically or in printed form. Since several types of mobile devices like PDA or Smartphones became highly available for students the demand of mobile learning scenarios is significantly stimulated.

   As part of a concerted activity for creating innovative e-learning environments the universities of Vienna, Linz and Klagenfurt and the Vienna University of Technology started the MobiLearn project[1]. It aims at offering digital content

---

[1] The project has been partially funded by the initiative "Neue Medien in der Lehre an Universitäten und Fachhochschulen" of the Austrian Federal Ministry for Education, Science and Culture.

C. Bussler et al. (Eds.): WISE 2004 Workshops, LNCS 3307, pp. 114–124, 2004.

from the domain of "Medieninformatik" composed in a form that specifically serves mobile learning teams and exploits the WLAN-enhanced infrastructure already provided at the university sites. The project is based on e-learning scenarios that take into account learning any time any where, i.e., providing digital content in the class room, at the PC or notebook of a student, at a PDA or Smartphone, depending on the needs of students and of course on the capabilities of the devices used. Students also should be supported in terms of collaborative learning in small teams.

The MobiLearn approach avoids creation of preorchestrated content, but allows to come up with highly modular content that can be combined as needed by teachers as well as students and that can be made available in proper form for the various output channels like online PC/notebooks, online or offline PDAs or Smartphones as well as for offline print products. MobiLearn content is not available in terms of single, downloadable files, but is accessible by means of different views, e.g., a view that very much fits the traditional way of presenting a subject in a class room at an European university, a view that meets the needs of students just starting out learning from examples, a view that prefers the presentation of definitions and concepts to focus more on models and theory, a view that only contains the essential issues by means of questions that may be part of an examination later on.

Given these application scenarios it is quite obvious that content needs to be structured such that it can be used for the various purposes of a any-time-any-where scenario. This paper addresses the approach taken to support the creation and management of such kind of structured content. Section 2 presents the approach taken for modelling and structuring the content. Section 3 presents architectural issues relevant for the realization of the approach. Section 4 addresses the open issues that need to be worked on or turned out to be critical for the overall success. Section 5 concludes the paper and gives some details on the first version of the prototype deployed at the participating sites.

2   Structuring Content

2.1   Structuring Courses: Learning Unit

In order to be able to process logical pieces of content according to the application scenario given above it is required to have well-defined means of structuring content. There are several approaches one can find in related projects, e.g., the LaMedica project[1], the Cardio-OP project[2][3][4] that already provide semi-structured content in some way. These approaches either follow some proprietary model or rely on (quasi) standards that facilitate structuring content, e.g., the approaches taken by ADL SCORM[5] or IMS[6], that mainly follow and are based on the IEEE LOM standard[7].

It is quite obvious and well accepted to structure content by means of "learning objects". But there is still no definite answer to the question of what a learning object is. The Learning Object Metadata Working Group of the IEEE

Learning Technology Standards Committee (LTSC) provides a very global definition: "Any entity, digital or non-digital, which can be used, re-used or referenced during technology supported learning"[7]. David A. Wiley in [11] - criticising the existing confusion created by the loads of definitions that are either too broad or too narrow - provides a more focused working definition for learning object: "any digital resource that can be reused to support learning".

To avoid any ambiguity, for the purpose of the MobiLearn project, we use the term of *"learning unit"* defined as self-contained unit of learning, ranging from 15 minutes to 45 minutes. Each learning unit is independent and can be reused as is in multiple contexts for multiple purposes ("black-box-reuse"). Learning units are aggregated to *modules*. The volume of a module corresponds to a typical class, i.e., it corresponds to about 1-2 ECTS points. Technically, the aggregation of learning units to modules is realized according to the IMS Content Packaging Specification[6]. Following the IMS Specification increases the interoperability of the learning content between different management systems. Furthermore, a collection of modules, called *course*, may be used to form a whole educational programme.

So far we rather have a very traditional structuring schema. The distinctiveness of the MobiLearn project is the way we structure learning units. The model considers the new learning paradigms without losing the connection to the traditional learning content. A student, on her way to exam, recalling the outlines of a given subject, using her PDA, is accessing the same content as some student, sitting at home and just starting to read a lecture about the same subject on his Notebook. Thus a single learning unit has to be deliverable at various devices, has to provide for varying degree of intensity of content and even for its semantic aspects at very low level. Fig. 1 shows the conceptual model of aggregating and structuring learning units in the MobiLearn project by means of an UML diagram. It shows that learning units are composed of presentation units characterized by a *level of detail (LOD)*, an indicator for the intended use of the material. Each presentation unit consists of blocks carrying an optional header and data (text, figures, etc.). Blocks are intended to be rendered for specific devices, e.g. PC, PDA or a Smartphone. Intuitive examples of types of blocks are *Definition* representing a formal definition of some subject, *Example* representing some example on a subject, *Interaction* representing some interactive element on a subject.

The subsequent sections describe the key concepts of the structuring scheme: structuring according to didactic aspects, multichannel delivery, and level of details.

2.2   The Concepts of Learning Units

Didactics. Didactic aspects of learning content gain in importance every day. Students look for direct access to certain parts of a lecture "on demand" during various phases of learning instead of going through all the material again and again. One way to solve this problem is to write really small learning units and to annotate them with proper metadata (e.g., according to Learning Object

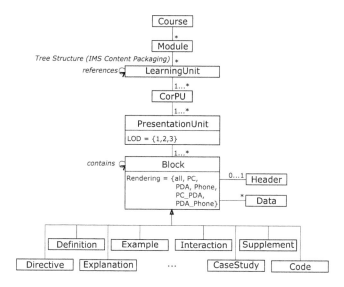

Fig. 1. Conceptual model of learning unitl

Metadata[7]. The way we choose to go is to tag every single paragraph or even whole section(*"Block"*) while writing the content. Authors don't have to annotated the material later on and users can easily filter the relevant aspects of the given learning unit or even of whole modules.

The following XML snippet shows and example of a proper annotated learning unit:

```
...
<LearningUnit>
    ...
    <Definition>
        <Header>XSLT</Header>
        <Data>
            Extensible Stylesheet Language Transformation (XSLT)
            is a language for expressing transformation of XML
            documents from one form into another.
        </Data>
        <Explanation>
            <Data>
                A transformation process expressed in XSLT describes
                rules for transforming a source XML tree into a
                result tree that can be another XML document, an
                HTML document, or any other text format...
            </Data>
        </Explanation>
    </Definition>
```

```
    . . .
</LearningUnit>
```

In the MobiLearn project we have defined a set of 16 didactic elements based on evaluation of existing didactic schemes and our rich teaching experience. Nevertheless the collection of elements is defined in such a way that it can be easily extended with minimal change of the XML Document Type Definition (DTD) that encodes the elements and without any destructive effects to existing content:

```
<!ENTITY % BlockType
  " CaseStudy | Code | Content | Definition
  | Directive | Example |  Exercise |  Explanation
  | Information | Interaction | Motivation | Quotation
  | References | Summary | Test | Theorem ">
```

Multichannel Delivery. The MobiLearn project considers three categories of devices - Notebooks and Personal Computer, PDA, and Smartphone - with different capabilities and limited resources related to display size, processing power and communication bandwidth. Thus the presentation of the content has to be adapted to the learning device on the fly. Automated transformations from XML-coded base content into *device-specific presentation* is supported (see Fig. 2 and Fig. 3).

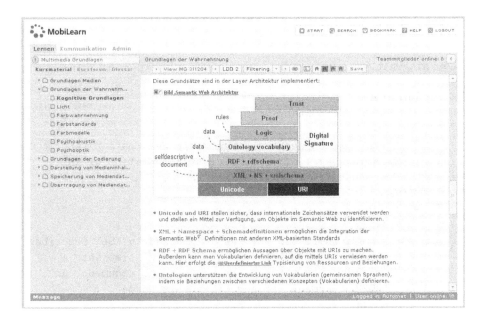

Fig. 2. Device-specific presentation for Notebook

Fig. 3. Device-specific presentation for PDA

Device types are annotated by appropriate attributes at the block level:

```
...
<LearningUnit>
    ...
    <Example Rendering="PC">
       [Encoding of content with e.g., big images, table]
    </Example>
    <Example Rendering="PDA">
       [Encoding of content only in textual representation]
    </Example>
    ...
</LearningUnit>
```

Again just a minor extension of the MobiLearn DTD with further attribute values allowed for the attribute "Rendering" is needed, if support of any further device is required.

Level of Detail. Learning units are sequential compositions of *presentation units*. A presentation unit is composed of one or more content blocks presenting given subject at the same level of granularity, encoded by means of - *Level of Detail*(LOD). The MobiLearn project considers three Levels of Detail:

1. *Level 1* gives an overview of the learning content. This level corresponds approxiamately to a slide view of the content used for lecture readings
2. *Level 2* represents the more comprehensive course material, a script format or maybe a kind of textbook of the learning content. This level is useful for students, who are not familiar with the subject and need to rely on more detailed material in order to understand the subject.
3. *Level 3* summarizes any additional information relevant to the subject and supporting the better understanding of the subject, including references to external materials and interactive elements.

Furthermore the three Levels of Detail are synchronized among each other, i.e. each Presentation Unit may have one or more corresponding presentation units at the other levels of detail. Thus switching between the available levels of detail is provided.

The following XML code illustrates the use of the LOD concept. Note, that the context of corresponding presentation units is established by the tag <CorPU> that contains presentation units assigned to different Levels of Detail.

```
. . .
<LearningUnit>
   <CorPU>
      <PresentationUnit LOD="1">
         [Content in a slide view, keywords]
      </PresentationUnit>
      <PresentationUnit LOD="2">
         [Content in a textbook or script style]
      </PresentationUnit>
      <PresentationUnit LOD="3">
         [Additional information, references, examples,
         interactive element]
      </PresentationUnit>
   </CorPU>
   . . .
</LearningUnit>
```

Users are able to choose content at different Levels of Detail depending on their current learning situation - e.g., learning at home or refreshing content while on the move.

3 Architectural Design

Content stored as XML has one essential aspect: using different transformation processes it is possible to convert any XML-coded data into various widely used structured document formats ((X)HTML, SMIL, PDF, etc.). In [12] a quite common architecture for multi channel delivery systems for e-learning is presented. In that model XML coded data is adapted to the capabilities of the requesting device via appropriate transformation processes. In the MobiLearn project we expanded the transformation part of that model as we needed transformation processes considering all the three key concepts of the project (see Fig. 4). Thus such a model of multi channel delivery systems enables the adaptation of learning content to device, desired level of details of content and semantic aspects.

The model proves some remarkable advantages:

1. MobiLearn learning units are XML coded data. Hence *interoperability* is guaranteed between systems understanding the MobiLearn approach and structure of learning units fixed by a pre-defined Document Type Definition (DTD).

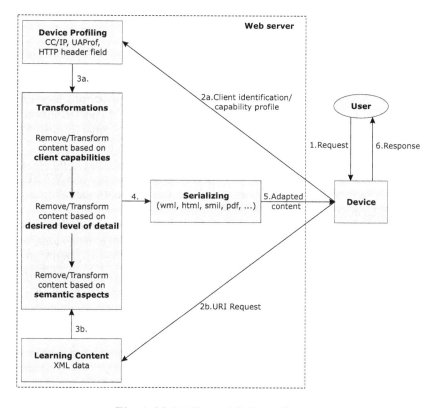

Fig. 4. Multi Channel Delivery System

2. The XML approach allows the definition of transformation processes (e.g. using the XML transformation language - XSLT[8], XSL-FO[9], or the XML query language - XQuery[10]). Such transformations enable easy *adaptation* of learning content to given requirements.

3. Transformation processes enable *delivery on the fly* as well as *delivery of offline content*. Delivery on the fly is used for online access to the content, where a quick adaptation to learners' requirements is requested. Still a lot of experts show significant preference for traditional printed material (see [13]) for reading, because learning online significantly reduces learning efficiency and speeds up the fatigues of the learners. An example for offline content are the traditional printed scripts (a kind of textbook). Still some advantages of the online content, i.e., its interactivity, potential animation, video or audio, are lost in printed material. For printed material, an easy connection to the lost multimedia elements was enabled by the idea of so called PaperLinks (see [14]). PaperLinks establish relationships between locations identified by e.g. barcodes in printed material and digital content.

4   Open Issues

Although the approach taken has been realized by the project consortium and a first version of the system has been put in operation, there are still many open issues that require further research and effort in order to find adequate solutions or improve existing solutions. One of the most important issues is the complexity and the degree of freedom of the Document Type Definition that specifies the details of the structuring according to the scheme given in Fig. 1. The richer the structuring primitives given by the various block types and their possible composition the more complex the authoring process. From the given experience of the project partners it is absolutely essential to have a WYSIWYG authoring system that fully supports the primitive concepts including level of details, rendering types, and didactic elements.

Another very important issue is to provide guiding rules during the authoring process that support an author in composing the blocks like definitions, explanations, or examples. Such guiding rules should not be "hard-wired" into the system, but should be configurable such that different didactic models can be supported. It should not be expected that teachers always agree on the pedagogical model and the underlying didactic building blocks. Hence, configurability of the composition schemes allowed is an essential requirement for the authoring system.

Another critical issue is the availability of an adequate e-learning platform. In our case we have available the SCHOLION system (see [15][16]) that has been initially implemented by the University of Linz and that has proved its applicability and usability already in the context of many classes. In the MobiLearn project that platform has been redesigned and extended to meet the specific requirements of the project. The platform needs to support the fine-grained structuring of the digital content in terms of it services, otherwise a user cannot exploit the added value of highly structured course material. Unfortunately, no one of the widely used and well known e-learning platforms provides enough support for structured content as given in the MobiLearn project. Even the possibility to import MobiLearn content by means of IMS compliant packaging does not solve the problem, as all the structuring within a presentation unit (see Fig. 1) is lost after importing and not made available for the user because of missing functionality of the e-learning platform.

These issues are considered to be most critical and there is significant further research effort needed to improve authoring tools and platform.

5   Conclusion

In this paper we presented a model for structuring content for a mobile e-learning environment. The structuring scheme incorporates didactically classified pieces of content (encoded by means of "Blocks"), that can be delivered to and rendered for individual device types (following the multi channel delivery approach and essentially covering PC or Notebook, PDA, and Smartphone), presented in different information intensity (encoded in terms of levels of detail), respectively.

The project follows a very modular approach: didactic elements can be easily defined and introduced by means of "Blocks" just by extending the predefined set of didactic XML elements in the MobiLearn DTD. Further device types can be easily supported by extending the set of attribute values allowed to be choosen for the rendering attribute at the block level. And even the level of semantic granularity of the content can be extended by introducing another level of detail in case the three levels of detail, currently choosen in the project, do not sufficiently fit particular learning needs.

We consider the openness and interoperability of the approach as a big advantage and strength compared to other approaches that either do not provide fine grained structuring of content or only provide hard-wired models that cannot always be adapted to specific needs.

Given our experience we can conclude that powerful tools are needed for authoring and presenting e-learning material composed according to our approach. Although we have specific tools available in our project environment, we consider the development of more suitable collaborative authoring tools as essential as the improvement of the e-learning platforms. Our future work will focus on these issues among the incorporation of the experiences resulting from operating the MobiLearn system in the teaching context of the different universities involved in the project.

Acknowledgement. We would like to thank all our colleagues from the Vienna University of Technology, the University of Klagenfurt and the University of Linz in the MobiLearn project for their collaboration in developing the MobiLearn approach and implementing the tools needed to run the system on a daily basis for our courses.

References

1. Friedl, R.; Preisack, M.B.; Klas, W.; Rose, T.; Stracke, S.; Quast, K.J.; Hannekum, A.; Godje, O.: Virtual Reality and 3D Visualizations in Heart Surgery Education. Heart Surg Forum. 2002; 5(3):E17-21. PMID: 12732500 (2002)
2. Klas, W.; Greiner, C.; Friedl, R.: Cardio-OP: Gallery of cardiac surgery. IEEE International Conference on Multimedia Computing and Systems 2:1092- 5 (1999)
3. Friedl, R.; Preisack, M.B.; Schefer, M.; Klas, W.; Tremper, J.; Rose, T.; Bay, J.; Albers, J.; Engels, P.; Guilliard, P.; Vahl, C.F.; Hannekum, A.: CardioOp: an integrated approach to teleteaching in cardiac surgery. Stud Health Technol Inform 70:76-82 (2000)
4. Friedl, R.; Klas, W.; Westermann, U.; Rose, T.; Tremper, J.; Stracke, S.; Godje, O.; Hannekum, A.; Preisack, M.B.: The CardioOP-Data Clas (CDC). Development and application of a thesaurus for content management and multi-user teleteaching in cardiac surgery. Methods Inf Med. 2003; 42(1):68-78. PMID: 12695798 (2003)
5. ADL Sharable Content Object Reference Model (SCORM) Version 1.3 (January 2004) http://www.adlnet.org/
6. IMS Content Packaging Specification v1.1.3 (July 2003) http://www.imsglobal.org/content/packaging/

7. 1484.12.1 IEEE Standard for Learning Object Metadata (June 2002)
   http://ltsc.ieee.org/wg12
8. W3C Recommendation. XSL Transformation (XSLT). Version 1.0 (November 1999). http://www.w3.org/TR/xslt
9. W3C Recommendation. Extensible Stylesheet Language (XSL). Version 1.0. October 2001. http://www.w3.org/TR/xsl/
10. W3C Working Draft. XML Query Language. November 2003.
    http://www.w3.org/TR/xquery/
11. Wiley, D.A.: Connecting Learning Objects to Instructional Design Theory. In D. A. Wiley (ed.), The Instructional Use of Learning Objects. Agency for Instructional Technology and the Association for Educational Communications and Technology. ISBN: 0-7842-0892-1. (2002)
12. Topland, K.O.: Mobile learning. Technological challenges on multi-channel e-learning services. Master Thesis. Agder University College, Norway (2002)
13. Mills, C.B.; Weldon, L.J.: Reading text from computer screens. ACM Computing Surveys 19/4 (1987)
14. Hitz, M.; Plattner, S.: PaperLinks - Linking Printouts to Mobile Devices. MLEARN 2004, Italy (2004)
15. Froschauer, B.; Stary, C.; Ellmer, M.; Pilsl, T.; Ortner, W.; Totter, A.: SCHOLION - Scaleable Technologies for Telelearning. Proceedings of the 2000 ACM Symposium on Applied Computing, Como, Italy, ACM (2000)
16. Auinger, A.; Stary, C.: Embedding Self-Management and Generic Learning Support into Courseware StructuresProceedings of the 35th Hawaii International Conference on Systems Sciences, IEEE (2002)

Smart Virtual Counterparts for Learning Communities

Mohan Baruwal Chhetri, Shonali Krishnaswamy, and Seng Wai Loke

School of Computer Science and Software Engineering, Monash University
{Mohan.Chhetri, Shonali.Krishnaswamy,
Seng.Loke}infotech.monash.edu.au

Abstract. Virtual learning environments can be greatly improved if they can provide location independent services and personalized interactions to the learning community. One way of achieving this is by having smart virtual counterparts to represent the users in the virtual learning environment. We propose that mobile agent technology is aptly suited for providing such smart virtual counterparts to represent learners, teachers and institutions in the virtual learning community.

1 Introduction

Education in the 21st century is undergoing a steady state of transition. There is a constant shift from the traditional view of regarding *teachers* as *content providers* and *transmitters* towards that of a *mentor* guiding and supporting *learners* through the process of knowledge acquisition [1]. This change is brought about by the need to adopt new approaches to teaching and learning in a world highly driven by technology. As a result of emerging computing paradigms such as ubiquitous computing, pervasive computing, and nomadic computing [10], learning can now be viewed as a global, life-long and flexible activity that can be carried in all environments with the learners themselves directing the learning process [1].

With the integration of technology into the learning process, universities are increasingly restructuring the educational system to support learning in virtual environments. A Virtual Learning Environment (VLE) can be defined a social space [2] in which teachers and students interact both synchronously and asynchronously. Its central concept is a virtual world in which participants can meet and interact. Users are represented in this virtual world by an avatar or a virtual counterpart [3]. It is important to remember that the driving force behind the notion of VLEs is the *learning* aspect and the virtuality refers to the technology, which is brought in to support learning in such an environment [1].

While numerous web-based educational systems have been deployed in recent years, most of these systems are non-interactive and non-adaptive [4]. They don't support features such as delivery of dynamic content, off-line learning and examinations, or user context awareness. Tools that assist learning in such passive virtual learning environments include e-mail, bulletin boards, chat rooms and whiteboards and can be considered as passive virtual counterparts of teachers and learners because they cannot provide the required level of autonomy, extensibility, re-configurability and rich personalized interactions required in virtual learning

C. Bussler et al. (Eds.): WISE 2004 Workshops, LNCS 3307, pp. 125–134, 2004.
© Springer-Verlag Berlin Heidelberg 2004

environments. Users aren't able to delegate tasks to these passive counterparts and some form of human intervention is necessary to initiate and supervise the teaching and learning process.

Virtual learning environments can be made as interactive and responsive to individual needs as learning in the physical environment if the virtual counterparts of teachers and learners can exhibit *smartness*. Mobile agent technology is particularly suited for developing intelligent virtual learning environments because mobile agents exhibit autonomous behaviour and can be engineered to decide the *when, why, with whom* and *whether at all* [5] of their interaction with other components in their environment. Mobile agents are also able to adapt to different working environments such as on-line mode, off-line mode and disconnected mode, and are particularly suited for building distributed applications involving *partially connected computing* [6]. This inherent distributed nature of mobile agents makes them ideally suited for developing educational applications for sharing resources on heterogeneous systems and platforms [7][17].

In this paper we propose that smart virtual counterparts can better represent users in virtual learning environments and can become a natural extension to human capabilities. They can work on heterogeneous networks and platforms and still be able to provide the users with personalized interactions in a persistent environment. We have designed the *Smart Seminar Room*, an application based upon the concepts of *virtual learning environments* [2] and *smart spaces* [8], in which mobile agents act as the *smart virtual counterparts* of *teachers* and *learners*. This application combines wireless technology and portable devices (mobile and stationary) to provide services to users of lecture theatres namely students and lecturers in universities. We have customized the service request, service presentation and negotiation process to support different kinds of users. We have adopted a *user-centred* approach in designing the Smart Seminar Room. Each user is represented in the virtual world by a software agent, which acts in accordance with the explicit/implicit input it receives from the user.

This paper is structured as follows. Section 2 discusses the smart virtual presence of real world entities. Section 3 describes the modelling of smart virtual counterparts while section 4 discusses the mapping of smart virtual counterparts to the learning/teaching environment. Section 5 discusses the implementation of the Smart Seminar Room and section 6 concludes the paper.

2   Smart Virtual Presence of Real World Entities

In the physical world, we can divide real world entities into three categories – *people, places* and *things* [9]. *People* are capable of moving between *places,* interacting with other *people*, and finding and using *things*. Technological advances enable enhanced access to people, places and things by augmenting them with useful IT functionality giving them a virtual presence [9] [10]. However the virtual world appears largely unstructured and it is difficult to associate real world entities with their virtual counterparts. This necessitates the need for dedicated representatives of real world entities in the virtual world, i.e. smart counterparts in the virtual world. Each real world entity can have several virtual counterparts (both active and passive) as shown in Figure 1. A virtual counterpart can represent several physical counterparts though not all virtual world entities need have a corresponding physical counterpart in the real world. However, we are more concerned with the active virtual counterparts of real world entities.

Services in virtual environments are supplied by, or based around *people, places* and *things*. Traditionally these services are confined to physical boundaries and are user-driven requiring user participation. Considerable research has been done on the concept of *smart spaces/smart environments* taking the approach that the *smart environment* has a finite physical boundary [9] [11] [12] within which services are offered by real world entities. Notable examples include Hewlett Packard's **CoolTown** project (www.cooltown.com) and AT & T laboratories' **Sentient Computing** project (www.uk.research.att.com/spirit/) among others.

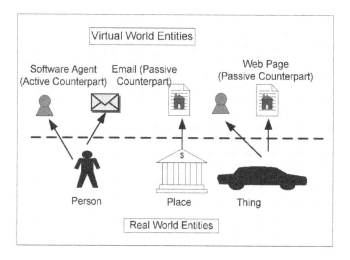

Fig. 1. Every real world entity has a virtual counterpart, which enables them to interact in the virtual world.

We take the approach that users can avail of services provided within smart spaces irrespective of their physical location. Both, the *people* and the *things* need not be required to physically enter the boundaries of the *smart environment* in order to provide services or to access the services offered. Users should be able to deploy their virtual counterparts who can access the services via logical mobility as if they were accessing the services locally. Moreover, the services offered to users should be at a much higher-level, which meet their needs irrespective of place and time. Such services include services providing remote access to people, places and things [9]. In smart environments, services are provided by the virtual counterparts of real world entities and are used by the virtual counterparts of real world entities. In an ideal situation, a smart environment would be able to provide two kinds of services – services that can be accessed from only within the physical boundaries, and services that can be accessed from both within and outside the smart space as shown in Figure 2.

This approach can be mapped to the notion of virtual learning environments as well. Technological advances have made it possible for the teaching community to provide teaching services within smart environments through their smart virtual counterparts. Similarly the learning community can also make avail of these services via their own smart virtual counterparts. The teachers have an opportunity to offer learning to those learners who are unable to participate in a traditional face-to-face environment [1]. Similarly smart virtual counterparts of students provide user support within the environment [3], allow sharing of educational resources [7][17] and optimize the learning process.

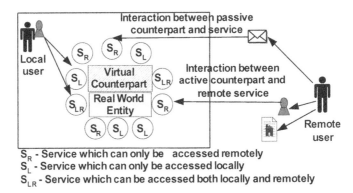

Fig. 2. An Ideal Smart Space should offer different kinds of services that can be accessed by active and passive counterparts of users.

3 Modelling Smart Virtual Counterparts

In order to achieve effective and personalized interaction with the learning environments, it is necessary to take the user's context into account. Keeping this in mind, we have adopted a user-centric approach while designing the smart virtual counterparts of users within the Smart Seminar Room. In our design, each user is represented by a software agent, which acts according to explicit/implicit input it receives from the user. This agent dialogues, communicates and negotiates with other agents within the learning environment on their behalf. These virtual counterparts represent the users in their interaction with the services available in the smart environment.

We have modelled three types of agents in our design of:

- **User Agents:** these are the smart virtual counterparts of the users (teachers and learners) that negotiate services with the smart environment on their behalf.
- **Service/System Agents:** these agents are also smart virtual counterparts of real world entities (representing a University lecture theatre in this particular case), which are specialized according to the kind of service they provide to the user agents.

- **Interface Agents:** these agents do not represent any real world entities in the virtual world. They interact with the user agents and the service agents and facilitate the interaction between the two.

In order to achieve effective personal interaction between the virtual counterparts and the corresponding real world entities, context awareness is of increasing importance. Since, with the mobility of users, their context changes constantly, the agents should be able to take into account, several factors such as the user's location, interaction device and time of day among others. From a learning perspective, a student can move between different environments (home, university, travelling) reflecting different learning modes (more participatory at university, more focussed while using the computer, or more passive while engaged in some recreational activity such as watching TV) [16]. Hence the interaction between the user and the user agent takes on added significance. The agent can take input from the user in two ways – explicitly from the user via different means such as a graphical user interface or speech, and implicitly from a *smart to do list* [8] which the agent developer has already prepared. This user input is then transformed into a service request, which is submitted to the smart environment.

4 Design of the Smart Seminar Room

The Smart Seminar Room is based upon the concept of *smart learning environments*. It aims to support the nomadic teaching and learning communities of the universities namely lecturers and students. The basic functionality of the Smart Seminar Room focuses on the ability of a user (teacher/student) to delegate agents from his/her device (such as palmtop, laptop or a desktop) to access the services about the lecture theatre such as making bookings, checking available facilities etc. In the Smart Seminar Room, all the real world entities including the users, and the seminar room system are represented by software agents – mobile and stationary, in the virtual world. Each interaction between the user and the seminar room is taken care of by their virtual counterparts.

There are three kinds of users of the Smart Seminar Room – students, lecturers and the administrator, represented by the *Student Agent, Lecturer Agent* and the *Administrator Agent* respectively. The *Seminar Room Agent* provides the services to the user agents in the Smart Seminar Room. It is the virtual counterpart of the lecture theatre. The services offered by the Smart Seminar Room differ according to the type of user request. Students can receive information about lecturers and the units they teach. The administrator performs database administration that includes insert, update and delete operations on the Smart Seminar Room database. The lecturers are the main users of the Smart Seminar Room. They can check up information about the seminar halls, make comparisons, make bookings on these seminar halls and cancel bookings. In the event that a lecture hall required by Lecturer A at a specific time slot has already been booked by another lecturer B, the user agent for A can negotiate the booking with the user agent of B by migrating to the user device of Lecturer B.

In addition to the user agents and the service agents, there are also interface agents such as the query agent, booking agent and the negotiation agent. These agents do not represent any real world entity but act as intermediaries between the user agents and the service agents. Table 1 shows the real world entities that interact with the Smart

Seminar Room and their virtual counterparts. Table 2 shows the services available to each type of user of the Smart Seminar Room. As mentioned previously, each user is offered different levels of services depending upon the user-type. Figure 3 shows the different users of the Smart Seminar Room and their virtual counterparts as well as the virtual counterpart of the seminar hall that offers the different services based upon user type.

Table 1. The different real world entities and their virtual counterparts in the Smart Seminar Room system

Real World Entity	Virtual Counterpart	Agent Type
Seminar Hall	Seminar-Hall Agent	Service Agent
Student	Student Agent	User Agent
Lecturer	Lecturer Agent	User Agent
Administrator	Administrator Agent	User Agent
	Query Agent	Interface Agent
	Booking Agent	Interface Agent
	Negotiation Agent	Interface Agent
	Update Agent	Interface Agent

Table 2. Services available to each type of user of the Smart Seminar Room

User Type	Services Available
Lecturer	• Check seminar hall Details • Make Bookings • Cancel Bookings • Negotiate Bookings
Administrator	• Add/update users • Add/update seminar halls
Student	• Check lecturer details • Check unit details

The following scenario demonstrates an interesting case of interaction of the smart virtual counterparts with each other and with their physical counterparts. Let us consider the case where a lecturer at location A wants to book a seminar hall for a particular time slot. So the lecturer can trigger the *Lecturer Agent*, which in turn invokes the *Booking Agent* that migrates to the Smart Seminar Room. This is represented in Figure 4 as '1'. It then interacts with the *Seminar Hall Agent* and tries to make the booking. If the seminar hall has been booked by another lecturer at location B, it returns back to its user device at location A and informs Lecturer A that the hall has been booked by lecturer B for that specific time slot. This movement is represented as '2' in the figure. If lecturer A wants to negotiate the booking with lecturer B, he/she instructs the *Lecturer Agent A* which then delegates the *Booking agent* to migrate to location B to negotiate the booking as indicated by '3' in Figure 4. On reaching the mobile device of lecturer B, *Booking Agent A* tries to negotiate the booking with the *Negotiation agent* at location B. If the negotiation is successful, the *Booking agent* once again migrates to the Smart Seminar Room, cancels the booking made by lecturer B and makes the new booking. This migration is indicated in the figure by '5'. Once booking has been made, the agent returns to back to location A along '2'. If the negotiation fails, then the agent returns back to location A from location B as indicated by '4' and informs the lecturer about the failed negotiation.

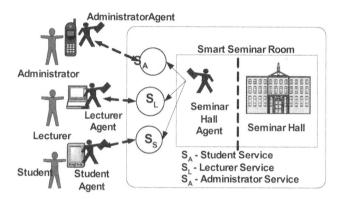

Fig. 3. The different users of the Smart Seminar Room and their virtual counterparts, and the different types of services offered by the Seminar Room Agent

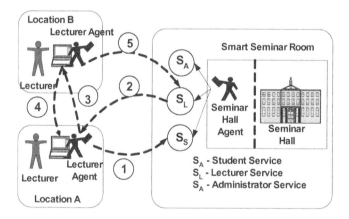

Fig. 4. Scenario showing the migration paths followed by the lecturer agent when the lecturer A wants to negotiate a booking made by lecturer B

This interaction shows how software agents (mobile and stationary) can be effectively deployed in the virtual learning environments to better represent the principal actors (teachers and learners) and provide a richer level of interaction within the virtual world.

5   Implementation of the Smart Seminar Room

The Smart Seminar Room was implemented using the Grasshopper Mobile Agent Toolkit [13]. Grasshopper is the first mobile agent toolkit, which has been developed compliant to the Mobile Agent System Interoperability Facility (MASIF) standards [14]. The Smart Seminar Room chiefly consists of two components – the user device on which the *Student, Lecturer* and the *Administrator Agents* are created and reside and the system device on which the *Seminar-Hall Agent* resides and offers services. Depending upon the type of user and the user needs, the *Query Agent,* the *Booking Agent, Negotiation Agent* or the *Update Agent* are initiated in the user device. These agents are mobile and migrate to the system device of the Smart Seminar Room and interact with the *Seminar Hall Agent* to process the queries input by the users. While the Seminar Hall device is always up and running, and is registered with a region registry, the users can start up their devices as and when they want to use the Smart Seminar System. Once they have finished using the services of the system, they can choose to close the application. However in the case of the lecturers, the agency on the user device has to be up and running throughout the life cycle of the system in order to facilitate the negotiation of bookings

Negotiation, which is one of the most important features that is facilitated by using mobile agent technology, is performed on the user device of the Lecturer. The first step in running this system is to have the Region Registry running. Once the Region Registry is started up and is running, the Server agency (representing the *Seminar Hall Agent*) has to be started on the system device. This is registered with the Region Registry. Similarly all the users of the system have to start up the Grasshopper agencies in their respective user devices and register with the Region Registry when they want to use the SSR system.

Once the agency has been registered, the user (in this case the Lecturer) is required to enter the login name and password and select from the list of options available. He/she is then required to enter the booking details and submit the request for processing. Once the lecturer has pressed the 'Submit' button, the *Booking Agent* migrates to the system device with the user request. The lecturer is informed of this migration via a message box. Once the booking has been confirmed, the *Booking Agent* returns to the user device of the lecturer and displays the booking results.

Once the lecturer books a lecture hall, it is possible that another lecturer requests the same hall at the same time and day. In such an event, negotiation takes place if the lecturer who originally booked the theatre is willing to swap the booking. The lecturer is asked if he/she wants to negotiate the booking with the other lecturer. If the lecturer decides to negotiate the booking, then the *Booking Agent* migrates to the agency of the other lecturer and tries to negotiate the booking. If the negotiation fails, the *Booking Agent* returns with the negotiation result and informs the lecturer. If the negotiation is successful, then the *Booking Agent* for the negotiating lecturer migrates from the user device of the other lecturer back to the system device and cancels the original booking. Then it makes the new booking and returns to its own user device. The *Negotiation Agent* informs the lecturer who made the first booking before cancelling the booking. The *Booking Agent* then goes from the other user device to the system device, cancels the original booking and makes the new booking. It then returns with the booking results.

6   Conclusion

In this paper we have stated that the concept of *intelligent environments* should not be confined to physical boundaries but should transcend them. Also with the availability of ubiquitous and mobile computing environments, it is possible to enhance *smart environments* by deploying the smart virtual counterparts of real world entities. Mobile agents can be used to link the physical world of people, places and things with the virtual world of services and applications. They can be used to provide personalized interactions with smart environments and provide location independent services to the user's mobile, portable computing device. This approach holds particularly true in the field of education where the entire teaching/learning experience can be enhanced by using mobile agents as the smart virtual counterparts of teachers and learners.

References

1. Barajas, Mario & Owen, Martin "Implementing Virtual Learning Environments: Looking for Holistic Approach" in *Educational Technology & Society* 3(3) 2000.
2. Dillenbourg, Pierre "Virtual Learning Environments" in *EUN Conference 2000: Workshop on Virtual Learning Environments*, 2000
3. Bouras, Ch., Philopoulos, A. and Tsiatox, Th., "A Neworked Intelligent Distributed Virtual Training Environment: A First Approach" in *5th Joint Conference on Information Sciences-JCIS'2000-1st International Workshop on Intelligent Multimedia Computing and Networking*, Taj Mahal, Atlantic City, New Jersey, USA, 2000, Vol. 2, pp. 604-607
4. Zakaria, Azizi., Siraj, Fadzilah., Ahdon, Mohd. Fadli., Hussin, Mohd. Zaidil Adha Mat, "PEAGENT: An Interactive Web-Based Educational System Using Animated Pedagogical Agent" in *Proceedings of International Conference on Artificial Intelligence Application in Engineering and Information Technology (ICAIET 2002)*, Hotel Sutera Magellan, Kota Kinabalu, Sabah. 17-18 June 2002.
5. Weiβ, G., "Agent Orientation in Software Engineering" in *Knowledge Engineering Review*, 2002, Vol 16, No 4, pp. 349-373
6. Gray, R., Kotz, D., Nog, S., Rus, D., Cybenko, G., "Mobile agents: the next generation in distributed computing" in *Proceedings of the Second Aizu International Symposium on Parallel Algorithms/Architecture Synthesis, 1997*, pp. 8-24.
7. Hong Hong and Kinshuk, "Mobile Agents in Adaptive Learning Systems" in the *Proceedings of the IEEE International Workshop on Wireless and Mobile Technologies in Education (WMTE'02)*, 2002.
8. Carolis De Berardina, Sebastiano Pizzutilo, "A MultiAgent Infrastructure supporting Personalized Interaction with Smart Environments", in *Proceedings of Workshop on Ubiquitous Agents on embedded, wearable, and mobile devices held in conjunction with the 2002 Conference on Autonomous Agents & Multiagent Systems (AAMAS 2002)*, 2002.
9. Kindberg, Tim, et.al., "People, Places, Things: Web Presence for the Real World" in the *3rd IEEE Workshop on Mobile Computing Systems and Applications*, pp. 19-28, 7-8 Dec 2000.
10. Romer, K., Schoch, T., Mattern, F., Dubendorfer, T.D., "Smart identification frameworks for ubiquitous computing applications" in *Proceedings of the 1st IEEE International Conference on Pervasive Computing and Communications (PerCom 2003)*, pp. 253-262, 23-26, March 2003.

11. Fox, B. Johanson, P. Hanrahan, and T. Winograd, "Integrating Information Appliances into an Interactive Workspace" in *IEEE Computer Graphics & Applications*, 20 (3), May/June 2000.
12. Kidd, G. Abowd, C. Atkeson, I.Essa, B. MacIntyre, E. Mynatt, T. Starner "The Aware Home: A Living Laboratory for Ubiquitous Computing Research" in *the Proceedings of the Second International Workshop on Cooperative Buildings – CoBuild'99.*
13. Grasshopper 2 – The Agent Platform at http://www.grasshopper.de/
14. OMG (1995), Common Facilities RFP3, Request for Proposal OMG TC Document 95-11-3, Nov. 1995, http://www.omg.org/; MASIF specification is available through http://ftp.omg.org/pub/docs/orbos/97-10-05.pdf
15. Saha, D.; Mukherjee, A.; "Pervasive Computing: a paradigm for the 21st century" in *Computer, Vol: 36 Issue: 3*, pp. 25-31, March 2003.
16. Mavrommati, Irene, "Situatied Interaction in an educational setting: Position paper" in http://www.teco.edu/chi2000ws/papers/25_mavrommati.pdf accessed on 11th February 2004.
17. Hong H., Kinshuk, He X., Patel A. & Jesshope C. "Application of Mobile agents in Web-based Learning environment" in *Proceedings of Ed-Media 2001*, Tampere, Finland. Montgomerie, C. and Viteli, J. (Eds). AACE, Vancouver, USA. ISBN 1-880094-42-8.
18. Pedro Perez, Gonzalo Mendez, Angelica de Antonio, "mIVA: Why to Use Mobile Agents in Virtual Environments and Wireless Devices" in *ECAI 2002, 15th European Conference on Artificial Intelligence. Workshop W6, Artificial Intelligence in Mobile System*, Lyon, France, July 2002.

Design and Implementation of Mobile Class Web Site for Promoting Communication

Yeonho Hong[1], Suk-ki[2], Woochun Jun[3], and Le Gruenwald[4]

[1] Seoul Usin Elementary School, Seoul, Korea
ddal_3@hanmail.net
[2] Division of Business & Economics, Dankook University, Seoul, Korea
skhong017@dankook.ac.kr
[3] Dept. of Computer Education, Seoul National University of Education, Seoul, Korea
wocjun@snue.ac.kr
[4] School of Computer Science, University of Oklahoma, Norman, OK, USA
ggruenwald@ou.edu

Abstract. This research is to develop mobile class Web sites for elementary schools. Even though traditional class Web sites have promoted the collaboration among teachers, students, and students' parents, their communication has been restricted to wired networks. However, with the development of wireless data transmission technologies, traditional class Web sites can be linked with wireless networks. Armed with wireless transmission handset devices such as cellular phones and PDA (personal digital assistants), students' parents can get class information directly through those devices. This research is to develop class Web sites that can be synergistically linked between wired and wireless networks. The communication through both wired and wireless networks enables students' parents to overcome the limitation of space and time, and further promotes better collaboration with teachers.

Keywords: Wireless Networks, Mobile Networks, Class Web Sites, Wireless Internet

1 Introduction

The development of information communication technologies has driven people to access information regardless of location and time, which can be summarized by three words, *anyone, anytime,* and *anywhere.* This trend has been also applicable to education environments. With the spread of the Internet, schools have provided class Web sites for the collaboration among students, teachers, and students' parents. However, the traditional Web sites have been usually developed on the wired networks, and parents must be in front of computers in order to get class information. Considering wired computers and their physical location, parents, especially working parents, sometimes have difficulties in accessing computer terminals. It means that limitation of space and time still exists in current educational systems.

Recently, the wireless Internet is growing fast all over the world and it has been also applied to education environments. The main advantage of the wireless Internet is in its mobility. In addition to handling voice transmission, smart phones such as cellular telephones and PCS (personal communication services) can handle voice mail, e-mail, and faxes, save addresses, and access the Internet to get information.

C. Bussler et al. (Eds.): WISE 2004 Workshops, LNCS 3307, pp. 135–144, 2004.
© Springer-Verlag Berlin Heidelberg 2004

Moreover, the wireless digital cellular handset enables to trade in e-marketplace. It overcomes the limitation of space, which is still common in the current on-line environments. Especially, wireless services through digital cellular handset and wired services through computers can be synergistically combined together.

Like business application areas, education is one of the domains where the wireless Internet through smart phones can be applied. Traditionally, schools have provided students' parents with class information through paper document [1]. With the development of the Internet, the class Web site is used as a more advanced communication tool. Most schools have used Web sites, but their contents were usually limited to overall school events and academic activities. Information on individual student cannot be sufficiently provided through traditional tools. Contents of paper document written by students are not sometimes accurate, especially by students in the lower classes, and computers for the Internet connection are not always available to parents, especially working parents.

Nowadays, smart phones are considered as effective communication tools in education environments. Above all, most people have smart phones equipped with micro browsers for the Internet connection, and the use of smart phones is not restricted by time and space. Parents can get their children's class information in timely manner, and share individual information with their teachers for achieving education goals.

In spite of growing spread of the wireless Internet, scant research has been conducted on the application of the wireless Internet to education environments. The main purpose of this research is to expand the wired class Web site to the wireless class Web site. In this system, the two class Web sites were linked to maximize both mobility and usability.

This paper is organized as follows. In Section 2, we present the theoretical background and prior works. In Section 3, we design our wired and wireless class Web sites. In Section 4, we describe the implementation of the sites. Finally, we give some conclusions and further research issues in Section 5.

2   Theoretical Backgrounds and Prior Works

2.1   School Education and Students' Parents

As home is the first social organization of human, parents are the first teachers. In the rapidly changing modern society, education is not responsible for schools only, but is based on the cooperation between schools and parents. Schools should provide parents with education information such as education philosophy, policies, curriculum, and teaching methods in a consistent manner for the consistent education environments. In addition, parents have to build a close relationship with teachers to resolve possible problems, which occur in home.

Parents traditionally have taken diverse roles such as teachers, participants in school activities, learners, and information consumers [2]. Especially, as information consumers, parents require effective tools to provide diverse education information.

The research is related to the application of the wired and wireless Internet to education environments. These tools were used to provide information on education in school, which eventually build parents' participation in school education and close cooperation with teachers.

2.2 Parents' Information Requirements

Although most schools provide the Web sites, students' parents do not frequently access the sites. In addition, a representative communication tool from schools to parents is paper document. However, the paper document is one-way communication method, and its contents may not be the information the parents require.

Especially, according to the degree of concerns, parents' awareness differs. While parents may be interested in the information on academic achievement, teacher's evaluation, and children's school life, they may be less interested in education goals, school budget, and facilities [3].

The research is related to providing information parents need through wire and wireless Internet technologies. In the situation that more than 90% of parents use smart phones (cellular phones and PCSs), the wireless Internet may be more effective as a communication tool. Therefore, according to the information requirements, the research seeks to link the class Web site with the wireless class Web sites.

2.3 Characteristics of the Wireless Internet

The wireless Internet is a way of accessing the Internet without physical connection through wires. Smart phones equipped with micro browsers can access Web pages formatted to send text or other information that is suitable for tiny screens. The focus of the wireless Internet is 'mobile' rather than 'wireless', and it usually means the Internet service through mobile devices such as smart phones, PDA, and notebook computers. Table 1 compares the characteristics of the wired Internet with those of the wireless Internet [4].

Table 1. Characteristics of the wired Internet and wireless Internet

Items	Wired Internet	Wireless Internet
Transmission speed	100 Mbps	2 Mbps
Information types	Diverse including multimedia	Text & small size multimedia
Access method	PC (space limitation)	Handset (less space limitation)
Access types	Bidirectional	Unidirectional
Usage time	Less time limitation	Short period
Usage types	Diverse sites, long period	Intermittent access with 1-2 sites
User Interface	User friendly screen	Small and limited screen size
Usage fee	Accustomed to free usage.	Accustomed to be charged
Languages	HTML, JavaScript etc	HDML, WML, mHTML etc.
Representative Biz.	Diverse e-commerce areas	Limited e-commerce area

Under the wireless Internet, information can be delivered correctly by reflecting the unique characteristics of the wireless Internet. For example, the limitations of screen size and accessing time by smart phones may require text-based compact information. Terms in menu should be user friendly and consistent, and numbers should be assigned to each of menu rather than scrolling the menu. In addition, the depth of links should not be deep, and movement by the arrow keys must be minimized. A method for returning to previous points should be provided [5]. Currently, SMS (short message service) is the most frequent wireless Internet service. Other services such as bell sound download, character download, and games are also used.

2.4 Prior Works

Abundant research has been conducted on the application of information communication technologies to education environments. Specifically, Web-based systems have been introduced to promote teaching-learning effectiveness. However, in spite of the spread of mobile handheld devices, scant research on the development of education systems under the wireless Internet has been conducted.

Some researches introduced applications of mobile devices to education. The wireless Internet site provides two types of class information; (1) announcement such as school schedule, school events, and placement, (2) student class information such as teacher's evaluation, attending status, academic record, and student school life. A system is developed by HDML (handheld device markup language) to link between wireless site and wired site [1]. However because HDML is not prevalent mark up language supported by most cellular phones, the system users are very limited.

A distance learning system was introduced in [6]. Based on the WAP (wireless application protocol) and Java middle ware, the systems provide animations and sound files. Based on mobile C, a system was developed to enhancing English listening abilities in [7]. Because listening and problem solving is possible through download function, learning can continue on the off-line.

Although ordinary adults usually have cellular phones, elementary students do not. Even more, phone fees for basic and supplementary services may be an economic burden of parents. The unfavorable conditions hinder the expansion of the wireless Internet application in education.

Considering the limitations of current systems, the system here is focused on followings. First, information on school events, attending status, school life and counseling is provided. Second, the system was implemented by diverse mark up languages such as WML (wireless markup language), mHTML (mobile hyper text markup language) and HDML, by which diverse users can utilize the system.

3   The Design of a Wireless Class Web Site

The research is to develop both wired and wireless Web system, through which parents can access education information *anytime* and *anywhere*. The system users are parents who usually need information on their children's school life in a convenient way.

3.1 Contents of the System

The contents of this system have following characteristics. First, brief information is provided in text format. Examples are school events related to first grade, homework and class preparation, attending status, class life, etc. Second, the system is very easy to use for parents, and provided information is accurate. Information is provided through wired and wireless Web sites and important information is also provided promptly by SMS. Third, community is provided for promoting users' participation. Class preparation is announced and guest book is also used for diverse interactions. Finally, information can be correctly provided by accommodating diverse cellular phones, and wireless Web site can be linked with wired one.

3.2 User Interface of the System

The user interface of this system has following characteristics. First, the menu is prepared for convenient operations of cellular phones. The view of menu is limited to a screen, and operation is possible by selecting numbers or pressing arrow buttons. Second, loading time is minimized. Information is text –based, and image is not used. Third, the wireless Web site is composed of text, and emoticon is used in initial screen to transfer user's emotion through icons.

3.3 System Configurations

While parents can search detailed information by using PC, they can also access wireless Web sites by cellular phones to get brief information timely in a convenient way. The wirelesses Web sites are composed of simple levels with core information to support user-friendly operations.

3.3.1 Design of Wireless Web Site

The wireless Web site is composed of WAP documents. The initial screen and menu are provided by index.asp. After users first access the initial screen of index.asp files according to default.asp and markup language compatible with cellular phones, they access the menu screen through the operation of down button.

Figure 1 shows the overall structure of the wireless Web site. The initial screen is the first screen the user accesses before the menu screen. Emoticons were used for friendly and positive interface. For the convenience of operations, menu can be selected by either assigned numbers or arrow keys.

3.3.2 Design of Wired Web Site

The wired Web site is designed to link with the wireless Web site. The primary purpose of the site is to provide information parents need. Parents can get information on "announcement" and "preparation notice", which are also provided through the wireless Web site. While some information is shared together in the wired and wireless Web sites, some information such as class album, resource center, directions of the wireless Web site and site tour is provided on the wired Web site only.

The Web site is managed through the wired Web site. Because cellular phone buttons are tiny, the complex operations like Web site management are not appropriate through cellular phones. The common parts linking two sites are also managed through the wired Web site.

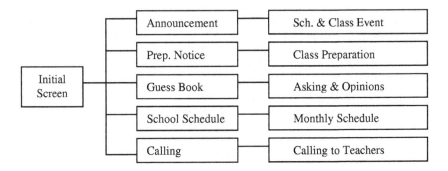

Fig. 1. Overall Structure of the Wireless Web Site

3.3.3 Design of SMS

The protocol of SMS is different from that of the wireless Internet. SMS does not need special network and works in existing network with the addition of a message center [1]. SMS is not linked with the wired Web site, but information requiring speedy delivery and/or being important is provided with parents by SMS.

Because most adults use smart phones, their usage is relatively easy, and message delivery is near to simultaneous transmission, SMS is well established as one of useful communication methods. Considering economic and technical aspects, commercial SMS server is used in the Web sites.

4   The Implementation of the Proposed Web Sites

4.1 Development Environments

The system configuration is shown in Figure 2.

WML was used as a markup language, and Namo and Anybuilder were used for site development. The wireless Web page is developed as shown in Figure 3. The tool provides convenience of development and enables to change to other languages beside WML. UP4.0 was used as a simulator, supporting SK-WML and UP-WML. Figure 4 shows the wireless Web page presented by the simulator.

After the Web server is established, the WAP server was developed. The WAP server was developed by setting up MIME (Multipurpose Internet Mail Extensions) types in the Web server.

4.2 The Wireless Web Site

The screen size of cellular phones is usually 120 to 128 pixels horizontally and 80 to 240 pixels vertically [8]. For the development of the wireless site, in addition to the screen size, the limitation of file size and transmission speed must be considered.

Figure 5 shows the initial screen of the wireless Web site, which uses emoticons.

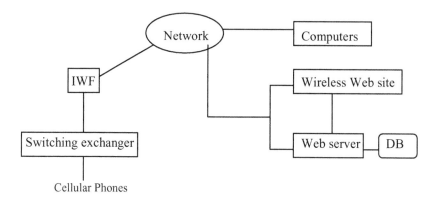

Fig. 2. System Configuration

Fig. 3. Wireless Web Page
by tools

Fig. 4. Wireless Web Page
by the Simulator

Figure 6 shows the menu screen. The menu is carefully determined so that they should be seen fully in a screen, and developed to access required information by 2-3 keystrokes only. The menu is composed of text rather than images for users' accurate and prompt understanding. The menu can be selected by either assigned numbers or arrow keys.

"Announcement" provides the relatively detailed information, of which school or class needs to inform parents. Examples are parents' meeting, school athletic meeting, class events, and other educational information. Parents can have more time to adjust their schedules through prompt announcement. Figure 7 shows "announcement" screen.

"Preparation notice" is related to information on the preparation of next classes. Because students sometimes write down the information on their notebooks inaccurately or do not write down at all, class preparation has been insufficient for quality education. However, the wireless Web site enables parents to share the information in advance through cellular phones. Figure 8 shows "preparation notice" screen.

Fig. 5. Initial Screen   **Fig. 6.** Menu Screen

Fig. 7. "Announcement" Screen   **Fig. 8.** "Preparation notice" Screen

"Gust book" is for parents who write to teachers. Because real name and telephone numbers are recorded in the cellular phone, direct calling is possible between a teacher and parents.

In addition to the functions mentioned above, "school schedule" and "calling" are available menu in the wireless Web site. Parents can confirm monthly school and class schedules, and call to the teacher teaching their children.

4.3   The Wired Web Site

Some common parts are linked between the wireless Web site and the wired Web site. Examples are "announcement", "preparation notice", "guest book", etc. Parents can access information whichever they are convenient, wired or wireless Web sites. Additionally, teachers can update Web contents in a convenient way through a computer rather than a tiny cellular phone.

Figure 9 shows the homepage of the wired Web site. Resource center, bulletin board, class album, and site tour are available in the wired Web site only, and unavailable in the wireless Web site.

"Resource center" consists of diverse multimedia files such as photos of class activities and teaching materials. Parents can access or download fast without fees through a computer. Otherwise, access and download speed would be slow with some service charge (phone fees) by using a cellular phone. "Bulletin board" is a communication tool as in other sites. "Class album" consists of students' class activity photos. Parents can access the class album to get information on their children's class activities. Parents are usually anxious to know how their children learn and act in classes. Figure 10 shows the class album. "Site tour" introduces various helpful Web sites to parents as well as students.

Fig. 9. Homepage of the wired Web site   **Fig. 10.** Class Album Screen

The wireless Web site can be seen by preview screen of the wired Web site. This function enables teachers to manage the wireless Web site in a simple and convenient way. In additional purpose, the fact that the wireless Web site is available to parents instantly, which will promote parents to use the wireless Web site. Figure 11 shows the preview screen. SMS is available to supplement the other communication ways. Because SMS is a fast and direct communication tool, it can induce parents' active participation. The effect is augmented when SMS is applied with other communication tools like paper document. Figure 11 and 12 show preview screen and SMS screen respectively.

Fig. 11. Preview Screen   **Fig. 12.** SMS Screen

5 Conclusions and Further Work

With the development of information communication technologies, a traditional communication tool like paper document has been expanded to the wired Web site, and further the wireless Web site. The wireless Web site in this research is linked with the wired Web site, and also uses SMS. The application of diverse information communication tools to education environments will get parents satisfied and promote their participation.

The following positive results are expected with the application of the proposed site.

First, parents can get information on their students in a convenient way through the wireless Web site as well as the wired Web site.

Second, parents can get class information faster and more accurately than ever, and help children prepare their classes accurately in a flexible schedule.

Third, diverse communication tools promote collaboration among students, their parents, and teachers.

In final, direct communication, especially in SMS and following calls, is available.

In spite of positive results mentioned above, the applications of the wireless Internet are not currently prevalent in education arena. Current applications of the wireless Internet seem to be focused on the communication and collaboration. However, educational applications beyond communication are more required and expected to be a major part in the near future. Above all, diverse educational contents for the wireless Internet should be developed.

References

[1]   Jang, B.: Design and Implementation of Educational Information Delivery System using Wireless Internet, Master's Thesis, Hanyang University, Seoul, Korea (2000)

[2]   Hamby, J. V.: The School-Family Link: A Key to Dropout Prevention. In Education and the Family, edited by Kaplan, L., Allyn and Bacon, Massachusetts, USA (1995)

[3]   Ahn, G.: Design and Implementation of Automatic Study Information Delivery System using Wireless Internet, Master's Thesis, Graduate School of Education, Shinra Univeristy, Korea (2002)

[4]   Kim, C.: A Study on the Development of Mobile Cultural Contents, Master's Thesis, Graduate School of Arts, Chungang University, Korea (2002)

[5]   Lee, B,: A Study on the Design Guide for Beginners in Mobile Internet, Master's Thesis, Dept. of Information & Industrial Engineering, Hongik University, Korea (2002)

[6]   Kim, D.: Design of a Distance Education System using Wireless Internet, Master's Thesis, Dept. of Computer Information, Konkook University, Korea (2002)

[7]   Park, K.: Design and Implementation of English Listening Study System in Mobile Environment, Graduate School of Education, Shinra Univesity, Korea (2002)

[8]   http://kr.ks.yahoo.com/service/question_detail.php?queId=46720

A Personal Knowledge Assistant for Knowledge Storing, Integrating, and Querying

Bogdan D. Czejdo[1], John Biguenet[1], Jonathan Biguenet[1], and J. Czejdo[2]

[1] Loyola University
New Orleans, LA 70118
czejdo@loyno.edu
[2] Edinboro University of Pennsylvania
Edinboro, PA 16412
jczejdo@edinboro.edu

Abstract. Using the underlying Unified Modeling Language (UML) for knowledge modeling, we discuss how to create a non-graphical interface to UML models and show how this interface can be used to capture knowledge from a sample domain specified in a natural language. We demonstrate the techniques of transforming a natural language text into standard sentences consisting of three tuples: known information—relationship—unknown information. We also discuss how to integrate the standard sentences with existing knowledge through a guided knowledge-discovery process in which more precise information is requested and added to the diagram in a controlled manner.

Based on this knowledge-processing methodology, a software prototype was developed. Using such software, existing PDAs or specialized hardware can allow the student to process the knowledge. These handheld devices can store, process, and retrieve knowledge from Knowledge Databases. We refer to such devices as Personal Knowledge Assistants (PKA).

1 Introduction

Handheld calculators, including graphic calculators and other equipment, have made dramatic changes in the way many subjects are taught [15]. There are several new technologies that will allow students in the near future to use small, handheld personal assistants to use Knowledge Databases covering a variety of subjects. There is, of course, an important role for larger, yet still mobile, PCs with big displays and huge memories that will allow students to keep long textbooks and other materials quickly available with unrivaled text-search possibilities. But we concentrate our discussion in this paper on small, handheld devices.

The appearance of the first Personal Digital Assistants (PDAs) several years ago did not cause the dramatic changes in education that calculators did. The educational use of PDAs in and outside the classroom is not very common. However, proper software and communication technologies such as WI-FI or BlueTooth provide a potential for the educational use of PDA-like devices. Such devices might contain Knowledge Databases.

A variety of approaches were used to store, process, and query the knowledge [1, 2, 3, 5, 10, 14, 23, 24, 25]. In this paper, we will use the underlying Unified

C. Bussler et al. (Eds.): WISE 2004 Workshops, LNCS 3307, pp. 145–158, 2004.
© Springer-Verlag Berlin Heidelberg 2004

Modeling Language (UML) for knowledge modeling. UML is traditionally used for visualizing, specifying, constructing, and documenting the artifacts of software-intensive systems [4, 11, 12, 13, 19, 20]. There have been some projects, however, that show the usefulness of UML modeling of systems not necessarily involving software [21]. James Rumbaugh, one of the authors of the UML, showed this in [21] examples of how to model the United States Constitution. We showed in several papers [6, 7, 8, 9] how we can use UML diagrams to capture classifications that constitute the basic knowledge about a variety of subjects. These classifications can be based on a subclass hierarchy, an aggregation hierarchy, named association relationships, or any combination of these. Such classifications can be used to develop a deeper understanding of the subject area, to guide in discovery of additional knowledge, and to support the learning process.

In this paper, we discuss how to create a non-graphical interface to UML models and show how this interface can be used to capture knowledge from a sample domain specified in a natural language. We show how to transform the underlying UML diagrams so that they represent a well-structured knowledge. This transformation is a guided knowledge-discovery process in which more precise information is requested and added to the diagram in a controlled manner.

Based on this knowledge-processing methodology, a software prototype was developed. Using such software, the existing PDAs can allow the student to process the knowledge. Alternatively, specialized hardware can be designed as a specialized PDA device with hardware buttons more convenient for knowledge manipulation. In both cases, we can use handheld device to store, process, and retrieve knowledge from Knowledge Databases. We will refer to such devices as Personal Knowledge Assistant (PKA).

PKA can be very useful for computer-assisted instruction (CAI) in many subject areas. In order to provide the best support for learning activities, the teaching system should consist of student PKAs and a teacher station being either another PKA or a regular mobile PC equipped with PKA software. We envision that PKA systems will provide a spectrum of learning services ranging from a self-contained learning mode with minimal communication with the teacher to a system that is guided externally with frequent communications with an instructor or an external Knowledge Database.

2   UML Diagrams for Knowledge Modeling

The UML, though created and used for software design, is not specific to software design. This kind of modeling is *object oriented*, meaning that whatever system is being modeled, its components become abstract objects that have some properties (also called *attributes*) and functions (also referred to as *responsibilities*). A *class* is a collection of these abstract objects. Generally, there are several types of UML diagrams that can be useful for knowledge modeling, including class diagrams and state diagrams. In this paper, we will concentrate on class diagrams.

Class diagrams contain classes and relationships. Classes can be described by their name, properties, and functions, and they are graphically represented as boxes. Lines or arrows are then drawn between classes to describe their relationships, the most common of which are aggregation, generalization, and named association. Typically, aggregation is treated as a special form of association [4, 20], but since aggregations play an important role in this paper, for convenience we will discuss aggregations separately from other associations, which are referred to here as *named associations*.

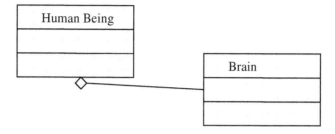

Fig. 1. Common Knowledge Represented by a UML Class Diagram

Let us consider a UML diagram describing common knowledge about our brain as shown in Fig. 1. The diagram simply states that there two important concepts (classes), Human Being and Brain, and that a brain is a part of Human Being. The diamond specifies an aggregation relationship. Similarly we can specify different relationships using different symbols as shown in Figure 2.

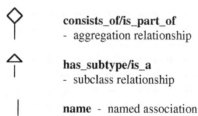

Fig. 2. UML Relationships

In order for UML diagrams to capture knowledge from various subject areas, two problems need to be resolved. The first problem is defining a consistent translation methodology for transferring information from a natural language into a diagrammatic form. The second problem is to extend the UML class diagram to allow the student to capture all knowledge in such a form.

3   Natural Language Modeling

The missing link in the process of transferring information from natural language to a form compatible with the storage, integration, and retrieval demands of a Knowledge Database has been a consistent and complete translation methodology. Fortunately, literary theorists have focused efforts over the last twenty-five years in the development of a relatively new area of research broadly known as translation studies [22]. Although some fundamental principles have emerged about the process of translating a text from one language to another, much work in the field has examined the complexity of the act of translation and the many factors influencing the decisions of the translator in transferring words, syntactical patterns, and literary structures to another language.

This research makes clear that if existing information in print-based natural language is to be translated accurately into a form such as Unified Modeling Language (UML) that is compatible with a Knowledge Database, rigorous attention must be paid to the analysis of the meaning of the original text. That analysis must extend well beyond the meaning of the vocabulary employed. For example, the elisions of thought a particular language allows through syntactical subtleties must be made explicit and represented in the UML translation. Just as importantly, the controlled ambiguities in the original text must be eliminated from the UML translation as it gradually refines meaning, but the elimination of these ambiguities must be sequenced so that a user of the translation is not overwhelmed from the outset by unnecessarily specific information.

Our approach has been to divide each natural-language sentence into three categories of information. We first identify what is already known to the reader, either through previous introduction of that material in the text or as a part of the body of common knowledge the original author anticipated the reader would bring to the text. The second element we identify is the relationship between the known and the unknown information in the sentence; this link is often expressed in the predicate of the sentence. Finally, we note which information in the sentence is new to the reader.

This approach mirrors the principles of effective argumentation taught in college freshman composition courses, in which the student author is urged to organize the evidence in an essay—even at the level of the sentence—from the known to the unknown. Similarly, a reader can expect that published authors will usually follow this pattern of organization in conveying information. So our analysis of the text imitates the strategy of interpretation the intended reader of the material would have likely employed and its author would have anticipated.

It should be noted that our analytical method has another benefit for manipulation of information within a database. If known versus unknown information is defined as new versus old information, the very sequencing of that information within the text allows an accurate identification of what is known to the reader and what is unknown. The data identified as unknown, or new, requires a further elaboration in UML, while old information does not trigger modification of the UML class diagram.

A simple example of our methodology will demonstrate its utility in moving from natural language to UML. We chose a simple paragraph to translate [26]:

> You have five senses—sight, hearing, smell, taste, and touch. Through these senses, your brain receives information about the world outside. A sense organ, for example the eye, contains many special receptor cells. These cells collect information and pass it to the sensory nerve cells which take it to the brain. Different receptors can receive information in the form of light rays, sound waves, chemicals, heat, or pressure.

Our analysis of the sentences of the paragraph sought to identify the following categories: Known Information—Relationship—Unknown Information. To simplify the explanation below, we have focused on only major elements of the sentences.

In the first sentence, we noted that the ambiguity of "You" as either a particular "You" or as representative of its class needed immediate clarification, which we indicated in brackets. As the reader's common body of knowledge includes an awareness of the existence of human beings, the subject of the sentence is known information. We delayed explicating the controlled ambiguity of "have," the predicate of the sentence, as either naming a constituent element or an object possessed, because the ambiguity did not bear on the meaning of the statement. Though the five senses might well be understood as common knowledge, we treated the remainder of the sentence as new information for the purposes of the paragraph.

>   You [human being]—have—five senses.
>   These senses— are—sight, hearing, smell, taste, and touch.

The analysis recognizes that in adjectival phrases like "your brain" (in the second sentence), "sense organ" (in the third sentence) or "Different receptor cells" (in the fifth sentence), a relationship of known and unknown information is implied in the linking of the adjective to the noun. We state that relationship in brackets just above the sentence in which it appears. The known information conveyed in the sentence includes the "senses," introduced in the previous sentence, and the common knowledge that a human being possesses a brain. The new data of "information about the world outside" is related to the old data through the predicate, "receives."

>   [A human being—has—a brain.]
>   Your brain—receives—information about the world outside through these senses.

The third sentence offers new information about the existence of "many special receptor cells" in "a sense organ."

>   [A sense—has—an organ.]
>   A sense organ—contains—many special receptor cells.

The fourth sentence is composed of two major relationships of known and unknown information. "These cells," introduced in the preceding sentence and therefore known to the reader, "collect information" and then "pass it to the sensory nerve cells." Because the reader is unfamiliar with this new term, a third relationship concludes the sentence and explains the function of these "nerve cells."

>   These cells [special receptor cells]—collect—information and
>   [special receptor cells]—pass—it [information] to the sensory nerve cells
>   which take it to the brain.

The final sentence offers new data about the specific forms of information that can be received by "Different receptor cells."

>   [Receptor cells—have—different categories.]
>   Different receptor cells—can receive—information in the form of light rays,
>   sound waves, chemicals, heat, or pressure.

Our analysis guides the creation of a UML class diagram and has implications for the entry of other types of information into Knowledge Databases.

4 Creating UML Diagrams for Knowledge Modeling

The UML class diagrams can be created explicitly or using a textual interface. Since in this paper we concentrate on the use of handheld mobile devices, let us describe in detail a textual interface, which is more appropriate for these handheld devices.

A sample interface for entering well-structured knowledge facts is shown in Fig. 3a. By well-structured knowledge facts, we mean tuples consisting of three components: first class name, relationship and second class name. The class name can be expanded by a multiplicity constraint that can be a typical numerical constraint or more descriptive such as "many," "always," "often," etc. Fig. 3b shows all tuples corresponding to the first sentence

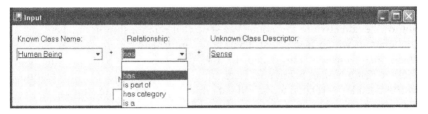

Fig. 3a. The Knowledge Database Interface to Enter Tuples.

human being—*has*—sense(s) (five)
sense– *has category*—sight
sense– ha*s category*—hearing
sense– *has category*—smell
sense– *has category*—touch

Fig. 3b. Tuples for the First Sentence from the Sample Text

human being—*has*—brain
your brain—*receives*—information about the world outside through these senses.

Fig. 4a. Tuples for the Second Sentence from the Sample Text

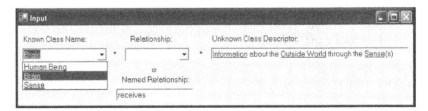

Fig. 4b. Knowledge Database Interface for Tuple with Complicated Unknown Class Descriptor

Similarly, the student can enter the first tuple corresponding to the second sentence as shown in Fig. 4. However, the second tuple is slightly different. If the second class name cannot be identified (e.g., more than one class), then the longer second class descriptor can be used. These longer class descriptors can contain many potential new classes. All of these are properly annotated so the information about them can be stored. On the interface, they are specified by underlining. These second class descriptors can be possibly transformed later into a standard tuple as discussed in the next section.

The underlying UML diagram is shown in Fig. 5. Please notice that all relationships and classes do not need to be identified fully in this step. We could stop accepting new knowledge and refine the diagram. However, to show explicitly the different phases of diagram creation, we discuss knowledge refinement in the next section.

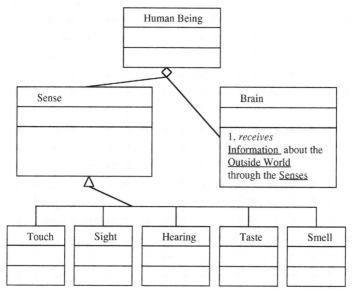

Fig. 5. The Intermediate UML Diagram for a Sample Text

We can continue the process of specifying the tuples for the third sentence as shown in Fig 6.

The fourth and fifth sentence will result in three tuples as shown in Fig. 7. Again the second and fourth tuples are in a nonstandard form and will need to be converted later. The third tuple is different since it does not contain any class name. However, this a special type of tuple describing the property of the class *receptor cell.*
The underlying UML diagram is shown in Fig. 8.

5 Processing and Integration of Knowledge Contained in UML Diagrams

In order to capture knowledge relatively quickly, we might want to postpone the process of knowledge integration and cleaning. The knowledge integration is mainly related to identifying common classes and refining nonstandard tuples. The

<u>sense</u>—*has*—<u>sense organ</u>
<u>sense organ</u>—*contains*—<u>receptor cells</u> (many special).

Fig. 6. Tuples for the Third Sentence from the Sample Text

<u>receptor cell</u>—*collects*—<u>information</u>
<u>receptor cell</u>—*passes*—<u>information</u> to the <u>sensory nerve cell</u>s which take it to the <u>brain</u>.
<u>receptor cell</u>—*has*—different categories.
<u>receptor cells</u>—*can receive*—<u>information</u> in the form of <u>light ray</u>s, <u>sound waves</u>, <u>chemicals</u>, <u>heat</u>, or <u>pressure</u>.

Fig. 7. Tuples for the Third Sentence from the Sample Text

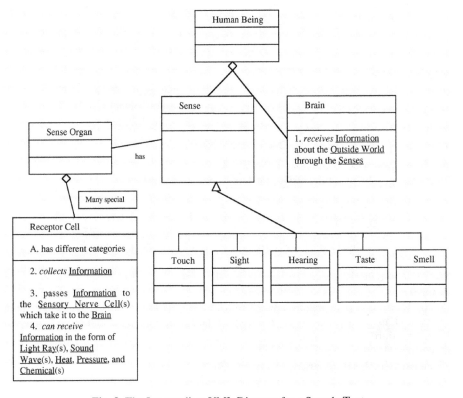

Fig. 8. The Intermediate UML Diagram for a Sample Text

knowledge cleaning is mainly related to finding similarity in functions/relationships and determining which are identical, which are refinements, and which are different.

Let us discuss first the translation of nonstandard class descriptors such as the one from Fig. 4: "<u>information</u> about the <u>world outside</u> through these <u>senses</u>." The system can interactively guide the student to identify whether the relationship is n-ary or whether it is a composite of many relationships. If the n-ary relationship is selected, the system can ask about:

1. active and passive classes;
2. the role (function) of each active class.

Classes in general are classified into active and passive. Even though the relationship is n-ary, meaning that it involves all n classes, only active classes have the function associated with the relationship.

Let us discuss it using the above example. Only the senses are identified by the student as active classes, and the roles are specified as shown in Fig. 9.

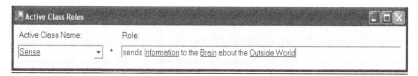

Fig. 9. N-ary Relationship Description with Roles

receptor cells—*pass*—information to the sensory nerve cells
sensory nerve cells—*take it to*—brain.

Fig. 10a. Composite Relationship Split into Two Tuples

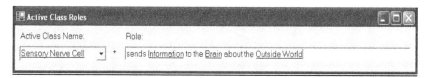

Fig. 10b. N-ary Relationship Description with Roles

The next nonstandard tuple, "cells—pass—information to the sensory nerve cells which take it to the brain," is refined differently since it is a composite function. It is simply split into two tuples, as shown in Fig. 10a. Then the first tuple is refined as an n-ary relationship as shown in Fig. 10b.

The last nonstandard tuple is left unchanged by not identifying any active classes.

receptor cells—*can receive*—information in the form of light rays, sound waves, chemicals, heat,
or pressure.

The necessary cleaning phase in our case required identifying similarity of functions/relationships like "send," "take," etc. The final standardized underlying UML diagram is shown in Fig. 11.

6   Querying Knowledge Contained in Underlying UML Diagram

The underlying UML diagram once constructed contains the knowledge about a specific subject or many subjects (e.g., about Senses). Therefore it can be used to answer queries in these subject areas. Again we will concentrate on textual interface for knowledge querying. The queries can be simple, complex, definition, comparison, or essay. The simple queries would deal with properties, functions, and direct relationships between class types. The complex queries can involve indirect relationships. The definition queries would require identifying all properties, functions and direct relationships for a chosen class. The comparison queries would request a comparison of classes. The essay queries would require extended definition of a chosen class identifying not only all direct relationships for this class but also all indirect relationships.

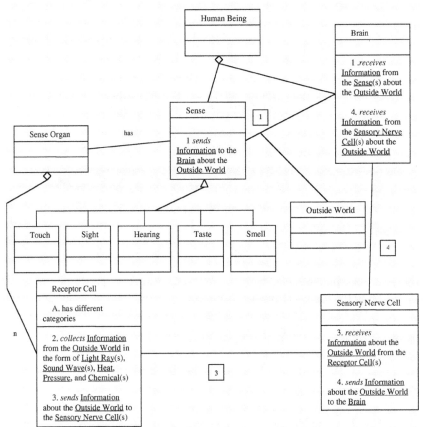

Fig. 11. The Refined UML Diagram for a Sample Text

An example of a simple query could involve an aggregation relationship (e.g., "What are the components of Sense Organ?"). Another simple query could involve subclass relationships: "What are the categories of Sense?" Yet another query can involve n-ary relationships (e.g., "What sends information to the brain about the outside world?").

An example of a complex query would be to identify the relationship between Human Being and Receptor Cell. The answer would be a "consists-of" relationship. An example of a definition query would be to ask for a definition of Sense. An example of a comparison query would be to ask: "What are similarities between Sense and Sense Organ?" Additionally, we could query a UML diagram to create an entire essay. The answer would be obtained by traversing the UML diagram from top to bottom, collecting all definitions.

The prototype of a Knowledge Database was implemented in Access. A query interface for the Knowledge Database is shown in Figure 12.

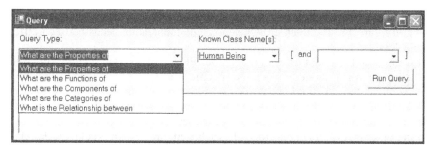

Fig. 12. Query Interface for Simple Queries for Knowledge Database

7 Computer-Assisted Instruction Using Personal Knowledge Assistant

The PKA systems allow for a spectrum of possibilities in learning ranging from a self-contained mode with minimal communication with the teacher to a system that is guided externally with frequent communications with an instructor or an external Knowledge Database.

Let us discuss first the least intrusive mode of operation of our teaching system requiring minimum communication in a mobile environment. In this mode, the PKA would accept the initial knowledge tuples (facts) from a student, for example the tuples discussed in Section 4. Next, the student would apply knowledge improvement rules guided by the PKA as described in Section 5. In each step the system would check significant constraints. Additionally, the CAI system can check if the UML diagram is well-formed. By "well-formed" we mean that all possible transformations have been considered. The architecture of such a system is shown in Figure 13.

Fig. 13. System Architecture for Less Intrusive CAI System

Let us discuss next a mode of operation of our PKA-based system using frequent communications with the outside world. The first reason for such a capability is the necessity to use common knowledge or additional knowledge available in the teacher's Knowledge Database. The need to integrate the specific knowledge provided by the teacher with knowledge more broadly available cannot be overestimated. The requirements for modern education stress the importance of such integration [16, 17].

The second reason to use frequent communications with the outside world is when the instructor feedback is important [16, 18]. In this mode, the PKA Knowledge Database would be frequently accessed by the teacher or teacher program to check the accuracy of recorded knowledge. The same process would be applied to knowledge processing in which the student would be allowed to apply only some of the transformation rules as indicated previously by the instructor. These two situations are shown in figure 14. The thick arrows denote communication needs between different mobile devices.

It is important to note that even though our PKA-based system requires the student in teacher-controlled mode to reach the specific well-formed knowledge, the order of application of the transformation rules is not imposed. In this way the student is allowed to discover new knowledge components that are tailored to his/her learning style. For example, he/she can choose the easiest sentences first or can pursue the learning process in some other order. In each step, the system would check not only significant constraints but also if the rules that the student applied belong to the set of answer rules previously stored by the instructor.

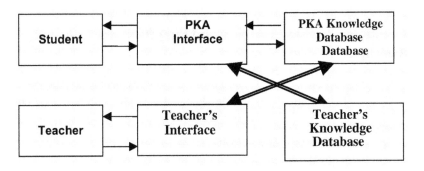

Fig. 14. System Architecture for More Intrusive CAI System

The third reason for frequent communication is related to potential student cooperation. Another requirement for modern education is to teach students teamwork in solving problems. We believe that a PKA-based teaching system would be most natural and effective in developing team-working abilities.

Within each of the communication modes, there are a variety of parameters that can be set by the instructor to control/relax the teaching activities. For example, as was described in section 3, the restriction can be imposed to allow the student to enter only the known class name as a first name in the knowledge tuple. That would mean a requirement to work with only one UML diagram. Alternatively this restriction can be relaxed allowing the student to start a new UML sub-diagram not linked with the existing one.

8 Summary

In this paper we discussed a methodology for creating a missing link between the information contained in natural language expressions into a form compatible with the storage, integration, and retrieval demands of a Knowledge Database. We used some experiences of an area of research broadly known as translation studies.

We showed the techniques of transforming a natural language text into what we called standard sentences consisting of three tuples: information known—relationship —information unknown. We also discuss how to design underlying UML diagrams to store this knowledge. Finally we showed how to integrate the standard sentences with the existing knowledge.

Based on this knowledge-processing methodology, a software prototype was developed. Using such software, the existing PDAs can allow the student to process the knowledge. Alternatively. a specialized hardware can be designed as a specialized PDA device with hardware buttons more convenient for knowledge manipulation. In both cases, we can use handheld device to store, process, and retrieve knowledge from a Knowledge Database. We referred to such devices as Personal Knowledge Assistant (PKA). The PKA systems allow for a spectrum of possibilities in learning, ranging from a self-contained mode with minimal communication with the teacher to a system that is guided externally with frequent communications with an instructor or an external Knowledge Database.

References

1. Arnheim, R.: Visual Thinking. University of California Press, Berkeley, CA (1969)
2. Bemers-Lee T., Hendler, J., Lassila, 0.: The Semantic Web. Sci Am 284(5). (2001) 34-43
3. Brachman, R.: On the Epistemological Status of Semantic Networks. In: Findlee, N.V. (ed): Associative Networks: Representation and Use of Knowledge by Computer. Academic, New York (1979) 3-50
4. Booch, G., Rumbaugh, J., Jacobson, I.: The Unified Modeling Language User Guide. Addison Wesley, Reading, MA (1999)
5. Chein, M., Mugnier, M.L.: Conceptual Graphs: Fundamental Notions. Rev Intell Artif 6 (4). (1992) 365-406
6. Czejdo, B., Mappus, R., Messa, K.: The Impact of UML Diagrams on Knowledge Modeling, Discovery and Presentations. Journal of Information Technology Impact, Vol.3 (1). (2003) 25-38
7. Czejdo, B., Czejdo, J., Lehman, J., Messa, K.: Graphical Queries for XML Documents and Their Applications for Accessing Knowledge in UML Diagrams. Proceedings of the First Symposium on Databases, Data Warehousing and Knowledge Discovery. Baden Baden, Germany (2003) 69 – 85
8. Czejdo, B., Czejdo, J., Eick, C., Messa, K., Vernace, M.: Rules in UML Class Diagrams. Opportunities of Change. Proceedings of the Third International Economic Congress. Sopot, Poland. (2003) 289-298

9. Czejdo, B., Sobaniec, C.: Using a Semantic Model and XML for Document Annotations. Lecture Notes in Computer Science. Springer-Verlag, Berlin Heidelberg New York (2000) 236-241

10. Delteil, A., Faron, C.: A Graph-Based Knowledge Representation Language. Proceedings of the 15th European Conference on Artificial Intelligence (ECAI), Lyon, France (2002)

11. Dori, D.: Object-Process Methodology -a holistic systems paradigm. Springer, Berlin Heidelberg New York (2002). www.ObjectProcess.org

12. Dori, D.: Why Significant Change in UML Is Unlikely. Commun ACM 45 (11). (2002) 82-85

13. Dori, D., Reinhartz-Berger, I., Sturm, A.: OPCAT—A Bimodal CASE Tool for Object-Process Based System Development. Proceedings of the IEEE/ACM 5th International Conference on Enterprise Information Systems (ICEIS 2003), Angers, France (2003) 286-291. www.ObjectProcess.org

14. Lehrnan, F. (ed): Semantic Networks in Artificial Intelligence. Pergamon, Oxford, UK (1999)

15. Mayer, R.E.: Multimedia Learning. Cambridge University Press, New York (2002)

16. McTear, M.F. (ed): Understanding Cognitive Science. Ellis Horwood, Chichester, UK (1998)

17. Novak, J.D.: A Theory of Education. Cornell University Press, Ithaca, NY (1977)

18. Novak, J.D., Gowin, D.B.: Learning How to Learn. Cambridge University Press, New York (1984)

19. OMG UML1.4. Object Management Group Unified Modeling Language v.l.4 (2001)

20. Rumbaugh, J., Jacobson, I., Booch, G.: The Unified Modeling Language Reference Manual. Addison-Wesley, Reading, MA (1999)

21. Rumbaugh, J.: Objects in the Constitution: Enterprise Modeling. Journal of Object Oriented Programming. (1993)

22. Schulte, R., Biguenet, J.: Theories of Translation. The University of Chicago Press, Chicago (1992)

23. Smith, M.K., McGuinness, D., Volz, R., Welty, C.: Web Ontology Language (OWL) Guide Version 1.0. W3CWorking Draft (2002)

24. Sowa, J.F.: Conceptual Structures: Information Processing in Mind and Machine. Addison-Wesley, Reading, MA (1984)

25. Sowa, I.F.: Knowledge Representation: Logical, Philosophical, and Computational Foundations. Brooks Cole, Pacific Grove, CA (1999)

26. Walpole, B.: Pocket Book of The Human Body. Wanderer, New York (1987)

Short Papers

Facilitating Collaborative Learning in Virtual (and Sometimes Mobile) Environments

Woojin Paik[1], Jee Yeon Lee[2], and Eileen McMahon[3]

[1] Dept of Computer Science, Konkuk University
322 Danwol-dong, Chungju-si, Chungcheongbuk-do, 380-701, Korea
wjpaik@kku.ac.kr
[2] Dept of Library and Information Science, Yonsei University
134 Shinchon-dong, Seodaemun-gu, Seoul 120-749, Korea
jlee01@yonsei.ac.kr
[3] Instructional Technology Center, University of Massachusetts Boston
100 Morrissey Blvd, Boston, MA 02125, USA
eileen.mcmachon@umb.edu

Abstract. Enrollment for online learning and virtual campuses is increasing in secondary education and higher education as educational institutions cope with an increased demand for specialized and asynchronous educational curricula. Our preliminary investigation shows approximately 50% of virtual groups formed online for the purpose of collaborative learning will encounter barriers that prevent them from forming an effective learning team. Our ongoing research is designed to identify the barriers that stand in the way of online learning groups in order to develop and test various intervention techniques, which can effectively remove the obstacles. Our secondary goal is to analyze the conversations of virtual group members using computational linguistics techniques and to develop a learning activity discourse model. The model is being used to construct an automatic system, which can be used to monitor the activities of the online learning group members to alert the instructors when the members encounter barriers.

1   Motivation

Online education is one of the most dynamic and enriching forms of learning that exist today. Online education is an appealing alternative for individuals balancing the demands of full time jobs and care of their families with the desire to advance in their careers and gain new skills. Online education is typically delivered through a learning management system, which facilitates the interaction of the students and instructor and the exchange of information. Learning management systems contain synchronous and asynchronous tools for interaction and input. Members of a learning community can exchange ideas and discuss course topics through a virtual discussion area using

C. Bussler et al. (Eds.): WISE 2004 Workshops, LNCS 3307, pp. 161–166, 2004.
© Springer-Verlag Berlin Heidelberg 2004

synchronous tools like Centra[1] while those who can't participate in a live event can use asynchronous tools like a threaded discussion to exchange ideas. The students are beginning to access these tools through mechanisms such as Short Message Service (SMS) available on mobile phones.

Online education has increased in popularity for many reasons: it offers the combination of asynchronous and synchronous communication tools, it addresses the fact that an instructor can't be available to students 24/7, and it appeals to the innate social need of humans, who want to work in teams and share knowledge. These features of online education have translated into a seismic shift in curriculum design away from a hierarchical approach centered around lectures and tests to peer-to-peer learning. Online curriculums are designed around constructivism and conversational learning pedagogies that are ideally suited to virtual learning communities.

One of the most difficult and challenging aspects of Internet based learning courses is social interaction. To be a successful member of an online learning group requires not only mature interpersonal and communication skills but also a carefully architected group design and a moderator to intervene when necessary. In a face-to-face classroom, individual group members call on a diverse set of informal strategies to form cohesion, while those used for aligning a virtual group are still being researched. For instance, Wiske [1] identified common purposes, shared trust, and interaction as aspects of dialogue that are important for constructive virtual interaction to occur. Ironically, however, current online learning systems do no facilitate or enhance these skills.

Intercultural collaboration presents another set of challenges to virtual learners. Harper [2] argues that "In the early years of internet adoption many people worried about a digital divide that would develop between those who had access and those who didn't…but it is the social, cognitive, and communicative factors that truly divide groups." The ability to listen and appreciate diverse perspectives is not innate and needs to be inculcated in any online learning activity. Others have identified additional requirements for successful online learning. Miltiadou and Savenye [3] examined social cognitive constructs of motivation to understand student success in online learning. In their review, they noted that self-regulated students who employ cognitive and metacognitive strategies involving planning, organizing, self-instruction, and self-evaluation will be more successful in learning online than those without these skills.

Clearly students who come to virtual communities with strong communication, social and cognitive skills are more likely to succeed in online environments than those with weak skills. If members of a group provide regular patterns in their written communication that they are failing to connect with group members, these signs can be identified, codified, and categorized, resulting in the creation of a smart teaching agent that can help an instructor create successful learning groups.

---

[1] Centra is an e-meeting tool provided by Centra Software (http://www.centra.com/index.asp)

2 Problem

Enrollment for online learning and virtual campuses is increasing in secondary education and higher education as educational institutions cope with an increased demand for specialized and asynchronous educational curricula. Based on our experience at Yonsei University and the University of Massachusetts Boston, approximately 50% of virtual groups formed online for the purpose of collaborative learning will encounter barriers that prevent them from forming an effective learning team. Strategies that are successful in a face-to-face classroom will not work in an environment that depends on the written word. Slower speed of expression, demand for clear unambiguous expression, and the permanency of written records are factors that impede the communication of virtual teams.

Our research questions are: 1) What characteristics are important for the formation of a successful online learning groups?; 2) What are the barriers for successful cohesion of online learning?; 3) What technology independent activity can be adopted by online faculty that will ensure successful group alignment and cohesion?; and 4) How can an intelligent computer agent technology be employed to facilitate the formation of online learning groups and prevent them from falling apart?

We are working to identify the barriers that stand in the way of online learning groups by analyzing the recorded conversational texts of both successful and unsuccessful groups. We looked for key words and key activities that signal problems. To collect the group conversation data, we developed an online test-based activity similar to ones that have been successful for real-time group cohesion. The activity was created with the facilitation of the cohesion of online learning groups in mind.

3 Research Design

The experiments to gather the research data were conducted at Yonsei University, which is one of the private Korean universities with about 52,000 students. The subjects of the experiments were four-hundred and fifty undergraduate students, who were taking two different sections of an introductory course in library and information science. There were about equal number male and female students. About 70% of the students were freshmen and the rest of the students were equally divided amongst sophomores, juniors, and seniors. The course was one of the liberal arts requirements for the undergraduate students. However, the students included wide variety majors including the ones from the natural science and engineering disciplines.

The experiments were conducted in a series of stages. Initially, we devised structured "warm up" team activities, which could involve synchronous and asynchronous communication, negotiation, and resolution. The activities were 1) find ways to resolve conflicts around the recent nuclear waste treatment construction site selection fiasco in Korea; 2) find ways to improve the rights of the gays and lesbians in light of the recent discussions regarding the same sex marriage issue; 3) find ways to increase the female employments; 4) find ways to reduce the number of people with bad credit and runaway adults; and 5) find ways to develop Korean movie industry in a balanced manner. Four-hundred and fifty students were randomly divided into ninety five-person teams. Each team was given a team activity and was told to carry out the activity by communicating with the team members either by using 1) email, 2) threaded discussion, or 3) email plus threaded discussion. The students were told not to meet in person to discuss the activity. At the end of the exercise, each team was asked to submit the results of the activity and the transcripts of their communication. In addition, the students were asked to provide narrative description of each message they wrote or read. The description should include the goal of sending, posting, or reading a message, reasons for carbon copying a message, appropriateness of the posted message, and/or problems the students perceived in the message.

All activity data were collected and the sample transcripts are currently being analyzed by using content and discourse analysis techniques. When the analysis is completed, we plan to build a prototype of "learning team agent" software. Then, we will conduct another set of activity based group problem solving experiments to determine whether a computer program can help students to become members of successful online learning groups.

3.1 Discourse Analysis Model

To develop a learning activity discourse model, we are manually coding a randomly chosen sample of transcripts with a pre-selected range of features that characterize successful linguistic interaction—features taken from the work of linguists and philosophers who have studied human communication systems.

Grice [4] proposed that all linguistic interaction is subject to four constraints that are part of what he terms the "cooperative principle." That is, when people communicate, there is an underlying agreement that interlocutors will:

(1)   Make their conversations as informative as possible by not saying too much or saying too little (maxim of quantity)

(2)   Insure that what they say is relevant to what is currently being discussed and does not digress from the topic at hand (maxim of relevance)

(3)   Strive to communicate in a clear and appropriate manner, avoiding ambiguity (maxim of manner)

(4)   Be truthful in what they say, avoiding falsehoods (maxim of quality)

To determine whether on-line communication follows these maxims, we are coding (a) the frequency that individuals contribute to communications and (b) the length of their contributions; (c) the number of times that individuals stay on the topic in discussions vs. the number of times that discussions lead to digressions; (d) the clarity of communications, measured by the extent to which individuals query each other concerning misunderstandings in their interactions; and (e) the number of times that individuals provide each other with accurate information vs. inaccurate information.

It is our hypothesis that it is possible to quantify successful vs. unsuccessful on-line interactions by coding the extent to which individuals adhere to or violate the maxims of the cooperative principles.

It is also possible to study human communication by identifying the intentions of interlocutors. Searle [5] classifies speaker intentions into the categories he identifies as "speech acts." Although Searle proposes a variety of speech acts, we see four acts—representatives, directives, commissives, and expressives—as particularly relevant to on-line communication. Representative speech acts are the statements of the facts that can be judged as true or false. Directive speech acts are, for instance, imperative sentences that are attempts to get somebody to do something. Commissive speech acts commit an individual to carrying out some activity. We hypothesize that successful on-line communication can be judged by the density of these three acts; that is, by the extent to which interlocutors present facts to one another, tell each other what to do, and commit themselves to actually doing something. But successful communication also has an affective dimension. Thus, we are also coding speech acts that are expressives: greetings, acts of thanking, congratulations. These kinds of speech acts indicate that individuals are comfortable with one another—an important characteristic of any human interaction.

4 Results

Our preliminary analysis of 921 randomly selected email messages yielded eighteen goal types and ten problem types. We also deduced twelve goal types and thirteen problem types based on the analysis of 1,073 randomly selected threaded discussion postings.

The most common type of problem identified while using email as the interaction medium was the speed of the communication namely the difficulty to communicate instantly. Out of one-hundred and fifty-five descriptions of the email messages by the students, which included any mention of the problems they perceived, there were forty-three occurrences of this problem type (i.e. twenty-eight percent). Other top problems included 1) problems with email service or Internet connectivity, which occurred nineteen percent of the time; 2) difficulty to reach a consensus occurred seventeen percent of the time; 3) the lack of other members' participation occurred fourteen percent of the time.

Similarly, seventy-one percent of the students described the slow rate of propagating his/her opinion as the top problem in using the threaded discussion as the only source of interaction to conduct the group project. The difficulty of keeping confidentiality of messages as the second most frequently identified problem (i.e. twenty-nine percent). There are a lot of data yet to be analyzed especially discovering when the group project participants become aware of the problems with respect to the group interaction or communication by correlating the goals or the contents of the messages with the reported problems. Once the correlation is discovered, we will be able to develop a prototype of "learning team agent" software.

5 Summary

The study reported in this paper is an ongoing effort. We reported a preliminary analysis of the data in the paper. The current experiments varied the subjects to conduct online group learning activities by the communication media such as email and threaded discussion. Although, we could have easily learned the impact of mobile devices in learning if we divided the subjects to use different hardware such as personal computers, personal digital assistant, or mobile phones, we believe our findings will still be able to provide useful insights on the difficulties that the mobile learners will face in solving problems as a group. Our analysis result will also provide baseline information on whether the traits of the successful or failed online groups are applicable to the mobile learners. For example, we expect the SMS will be a better medium to overcome the major problem of instant communication or the rapid propagation of the information as the mobile phones have built-in mechanism to remind the users of the incoming new messages and also the mobile phone users are expected to be interrupted for the incoming messages. However, we need further investigation of other problems, which hinder the optimum online group work. For example, 'accuracy of the transferred information' was identified as one of the problems of using emails as the communication medium. Personal Digital Assistant (PDA) or SMS are more apt to deliver shorter messages than the typical emails. Thus, we do not expect the PDA or SMS will serve as better platforms to deal with the accuracy problem if we assume that there is a strong correlation between the accuracy and the length of the messages. Our next set of experiments will include the exclusive use of SMS to conduct group projects to accurately determine the appropriateness of the mobile devices in group-based e-learning activities.

References

1. Wiske, S.: New Technologies for School / University Collaboration, http://learnweb.harvard.edu/ent/library/wiskefeb/sld005.htm retrieved on June 30, 2004
2. Harper, V.: The Digital Divide (DD): A Reconceptualization for Educators The Educational Technology review Vol. 11, No. 1, 2003, http://www.aace.org/pubs/etr/issue4/harper retrieved on October 29, 2003
3. Miltiadou, M. and Savenye, W.C.: Applying Social Cognitive Constructs of Motivation to Enhance Student Success in Online Distance Education The Educational Technology review Vol. 11, No. 1, 2003 http://www.aace.org/pubs/etr/issue4/miltiadou.cfm retrieved on October 29, 2003
4. Grice, H.P.: "Logic and Conversation." In Peter Cole and Jerry L. Morgan (eds.) Syntax and Semantics 3: Speech Acts. New York: Academic Press. (1975) 41-58.
5. Searle, J.: A Classification of Illocutionary Acts. Language in Society 5. (1976) 1-23.

A Fundamental Web-Board System Toward the Adaptive Mobile School Web Site

Suk-Ki Hong[1] and Woochun Jun[2]

[1] Division of Business & Economics, Dankook University, Seoul, Korea
skhong017@dankook.ac.kr
[2] Dept. of Computer Education, Seoul National University of Education, Seoul, Korea
wocjun@snue.ac.kr

Abstract. With the advance of information communication technology, specifically the Internet technology, most schools have developed their own sites for the communication of diverse parties such as students, their parents, teachers, and others. The purpose of this research is to develop the Web-board system for schools, which can be applied to the adaptive school Web site. It would the foundation for the mobile school Web site. This Web-board system is designed to reflect the educational environments as well as the user characteristics under the idea of customization and optimization. The main advantage of this Web-board system is that it can allow the easy access to the system through user-friendly interface, and also promote interactions among users through their personalized Web pages.

Keywords: Web-board, Bulletin Board, Adaptive Web Site, Mobile Web Site

1 Introduction

With the rapid development of information communication technology and heavy investment on information systems, many schools have developed their own Web sites. However, the school Web sites have evolved in terms of their contents as well as the functions of the system, and became a space to induce interactions among relevant parties, students, their parents, teachers and others [4,8,9]. Interactions can be conducted in diverse forms such as bulletin boards, e-mail, chatting, and other electrical media. Especially, bulletin boards have become a major role of sharing materials and communication in school Web sites.

The research is to develop the Web-board systems for the adaptive Web site that can reflect educational environments and users' characteristics on system usages. It would the foundation for the mobile school Web site. For this research, theoretical backgrounds are introduced in Section 2. Adaptive Web site and the types of bulletin boards are explained in this Section. Section 3 is related to the design of the Web-board system for the adaptive school Web site. It includes an algorithm of the adaptive school Web site. The implementation of the Web-board system is described in Section 4. Finally, some conclusions and future work are in Section 5.

C. Bussler et al. (Eds.): WISE 2004 Workshops, LNCS 3307, pp. 167–172, 2004.
© Springer-Verlag Berlin Heidelberg 2004

2   Theoretical Backgrounds

2.1   Definition of Adaptive Web Sites

One of the major problems in current Web sites is that the initial sites are seldom updated timely and in the right forms. In order to overcome this problem, the concept of adaptive Web sites applying artificial intelligence techniques is introduced [1,5,7]. According to Etzioni, an adaptive Web site can be defined as a Web-based system that improves its own structures and/or forms through learning visitors' accesses [3,6]. An adaptive Web site can be eventually the foundation to reduce users' operation burdens, which are usually issues in mobile environments.

2.2   Implementation Approaches of Adaptive Web Sites

Two major approaches for adaptive Web sites are *customization* and *optimization* [2,5,10]. Customization means that information is provided in timely manner according to user's (visitor's) requirements and interests. Because the interface is designed individually for users, users can be more satisfied. The adaptive Web sites induce users to select their needed information, or automatically expect users' navigation paths through internal processes.

While *customization* is relevant to the effective navigation of individual user, *optimization* is for every user. The adaptive Web sites learn (past and potential) visitors' characteristics, and adaptively change their structures and/or forms.

The implementation of the adaptive Web sites consists of two phases, monitoring and transformation. The former is related to information on access frequencies, navigation, visitors' profiles, and unexpected operation problems. The latter is concerned with the actual transformation of structures and/or forms by using monitoring results. Customization and optimization is more emphasized in mobile environments.

2.3   Web-Board and Bulletin Board System

Web-board is the program that enables users to generate and manage bulletin board systems in a Web server through interworking with databases. Bulletin board system (BBS) is the two-way media that have searching, posting, and replying functions. Because it is usually open to every user, its purpose is to share information rather than exchanging private messages. According to the usage of bulletin boards, bulletin board systems can be classified into free bulletin board, Q&A bulletin board, FAQ bulletin board, announcement bulletin board, resource center, and visitors' book. In other way, bulletin board systems can be classified into three types by their forms, data-type board, reply-type board, and comment-type board.

Prior research on adaptive Web sites and Web-board shows that they were independently treated. Moreover, the application domain, educational environments, is not reflected in developing Web-board for the adaptive Web site. The research is to develop the Web-board system for the adaptive Web site that can reflect educational domains and users' characteristics on system usages.

3   The Design of Web-Board System for Adaptive School Web Sites

3.1   The Characteristics of the Proposed Web-Board System

The characteristics of the proposed Web-board system are as follows.

First, individual Web utilization for customization and optimization is classified by the algorithm of a step function, which generates index pages. Individual index page is generated for closed user groups, while index pages through analyzing utilization of total visitors are presented for guests. Second, most prevalent bulletin board type is identified through in-depth analyses of school bulletin board systems, and it is generated by the proposed Web-board system. Third, a Web master has a separate page for generation, modification & deletion of bulletin board as well as membership management. Fourth, members are classified into a Web master, teachers, students, and their parents. In final, for the consistent design, the environments for SSI (Server Side Include) application are presented.

3.2   Algorithm for Adaptive Pages

Individual index pages of this Web-board are based on the utilization of the sites. Users' activities such as reading and posting contents on the bulletin board are analyzed for producing individual index pages. Although a simple way of analysis is to count the number of clicks, it is not widely accepted as a measure of the bulletin board utilization. In the Web-board system of this research, individual index pages were generated by the step function below.

$$ka = \left[\frac{\sum_{i=0}^{n} Rai}{10(1-Rt)} \right] + \left[\frac{\sum_{i=0}^{n} Wai}{10(1-Wt)} \right]$$

$$(* \; 0 < Rt < 1, \; 0 < Wt < 1)$$

Where,
ka: Degree of reflection for creating individual index page,
a: Bulletin board,
i: Contents posted in bulletin board,
Rai: Score of reading contents i in bulletin board a,
Wai: score of writing contents i in bulletin board a

The shape of this function is determined by Rt and Wt. A Web master can assign adjusting scores for different activities, that are, reading, frequent but less active participation, and writing, less frequent but active participation. It assumes that the higher is the value of reflection, the more the bulletin board is utilized. Individual pages are presented according to the order of values. The assigned hyperlinks enable clicks to move to the desired pages.

3.3 Types of Web-Board System

Bulletin board types, their purposes, and detailed items were determined by in-depth analysis of the current bulletin board systems used in various schools. Table 1 shows the analysis result, which is applied for the research.

Table 1. Bulletin Board Systems for Schools

Classification	Detailed Items	BBS Types
Basic Public Relations	Announcement	Announcement BBS
	School Album	Image BBS
Teaching - Learning	Teaching-Learning Materials	Materials BBS
	Education Sites	Links BBS
Information Sharing	Resource Center for Teachers	Materials BBS
	Resource Center for Guests	
	Resource Center for Students	
Communications	Free Bulletin Board	Generic BBS
	Visitors' Book	Visitors' Book BBS
	Alumni Bulletin Board	Generic BBS
	Counseling	Privacy BBS
	Suggestion	Generic BBS
	Questions and Answers	Generic BBS
	Discussion Rooms	Discussion BBS

According to the types of bulletin board systems, different items are shown. The relationship between bulletin boards types and items are shown in Table 2.

Table 2. Types of Bulletin Board Systems and their Items

Types	Title	Writer	Writer e-mail	Cont.	Reply	Ans.	Up-load	Pass-word	Link	Small Image	Mark-ing
Generic	⊙	⊙	⊙	⊙	⊙	⊙					
Materials	⊙	⊙	⊙	⊙	⊙	⊙	⊙				
Announ.	⊙			⊙							
Visitors'	⊙	⊙	⊙	⊙							
Privacy	⊙	⊙		⊙	⊙	⊙		⊙			
Links	⊙	⊙	⊙	⊙	⊙	⊙			⊙		
Image	⊙	⊙	⊙	⊙	⊙	⊙				⊙	
Discuss.	⊙	⊙	⊙	⊙							⊙

3.4 Web-Board Administration

A Web master installs and manages Web-board systems. Information on databases is installed in the process of initialization, and databases required for bulletin board generation are automatically created. After that, Web master input his or her information. After logging in, a Web master have the authorization for membership management such as grading adjustment and deletion of members, and also bulletin board administration such as generation, modification, and deletion of bulletin board.

4 Implementation of the Proposed Web-Board System

Implementation environments for this research are as follows. IIS 5.0 for Windows 2000 as a Web server, ASP 3.0 as server script language, VBscript and JavaScript as client script language, SQL-Server 2000 as relational database management systems, Namo 5.0 and Edit plus as an authoring tool.

4.1 Web-Board System Installation

Execution of ./setup/setup.asp, the compressed Web-board program, generates the screen for accessing databases. Inputting IP address, name, administrator name, passwords to the database established by ODBC automatically generates tables for creating bulletin boards. By applying OLE-DB type in linking databases, a Web server and a database server can be used in a distributed manner.

After completing database linkage and table generation, a screen for administrator's logging in is generated. The administrator has the authorization of every screen by session, and any accesses without the authorization automatically move back to administrator screen. Figure 1 & 2 show the database environment input screen and administrator login screen, respectively.

Fig. 1. DB Environment Input Screen   **Fig. 2.** Administrator Login Screen

4.2 Administrator Screen

Membership management and bulletin board management are performed in the administrator screen. Bulletin board can be generated, and the preview of generated bulletin board provides its forms and styles, IP address. Modification of bulletin board types and other options is available, and also entire bulletin board can be deleted.

Clicking the button of 'creating bulletin board' generates a screen for generating a bulletin board. Bulletin board types, title, name, color, and other options can be set up in the screen. Width adjustment to the screen size, file and text inputs for consistent design through SSI, and the number of posting materials are established.

4.3 Customization Pages

Based on users' utilization, customization pages are presented after member's logging in the system. Bulletin boards are presented in the order of users' utilization, and linkages by hyperlink allow users to move to the relevant items. Periodic refresh provides the latest information.

5 Conclusions and Further Work

Based on the in-depth analyses of current school bulletin boards, a Web-board system is developed for adaptive school Web sites. Especially, customization is achieved through the algorithm of a step function. The following desirable results are expected from this research.

First, friendliness and customization of bulletin board systems will motivate students to utilize school sites frequently. Second, the bulletin board fitting to educational environments will promote interactions among relevant parties. Finally, Web-board is easy to install and manage, which will save Web master's time and efforts.

The study should be expanded to mobile environment, linking the adaptive Web-board to mobile devices in the future. Further, it should encompass more diverse educational environments. For example, customization on the other pages of the sites in addition to bulletin boards can be a future research subject.

References

[1] Anderson, T. and McKell, M.: A Component Model for Standardized Web-based Education, Journal of Engineering Resources in Computing, Vol. 1 No. 2, (2001)

[2] Bauer, J. F.: Assessing Student Work from Chatrooms and Bulletin Boards, New Directions for Teaching & Learning, No.91 (2002) 36-46

[3] Brusilovsky, P. and Rizzo, R.: Map-based Horizontal Navigation in Educational Hypertext, Proceedings of 13th ACM International Conference on Hypertext and Hypermedia (2002) 1-10

[4] Curran, K.: A Web-based Collaboration Teaching Environment, IEEE MultiMedia, Vol. 9, Iss. 3, July (2002) 72-76

[5] Papanikolaou, K. A. et. al.: Personalizing the Interactions in a Web-based Educational Hypermedia System: the case of ISPIRE, User Modeling and User Adapted Interaction, Vol. 13, Iss. 3, Aug. (2003) 213-267

[6] Perkowitz, M. and Etzioni. O,: Adaptive Sites: an AI Challenge, Proceedings of the 15th International Joint Conference on AI (1997)

[7] Ray, U.: Prepare Engineers for a Future with Collaborative Technology, Computer Applications in Engineering Education, Vol. 6, No.2 (1999) 99-104

[8] Spence, L. J. and Wadsworth, D.: Using an Electronic Bulletin Board in Teaching Business Ethics: En Route to a Virtual Agora, Teaching Business Ethics, Vol. 6 No. 3, Aug. (2002) 335-354

[9] Slator, B. M. et. al.: Virtual Environments for Education, Journal of Network and Computer Applications, Vol. 22, Iss. 3, July (1999) 161-174

[10] Tetiwat, O. and Lgbaria, M.: Web-based Learning and Teaching Technologies: Opportunities and Challenges, Journal of Engineering Resources in Computing, Vol. 1, No. 2 (2000) 17-32

Mobile Computer-Assisted Language Learning Courseware for Korean Language Learners*

Su-Jin Cho[1], Junhyung Kim[2], and Seongsoo Lee[2]

[1] Department of Korean Language Education, Seoul National University, 151-742, Korea
chosoojin@chollian.net
[2] School of Electronics Engineering, Soongsil University, 156-743, Korea
sslee@ssu.ac.kr

Abstract. This paper presents M-CALL, a mobile computer-assisted language learning courseware for Korean language learners. Since conventional computer-assisted language learning is often boring, it exploits a cyber pet game to increase the learner's interest. M-CALL runs on a personal digital assistant with public wireless LAN for mobile learning. It grows a cyber pet by solving problems of Korean language learning. Korean Proficiency Test (KPT), a nationally certified Korean language test, was used as problem sets. It consists of cyber pet game, mobile learning courseware, mobile learning system, and mobile tutoring. It provides various functions for Korean language learning. Currently, the prototype M-CALL was designed and partly implemented between mobile PDA and personal computer.

1 Introduction

Mobile learning on wireless devices such as personal digital assistant (PDA) with wireless local area network (wireless LAN) overcomes spatial and temporal limitations of traditional education. In Korea, the information infrastructure is well provided for mobile learning, and people can connect their PDAs or notebook computers to Internet on many places such as libraries, schools, offices, department stores, theaters, and restaurants. There are several public wireless LAN services covering more than 100,000 spots all over the country.

In Korea, there are a large number of foreign students studying Korean language. They learn Korean language in Korean language institutes. However, most of them have little chances to learn Korean language once they go out of their language institutes. Computer-assisted language learning (CALL) gives them more chances to learn when they are home with their PCs, but it is of little use when they are in the bus or they do their part-time jobs. Mobile learning can help them to learn everywhere they are. Most of the students stay in the metropolitan area, where public wireless LAN is available.

---

* This work was supported by the Soongsil University Research Fund.

C. Bussler et al. (Eds.): WISE 2004 Workshops, LNCS 3307, pp. 173–178, 2004.

A serious problem of CALL is lack of interest. Most CALL courseware is just a computerized textbook, so learners often feel bored. One possible solution is exploiting computer game [1],[2]. In this paper, we propose and implement M-CALL, a mobile CALL courseware on the PDA with public wireless LAN. It is basically a cyber pet growing game, where a learner solves some problems to feed or bathe a cyber pet. When the learner encounters a difficult problem, he/she can ask a tutor to help him/her. He/she can listen to written problems in Korean or reads its English version. His/her score is analyzed and reported to the tutor for efficient learning.

2 M-CALL Courseware

Fig. 1 shows a prototype M-CALL courseware. It is written in C# programming language, and runs on the PDA with Pocket PC operating system. It is connected to Internet via NESPOT public wireless LAN on 11Mbps. Fig. 2 shows a network configuration. All learners are connected to a learning center that performs CALL. Learning center also connects a tutor to a learner in need of help. Usually, there are many volunteers who wish to teach Korean language to foreigners, but most of them cannot do it due to the special and temporal limitation. In the proposed M-CALL, they can easily help and teach learners while doing their jobs. Fig. 3 shows the M-CALL system architecture. It consists of cyber pet game, mobile learning courseware, mobile learning system, and mobile tutoring.

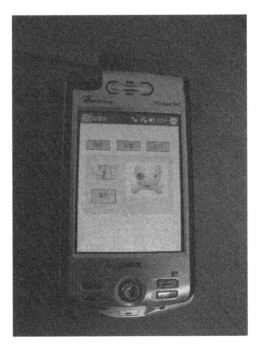

Fig. 1. Prototype M-CALL courseware on mobile PDA with public wireless LAN.

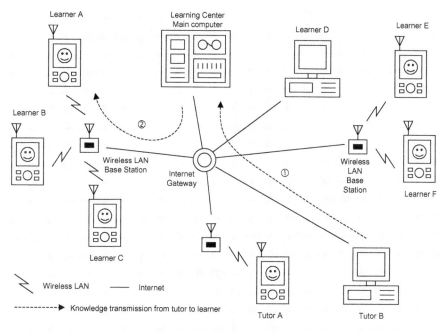

Fig. 2. M-CALL network configuration.

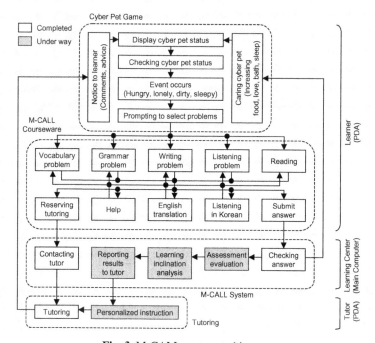

Fig. 3. M-CALL system architecture.

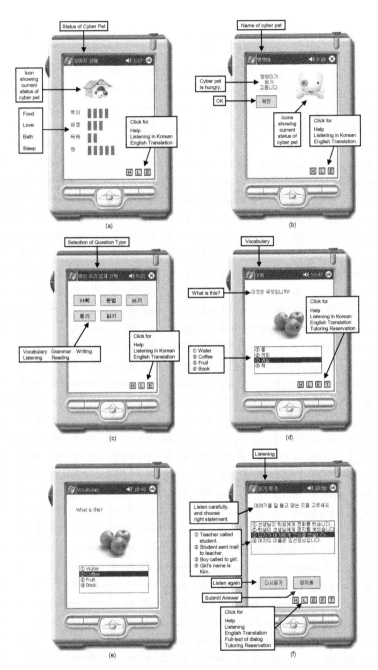

Fig. 4. Operation of M-CALL courseware. (a) Status of cyber pet when no event occurs. (b) Event occurs when cyber pet is hungry. (c) Learner should choose and solve problems to feed cyber pet. (d) Vocabulary problem. (e) English translated version of vocabulary problem. (f) Listening problem.

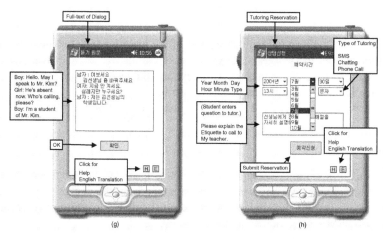

Fig. 4. (continued) (g) Learner can see full-text of dialog. (h) Learner can make a reservation for tutoring.

2.1 Game

The cyber pet game runs on the learner's PDA. Learner grows a cyber pet by feeding, loving, bathing, and lodging (Fig. 4(a)). When the cyber pet is hungry, it sends an alarm on the screen (Fig. 4(b)). A learner can feed the cyber pet by solving problems. When the learner gets a good score, the cyber pet grows up fast, but it dies or gets weaker when he/she repeatedly fails the problems. Feeding and other cyber pet caring occurs sparsely in order not to disturb the learner's daily life.

2.2 Courseware

M-CALL courseware runs on the learner's PDA. It shows the problems (Figs. 4 (c) and (d)) and gets learner's answer (Fig. 4(f)). Korean Proficiency Test (KPT), a nationally certified Korean language test, was used as problem sets. These problems are classified into five categories, i.e. vocabulary, grammar, writing, listening, and reading. The problems themselves are stored in the learning center due to the storage limit of PDA.

The courseware provides tutoring reservation, where the learner can make an appointment with the tutor (Fig. 4(h)). The tutor can help the learner by short message service (SMS), chatting, or phone call. When the learner wants to read the menus or problems written in Korean, he/she can see their English versions (Fig. 4(e)). The learner can listen to the menus or the problems in Korean. In the listening problems, the learner can see the full-text of the problems or dialogs (Fig. 4(g)). When the learner feel difficulty using the courseware, he/she can see the help.

2.3 System

M-CALL system runs on the main computer of the learning center. When the answer is transmitted from the learner's PDA, it checks the answer whether it is correct or not. The score is recorded, and the assessment and the evaluation are analyzed to get the learning inclination of the learner. This information is useful for future tutoring. It also connects the learner and the tutor, and makes a reservation for tutoring.

2.4 Tutor

Tutor is usually a volunteer helping the learner to learn Korean language. When the tutor has some knowledge on the instruction method, he/she can gives personalized instruction based on the learning inclination of the learner. Most tutors prefer tutoring the learner by SMS, since most tutors are volunteers.

2.5 Design, Implementation, and Future Work

Currently, we designed the whole M-CALL except for assessment/evaluation module, learning inclination analyzer module, analyzed result reporting module, and personalized reporting module. The prototype M-CALL was partly implemented on PDA (cyber pet game, courseware, and tutoring) and PC (system) with public wireless LAN. M-CALL including missing modules is expected to be finished at the end of 2004.

3 Conclusion

In this paper, M-CALL, a mobile computer-assisted language learning courseware for Korean language learners, is proposed. It runs on PDA with public wireless LAN. To increase the learner's interest, it employs a cyber pet game where the learner feeds, loves, bathes, and lodges. It consists of cyber pet game, mobile learning courseware, mobile learning system, and mobile tutoring. The prototype M-CALL was designed and partly implemented between mobile PDA and personal computer. We expect that M-CALL is useful for foreign students who learn Korean language.

References

1. Hubbard, A.: Evaluating Computer Games for Language Learning, Simulation and Gaming, **22** (1991) 220-223
2. Rosas, R., Nussbaum, M., Cumsille, P., Marianov, V., Correa, M., Flores, P., Grau, V., Lagos, F., Lopez, X., Lopez, V., Rodriguez, P., Salinas, M.: Beyond Nintendo: Design and Assessment of Educational Video Games for First and Second Grade Students, Computers and Education **40** (2003) 71-94

Workshop on
Web Information Systems

Track1: Fragmentation Versus Integration
– Perspective of the Web Information
System Discipline (FIPWIS)

The Co-design Approach to WIS Development in E-business and E-learning Applications

Klaus-Dieter Schewe[1] and Bernhard Thalheim[2]

[1] Massey University, Department of Information Systems &
Information Science Research Centre
Private Bag 11 222, Palmerston North, New Zealand
k.d.schewe@massey.ac.nz
[2] Christian Albrechts University Kiel
Department of Computer Science and Applied Mathematics
Olshausenstr. 40, D-24098 Kiel, Germany
thalheim@is.informatik.uni-kiel.de

Abstract. We argue that the generic co-design approach to the development of web information systems is powerful enough to cover diverse applications. We illustrate the validity of this claim by comparing the key features of the approach with needs arising in e-business and e-learning applications. While this does not exclude that there still exist application-specific features that need to be handled separately, it underlines that it is advisable to consider the most generic approach first. In addition, it is recommendable trying to generalise specific features that arise in e-business and e-learning to the whole area of web information systems.

1 Introduction

Data-intensive information systems are a well-researched field that has found a lot of applications. Over the last decade there has been a shift of interest toward web information systems (WISs), i.e. information systems that are made available via the world-wide web. This area also has found a lot of applications in information services [13], electronic learning [5,4,3,14,16,22], electronic business [18,19], and others.

In these application fields, in particular in Electronic Business (EB) and Electronic Learning (EL) we now find groups of researchers claiming the field to be not just a field of application but a genuine research area in its own right. Of course, both areas have to link to business or education, respectively, but the question is, whether there are enough research problems that would lead to substantively different results than those achieved for WISs, i.e. on a more generic level.

In this position paper we argue that it is better to treat them still as application areas for WISs and not as separate fields in their own right. In order to present evidence for this claim we will briefly sketch the key concepts of the generic co-design approach to the development of web information systems [20],

C. Bussler et al. (Eds.): WISE 2004 Workshops, LNCS 3307, pp. 181–189, 2004.

i.e. storyboarding [11] and media types [12]. Both components have been deeply analysed with respect to their expressive power in [21,20] and [17,20], respectively. Both approaches have also been tailored to applications in EB [19] and EL [22].

We will demonstrate that key features such as story spaces, actors, media types and adaptivity each have a specialisation in EB and EL. That is, the generic co-design is very well reflected in the application area, and most of the specific needs arising from the application will already be captured by the approach. While this does not exclude that there still exist application-specific features that need to be handled separately, it underlines that it is advisable to consider the most generic approach first.

For instance, in e-learning didactic design is extremely important as strongly emphasised in the literature [9,10,7]. We do not argue that the arrangement of course material is enough for e-learning, but it is at the core of systems design for e-learning. In addition, our model for actors including roles, profiles, a deontic logic for obligations and rights, and intentions puts a strong emphasis on users, i.e. in e-learning on the learners and their behaviour. This addresses what might be called a model of the "learning experience". Of course, defining learner profiles, anticipating learner behaviour and arranging the course material, the learning steps and personalisation procedures exceeds the limits of a pure technologically focussed approach. In fact, it is one of the major differences in our work in comparison to others, e.g. [8]. Nevertheless, the modelling approach is still a generic one.

There are lots of other generic approaches to the development of WIS such as ARANEUS [1,2], WebML [6,8] and OOHDM [23]. We do not want to discuss the individual merits of these approaches, their advantages and disadvantages (see [17,20] for some comparison). We are confident that our argument will also hold largely for these other approaches.

2   Story Spaces

On a high level of abstraction we may think of a WIS as a set of abstract locations, which abstract from actual pages. A user navigates between these locations, and on this navigation path s/he executes a number of actions. We regard a location together with local actions, i.e. actions that do not change the location, as a unit called *scene*.

Then a WIS can be decribed by a edge-labelled directed multi-graph, in which the vertices represent the scenes, and the edges represent transitions between scenes. Each such transition may be labelled by an action executed by the user. If such a label is missing, the transition is due to a simple navigation link. The whole multi-graph is then called the *story space*. A *story* is a path in the story space. It tells what a user of a particular type might do with the system.

The combination of different stories to a subgraph of the story space can be used to describe a "typical" use of the WIS for a particular task. Therefore, we call such a subgraph a *scenario*. Usually storyboarding starts with modelling scenarios instead of stories, coupled by the integration of scenarios to the story space. At a finer level of details we may add a triggering *event*, a *precondition* and a *postcondition* to each action, i.e. we specify exactly, under which conditions an action can be executed and which effects it will have.

Looking at scenarios or the whole story space from a different angle, we may concentrate on the flow of actions:

- For the purpose of storyboarding actions can be treated as being atomic, i.e. we are not yet interested in how an underlying database might be updated. Then each action also belongs to a uniquely determined scene.
- Actions have pre- and postconditions, so we can use annotations to express conditions that must hold before or after an action is executed.
- Actions can be executed sequentially or parallel, and we must allow (demonic) choice between actions.
- Actions can be iterated.
- By adding an action `skip` we can then also express optionality and iteration with at least one execution.

These possibilities to combine actions lead to operators of an algebra, which we will call a *story algebra*. Thus, we can describe a story space by an element of a suitable story algebra. We should, however, note already that story algebras have to be defined as being many-sorted in order to capture the association of actions with scenes.

In the area of EL the story space corresponds to the curriculum, which can be modelled by an *outline graph* that describes the navigation of learners through an e-learning system [3]. Formally, an *outline graph* is a finite, directed graph $\mathcal{G} = (V, E)$, i.e. V and E are finite sets with $E \subseteq V \times V$. The vertices, i.e. the elements of V, are called *learning units*, and the edges, i.e. the elements of E are *links* between these units. Thus, scenes in story spaces correspond to learning units in EL systems.

Take for example a course dealing with e-learning systems. Then we might have learning units such as Introduction, Learner Profiling, Course Outlining, Data Management, Adaptivity, Style Definition, and Implementation.

Actions on a learning unit may depend on the successful completion of the learning unit by the learner. According to our view this is part of the action specification, and should be left for further refinement of the outline.

From a more conceptual point of view we model learner interaction with an e-learning system according to two primitives: transition between learning units and using the functionality offered at a given learning unit. This allows for a two-step modelling procedure to be applied. First at a coarse-grained level learning units and navigation links are modelled. Then in a refinement step the actual activities of the the learners are added. This procedure allows for a good separation of concern with respect to personalisation and localisation.

In the area of EB, the notions of story space and scenario have been adopted directly [18]. Describing the application story for e-business systems permits concentration on the business aspects. In particular, the accentuation of the communication aspects can be more easily approached on such a level of abstraction. Thus, it satisfies the primary criterium for conceptual modelling of not being implementation-biased. Furthermore, the approach is both grounded in solid mathematical theory such as Kleene algebras and deontic logic [20], and in the sophisticated pragmatics of a successful business branch – movie production – which may be considered a godfather for the approach.

3   Actors

A second key feature of storyboarding concerns the description of the *actors*, i.e. groups of users with the same profile. Users can be classified according to their roles, intentions and behaviour. We use the term *actor* for such a group of users. The *role* of an actor indicates a particular purpose of the system. As such it is usually associated with obligations and rights, which lead to deontic integrity constraints. Roles are also connected with the *tasks*, but tasks will be handled separately. The *intention* of an actor can be modelled by goals, i.e. postconditions to the story space. Modelling the behaviour of an actor leads to *user profiles*, which can be modelled by giving values for various properties that characterize a user. Furthermore, each profile leads to rules that can again be expressed by constraints on the story space.

In addition, each actor has an *information portfolio*, which specifies the information needs as well as the information entered into the system. We do not model the information portfolio as part of an actor, but instead of this we will model the information "consumed" and "produced" with each more detailed specification of a scene. However, we associate information consumption and production with each scene of the story space. Assuming that there is a database for the data content of the WIS with database schema $\mathcal{S}$, information consumption on a scene s definitely accounts for a *view* V_s over $\mathcal{S}$. That is, we have another schema $\mathcal{S}_V$ and a computable transformation from databases over $\mathcal{S}$ to databases over $\mathcal{S}_V$. Such a transformation is usually expressed by a query q_V. Such views will form the basis of the theory of media types.

The presence of roles indicates a particular purpose of the system. For instance, in a web-based conference system we may have roles for the programme committee chair(s), the programme committee members, and for authors. On the other hand, in an on-line loan system we may not wish to distinguish roles, as all actors will only appear in the one role of a customer.

A *role* is defined by the set of actions that an actor with this role may execute. Thus, we first associate with each scene in the story space a set of role names, i.e. whenever an actor comes across a particular scene, s/he will have to have one of these roles. Furthermore, a role is usually associated with obligations and rights, i.e. which actions have to be executed or which scenes are disclosed.

An *obligation* specifies what an actor in a particular role has to do. A *right* specifies what an actor in a particular role is permitted to do. Both obligations and rights together lead to complex deontic integrity constraints. The *intention* of an actor can be expressed by goals, which can be modelled by postconditions to the story space.

Modelling the behaviour of an actor leads to *user profiles*. We may ask which properties characterize a user and provide values for each of these properties. Each combination of such values defines a profile, but usually the behaviour for some of these profiles is the same. Furthermore, each profile leads to rules that can again be expressed by constraints on the story space.

The dimensions used in user profiles depend on the application. Formally, in order to describe such user profiles, we start with a finite set Δ of *user dimensions*. For each dimension $\delta \in \Delta$ we assume to be given a scale $sc(\delta)$. Formally, a *scale* is a totally ordered set. If $\Delta = \{\delta_1, \ldots, \delta_n\}$ is a set of user dimensions, then the *set of user profiles* is $gr(\Delta) = sc(\delta_1) \times \ldots \times sc(\delta_n)$. A *user type* is a convex region $U \subseteq gr(\Delta)$.

The analogue of the actor in EB and EL applications are the *customer* and the *learner*, repectively. In particular, user types become customer types or learner types, respectively. The only decisive feature in both application areas is the decision on the relevant user dimensions and the associated scales. Formally, however, there is no need to introduce a particular new theory.

4   Media Types

The central concept for modelling the content and the functionality of a WIS is the *media type*. We may assume that we have an underlying database. On the basis of a given database schema we may introduce *interaction types* as views that are extended by operations. This permits to apply completely different design criteria for the database schema and the interaction schema. One major facility used in interaction types is the possibility to create a navigation structure via URLs and links. *Media types* arise from tailoring the information types in such a way that different presentation options will be enabled.

A *media type* is an interaction type M together with an cohesion order $\preceq_M$ (or a set of promimity values) and a set of hierarchical versions $H(M)$.

Cohesion introduces a controlled form of information loss. Formally, we define a partial order $\leq$ on content data types, which extends subtyping. If $cont(M)$ is the content data type of a interaction type M and $sup(cont(M))$ is the set of all content expressions exp with $cont(M) \leq exp$, then a preorder $\preceq_M$ on $sup(cont(M))$ extending the order $\leq$ on content expressions is called an *cohesion preorder*.

Small elements in $sup(cont(M))$ with respect to $\preceq_M$ define information to be kept together, if possible. Clearly, $cont(M)$ is minimal with respect to $\preceq_M$. This enables a controlled form of information decomposition. If we want to decompose an interaction type or if we are forced to decompose according to user requirements or technical restrictions, then we may choose a minimal elements $t_1 \in sup(cont(M))$ with respect to $\preceq_M$ such that it satifies the representation requirements. Note that if we only provide a preorder, not an order, then there may be more than one such t_1.

Taking just t_1 instead of $cont(M)$ means that some information is lost, but this only refers to the first data transfer. When transferring t_1, we must include a link to a possible successor containing detailed information. In order to determine such a successor we can continue looking at all content types $t' \in sup(cont(M))$ with $t_1 \not\preceq_M t'$. These are just those containing the complimentary information that was lost. Again we can choose a least type t_2 among these t' with respect to $\preceq_M$ that requires not more than the available capacity. t_2 would be the desired successor.

Proceeding this way the whole communication is broken down into a sequence of suitable units $t_1, t_2, \ldots, t_n$ that together contain the information provided by the interaction type. Of course, the cohesion pre-order suggests that the relevance of the information decreases, while progressing with this sequence. The user may decide at any time that the level of detail provided by the sequence $t_1, \ldots, t_i$ is already sufficient for his/her needs. An alternative to cohesion preorders is to use *proximity values*, which we do not discuss here.

Another possibility to tailor the information content of interaction types is to consider dimension hierarchies as in OLAP systems. Flattening of dimensions results in information growth, its converse in information loss. Such a hierarchy is already implicitly defined by the component or link structures, repectively.

For an interaction type M let $\bar{H}(M)$ be the set of all interaction types arising from M by applying a sequence of flat-operations or their converses to interaction types or underlying database types. A *set of hierarchical versions* of M is a finite subset $H(M)$ of $\bar{H}(M)$ with $M \in H(M)$. Each cohesion order $\preceq_M$ on M induces an cohesion order $\preceq_{M'}$ on each element $M' \in H(M)$.

Media types are used directly in EL applications [16] and in EB applications [17].

5   Adaptivity

In order to avoid an unnecessary replication of WISs with the undesired increase in maintenance costs we prefer to have a single server-side specification of the system, which adapts itself to various needs of the clients. Basically, we see two dimensions of this adaptivity problem.

The first one concerns the distinction between the adaptivity of content and process. Processes determine which functionality becomes available to users and which not. Process adaptivity thus results in discarding access to part of the system and to reduce the number of available actions. Content adaptivity on the other hand refers to tailoring the data content that is presented to a user. This may result in reducing the content, splitting or merging it, or aggregate it to a more compact representation.

The second dimension of adaptivity concerns the parameters that determine the adaptation. Here we distinguish between adaptivity to users, locations, channels and devices. With respect to the users we consider preferences of users and requirements resulting from profiling characteristics of users. With respect to locations we consider the actual location of a user. With respect to channel we consider the communication channel used by a user, e.g. fixed line, telephone, broadband, mobile, TV cable-net, etc. With respect to devices we consider the end-device used by a user, e.g. PCs, PDAs, cellphones, TVs, etc.

Content adaptivity can be approached on the level of media types. In fact, that is exactly the purpose of cohesion. We already described the adaption procedure. Obviously, there is no need for a particular theory in the areas of EL or EB.

Process adaptivity to can be obtained on the level of the story space. For this we may exploit the fact that a story space can be described by an expression in a many-sorted Kleene algebra with tests (MKATs) [15,20]. The general approach is as follows. We express the story space or parts of it by some process expression p. We then formulate a problem by using equations or conditional equations in this MKAT. Furthermore, we obtain equations, which represent application knowledge. This application knowledge arises from events, postconditions and knowledge about the use of the WIS for a particular purpose. We then apply all equations to solve the particular problem at hand.

The equations that define the application knowledge formulate preferences of a user. Furthermore, we formalised the intention of a user by some propositional formula ψ. Then the problem is to find a minimal expression p' in the MKAT such that $p\psi = p'\psi$ holds.

The equational reasoning with MKATs used for process adaptivity is independent from the application. The application area only determines the equations and the goal formulae. In EL these correspond to learning style and learning goals [14]. In EB no particular notions were introduced.

6 Conclusion

In this position paper we claimed that the generic co-design approach to the development of web information systems is powerful enough to cover diverse applications, in particular in EB and EL, and therefore it would not be justified to treat EB and EL as fields in their own right. We demonstrated the validity of this claim by comparing the key features of the approach with corresponding features in these two application areas.

From this we may conclude that a generic theory for WISs is needed, and that the development of such a theory is the preferable scientific approach. This does not exclude that there still exist application-specific features that need to be handled separately. In addition, it is recommendable trying to generalise specific features that arise in applications to the whole area of WISs.

Acknowledgement. We would like to thank the anonymous reviewers for their valuable comments. According to the theme of the FIPWIS workshop this paper is written as a position statement emphasising that there is a generic approach that covers quite well various applications, which we illustrated by the two areas of e-learning and e-business. We admit of course that in a concrete application context expertise from other areas such as teaching or business knowledge has to come in as well, but this is nothing new, as systems development has always been an inter-disciplinary effort. To that end some statements in our paper are meant to provoke the discussion about the respective merits of generic versus specific theories in web information systems. From the comments of the reviewers we conclude that this provocation was quite successful.

References

1. ATZENI, P., GUPTA, A., AND SARAWAGI, S. Design and maintenance of data-intensive web-sites. In *Proceeding EDBT'98*, vol. 1377 of *LNCS*. Springer-Verlag, Berlin, 1998, pp. 436–450.

2. BARESI, L., GARZOTTO, F., AND PAOLINI, P. From web sites to web applications: New issues for conceptual modeling. In *ER Workshops 2000*, vol. 1921 of *LNCS*. Springer-Verlag, Berlin, 2000, pp. 89–100.

3. BINEMANN-ZDANOWICZ, A., SCHEWE, K.-D., AND THALHEIM, B. Adaptation to learning styles. In *Proceedings ICALT 2004* (2004), IEEE Computer Society.

4. BINEMANN-ZDANOWICZ, A., SCHULZ-BRÜNKEN, B., THALHEIM, B., AND TSCHIEDEL, B. Flexible e-payment based on content and profile in the e-learning system DaMiT. In *Proceedings of E-Learn 2003* (Phoenix (Arizona), USA, 2003), Association for the Advancement of Computing in Education.

5. BINEMANN-ZDANOWICZ, A., THALHEIM, B., AND TSCHIEDEL, B. Logistics for learning objects. In *Proceedings of eTrain 2003* (2003).

6. BONIFATI, A., CERI, S., FRATERNALI, P., AND MAURINO, A. Building multi-device, content-centric applications using WebML and the W3I3 tool suite. In *ER Workshops 2000*, vol. 1921 of *LNCS*. Springer-Verlag, Berlin, 2000, pp. 64–75.

7. BRANSFORD, J. D., BROWN, A. L., AND COCKING, R. R., Eds. *How People Learn – Brain, Mind, Experience, and School*. National Academy Press, 2003.

8. CERI, S., FRATERNALI, P., BONGIO, A., BRAMBILLA, M., COMAI, S., AND MATERA, M. *Designing Data-Intensive Web Applications*. Morgan Kaufmann, San Francisco, 2003.

9. DAMASIO, A. *The Feeling of What Happens – Body and Emotion in the Making of Consciousness*. Hartcourt Inc., 1999.

10. DAVIS, B., SUMARA, D., AND LUCE-KAPLER, R. *Engaging Minds – Learning and Teaching in a Complex World*. Lawrence Erlbaum Associates, 2000.

11. DÜSTERHÖFT, A., AND THALHEIM, B. SiteLang: Conceptual modeling of internet sites. In *Conceptual Modeling – ER 2001*, H. S. K. et al., Ed., vol. 2224 of *LNCS*. Springer-Verlag, Berlin, 2001, pp. 179–192.

12. FEYER, T., KAO, O., SCHEWE, K.-D., AND THALHEIM, B. Design of data-intensive web-based information services. In *Proceedings of the 1st International Conference on Web Information Systems Engineering (WISE 2000)*, Q. Li, Z. M. Ozsuyoglu, R. Wagner, Y. Kambayashi, and Y. Zhang, Eds. IEEE Computer Society, 2000, pp. 462–467.

13. FEYER, T., SCHEWE, K.-D., AND THALHEIM, B. Conceptual modelling and development of information services. In *Conceptual Modeling – ER'98*, T. Ling and S. Ram, Eds., vol. 1507 of *LNCS*. Springer-Verlag, Berlin, 1998, pp. 7–20.

14. KASCHEK, R., SCHEWE, K.-D., THALHEIM, B., KUSS, T., AND TSCHIEDEL, B. Learner typing for electronic learning systems. In *Proceedings ICALT 2004* (2004), IEEE Computer Society.

15. KOZEN, D. Kleene algebra with tests. *ACM Transactions on Programming Languages and Systems 19*, 3 (1997), 427–443.

16. ROSTANIN, O., SCHEWE, K.-D., THALHEIM, B., AND TRETIAKOV, A. Managing the data in electronic learning systems. In *Proceedings ICALT 2004* (2004), IEEE Computer Society.

17. SCHEWE, K.-D. The power of media types. In *Proceedings WISE 2004: Web Information Systems Engineering*, LNCS. Springer-Verlag, 2004.

18. SCHEWE, K.-D., KASCHEK, R., WALLACE, C., AND MATTHEWS, C. Modelling web-based banking systems: Story boarding and user profiling. In *Advanced Conceptual Modeling Techniques: ER 2002 Workshops* (2003), vol. 2784 of *LNCS*, Springer-Verlag, pp. 427–439.

19. SCHEWE, K.-D., KASCHEK, R., WALLACE, C., AND MATTHEWS, C. Emphasizing the communication aspects for the successful development of electronic business systems. *Information Systems and E-Business Management* (2004). to appear.

20. SCHEWE, K.-D., AND THALHEIM, B. Conceptual modelling of web information systems. Tech. Rep. 3/2004, Massey University, Department of Information Systems, 2004. available from
http://infosys.massey.ac.nz/research/rs_techreports.html.

21. SCHEWE, K.-D., AND THALHEIM, B. Reasoning about web information systems using story algebras. In *Proceedings ADBIS 2004* (Budapest, Hungary, 2004).

22. SCHEWE, K.-D., THALHEIM, B., BINEMANN-ZDANOWICZ, A., KASCHEK, R., KUSS, T., AND TSCHIEDEL, B. A conceptual view of electronic learning systems. submitted for publication.

23. SCHWABE, D., AND ROSSI, G. An object oriented approach to web-based application design. *TAPOS 4*, 4 (1998), 207–225.

Using KCPM for Defining and Integrating Domain Ontologies[1]

Christian Kop, Heinrich C. Mayr, and Tatjana Zavinska

Institut für Wirtschaftsinformatik und Anwendungssysteme,
IWAS University of Klagenfurt

Abstract. The paper discusses the representation and integration of domain ontologies using the Conceptual Predesign Model KCPM. This model initially was developed as a means to bridge, within the information system design cycle, the 'impedance mismatch' between natural language requirements specifications and abstract conceptual models (schemas) by an user centered interlingua: Requirements are represented in a formalized fashion by focusing the structural, functional and behavioral terminology of an application domain. Methods and tools have been developed so far, to derive KCPM schemas out of natural language specifications by natural language processing and interpretation techniques, and, to map these schemas, after validation, to any conceptual representation. We introduce the main KCPM modeling concepts and demonstrate, how these may be used to define domain ontologies. Based here-on, aspects of reuse, extension and integration are discussed.

1 Introduction

Today the development of ontologies is no more reserved for a narrow circle of specialists in Artificial Intelligence but has been moving to the desktops of domain experts. Many disciplines are occupied with the discussion and development of standardized ontologies, the evolvement of the Semantic Web will even accelerate that trend. Using ontologies domain experts can share conceptualizations of their domain and annotate information about their understanding of the particular concepts resp. notions and their interrelationships. Represented in an machine-interpretable form ontologies are the key means for a more semantic-driven communication between (partly) autonomous software systems.

We concentrate here on so-called *domain ontologies* which focus on a specific application domain. Developing such ontologies is not at all a trivial task for the application expert. He/she has to reveal the concepts to be specified, to choose between an increasing number of different approaches and thus languages for ontology representation, to associate the right notions (e.g. 'concept', 'class', 'attribute', 'property', 'facet', 'rule' etc.) to his/her concepts, and to iteratively validate the results. Thus, guidelines and process models are needed, as discussed e.g. in [4], [12], that support these tasks from planning to validation. For eliciting ontology constructs from natural

---

[1] The work underlying that paper has been financed partly by the Klaus-Tschira-Stiftung, Heidelberg.

C. Bussler et al. (Eds.): WISE 2004 Workshops, LNCS 3307, pp. 190–200, 2004.

language texts different techniques are proposed (repertory grids, clustering methods, frequency-based approaches, CommonKADS), see [13].

This work proposes an application expert centered approach by using the Klagenfurt Conceptual Predesign Model (KCPM) [9], [10] as a means for domain ontology development by the 'business owner'. KCPM initially was developed to bridge, within the information system design cycle, the 'impedance mismatch' between natural language requirements specifications and abstract conceptual models (schemas). Requirements are represented in a formalized fashion by focusing the structural, functional and behavioral terminology of an application domain. As such KCPM meets the increasingly postulated 'verbalization' of specifications w.r.t. to the 'business owner's' needs (see, e.g. [7]).

Methods and tools have been developed so far to derive KCPM schemas out of natural language specifications by natural language processing and interpretation techniques, and, to map these schemas, after validation by the users and stakeholders, to any conceptual representation². Thus, KCPM acts as an interlingua, i.e.as an intermediate language, on both, the conceptual and the technical level. It turned out that this approach comes with two further benefits: First, KCPM schemas may be used as a kind of reusable knowledge base [2], [8] describing a certain domain (Universe of Discourse, UoD) which evolves, by repeated application, extension and generalizations, to a domain reference model, i.e. what is called usually a "domain ontology". Secondly, due to the nature of the KCPM modeling concepts, the integration of different, possibly distributed schemas representing partial knowledge is a quite straight forward process which may be executed by domain experts independently from system analysts or design specialists.

The paper consists of 5 sections. Section 2 outlines the most important notions in the context of ontologies. Section 3 introduces KCPM and shows how it can be used for the development and representation of domain ontologies. Section 4 is devoted to the integration, sharing and reuse of ontologies. The paper closes with a short summary and the reference list.

2 Ontologies

A quite commonly used definition of the term ontology is that of Fensel [6] who defines an ontology to be a formal and explicit specification of a shared conceptualization. Typical ontology components supporting that conceptualization are the following:

- **Concepts,** also called *classes* or *frames*, are the key elements of most ontologies. They specify any abstract or concrete, elementary or compound, real or fictitious thing of interest. I.e., a concept could also specify a task, action, strategy, reasoning process, etc.

---

² The reader who is interested in more details is referred to: www.ifi.uni-klu.ac.at/IWAS/HM/Projects/NIBA

- **Slots** specify features, characteristics, and aspects of relations between concepts.
- **Taxonomies**: Most widely used are *generalization/specialization* relations which serve to establish taxonomies and provide simple and/or multiple inheritance. They are not defined by slots but by separate relationship definitions (e.g. sub-class–of in OIL).
- **Rule types** or **Constraints** specify valid dependencies (e.g. restrictions, causalities) between concepts and relations.
- **Facets** are associated with slots and specify their properties, e.g. value type and value type restrictions, min-cardinality or max-cardinality. Some languages also allow the definition of *axioms* and *production rules*.
- **Facts** relate instances to concepts and relations.

For ontology development Cristani and Cuel [4] propose the following (iterative) phases:

- *plan phase*: definition of the goals and limitations, determination of the (amount of) resources needed,
- *introspective phase*: definition of the draft schema, such as the general concepts and relations, their formalization into a chosen formal language and its demonstration; this phase is based on references to literature and on 'arm-chair research',
- *bottom up phase*: the draft terminology is constructed and refined; relationships among terms are established. This process might be supported by automated tools, i.e. for lexical text analysis and data mining,
- *provision of basic axioms*: by domain experts interviews or participation,
- *validation phase*: the obtained set of specifications is tested, corrected, refined, validated, and used.

3   KCPM

3.1   KCPM Modeling Notions

An important aim for the development of KCPM was to harmonize the developer's and the end-user's ('business owner) view of a given UoD, i.e. to provide an interface for their mutual understanding. To enforce that understanding, two kinds of KCPM schema representations have been developed: A graphical one and a tabular one using glossaries adopted from [3]. Within this paper we restrict ourselves to the latter. Especially for business people dealing with ontologies, glossaries seem to be more easy read and checked, in particular in the case of large schemes where tool supported groupings and aggregations are not interfered with layout rearrangements as may happen in graphical representations. The column headers of the glossaries represent KCPM meta-attributes of the resp. modeling notions. Traceability between all the glossary entries and their source (the natural language text of the business owners) is given by means of so-called requirement source references.

KCPM provides modeling notions for both static and dynamic aspects of an UoD. However, it suffices to concentrate here on the former since we do not deal with operations on ontologies within that paper. The most important KCPM notions for modeling static aspects are: *thing-type*, *connection-type* and *perspective*:

Thing-type is a generalization of the ontology notions *concept* and *value-type*. Thus, typical things (instances of thing-types) are

- natural or juridical persons,
- material or immaterial objects,
- abstract notions as well as
- descriptive characteristics of the above mentioned examples (e.g. a *customer name, a product number, a product description*) which can be seen as attributes or as specific legal domain determiner.

Thing-type glossary meta-attributes help to specify synonyms belonging to a thing-type as well as quantity descriptions, restrictions on values of a thing-type (see column value domain). Example instances of a thing-type are named in the examples meta-attribute.

UoD: publishing								
Id#	name	classi-fication	quantity descrip-tion	examples	value do-main	syno-nyms	textual descrip-tion	require-ment sources
D001	author	thing-type		Arthur Miller		D007	An author is a writer of any text	S1, S2
D002	book	thing-type	500					S1, S2, S3
D003	ISBN	thing-type	500	3-540-65470-4	string		The interna-tionally unique code for listed publications	S3
.....	.....	.....	.....	.....	.....	.....	.....	.....

Fig. 1. Part of a thing-type glossary

Things are related within the real world. This is captured by the notion of **connection-type**. Two or more thing-types can be involved in a connection-type. To define a connection-type completely, it must be described from the point of view (**perspective**) of all of the involved thing-types. This corresponds to the NIAM object/role model [11]. Sentences leading to connections (and perspectives) are e.g. the following:

(S1) *Authors write books.* (perspective of *author*)
(S2) *Books are written by authors.* (perspective of *book*)
(S3) *An ISBN number identifies a book.*

3.2 Ontology Modeling Using KCPM

We now will show how KCPM can be used as an ontology modeling language by associating the KCPM notions with the corresponding ontology notions *concept, slot, taxonomy, constraint, axiom* and *production rule* as introduced in section 2.

UoD: book publishing								
		connec-tion-type deter-miner	**Perspective**					require-ment sources
c-id#	name		p-id#	involved thing-type	name	min/max	perspec-tive deter-miner	
C001	write/ is_written	<optional reference to a concept capturing the relationship; similar to the association class in UML>	p001-1	D001, author	write	0..n	<optional reference to a concept capturing the perspective>	S1, S2
			p001-2	D002, Book	is_writ-ten	0..n		
C002	identification		p002-1	D004, ISBN	Identi-fies	0,1		S3
			p002-1	D002, Book	is_iden-tified-_by	1,1		
.....	.....	.....	.....	.....	.....	.....	.....	.....

Fig. 2. Part of a connection type glossary

As has been said already, thing-types generalize the ontology notions concept and value-type, i.e. may be used for the specification of concepts and value types. Connection-types may be used as follows:

- If the involved thing-type of a perspective specifies a concept, the perspective corresponds to a slot of that concept, and its min-/max-cardinalities correspond to facets of that slot.
- If the involved thing-type of a perspective specifies a value type, it corresponds to a slot facet (value type) of a concept specifying the (or in case of multidimensional connection-types of an) other involved thing-type of that connection-type. This implies that at least one of the involved thing-types has to be related to a concept. Such a restriction, however, is not generally imposed by KCPM which, as an interlingua, also complies with e.g. the ER model that allows for relationships between attributes.

The abstractions *generalization* (to build „is-a" taxonomies with set inclusion on the instance level; i.e. extensional) and *component/object* („is part of") are treated by KCPM as specific connection-types. An example for a generalization resulting from the sentence

(S4) *an author is a person.*

is given in figure 3. These abstractions correspond to ontological 'subset-of' (or 'kind-of') relations and 'part-of' relations, respectively.

Note that these interrelationships between KCPM and ontological notions may be used as heuristic mapping rules for an automated tool transforming KCPM schemes into statements of an ontology language (similar to the mapping of KCPM requirements schemes to UML models as discussed in [10]). Clearly, for a specific ontology language, these rules have to be refined. E.g., if the 'part-of' relation is not supported by an ontology language, it can be mapped to slot definitions.

UoD: book publishing								
			Perspective					
c-id#	Name	connec-tion-type determiner	p-id#	Invol-ved thing-type	name	min/max	perspec-tive deter-miner	require-ment sources
C001	generali-zation		p001-1	D004, person	genera-lization	0..1		S4
			p001-2	D001, author	specia-lization	1..1		

Fig. 3. Part of a connection type glossary with Generalization

KCPM is open for further semantic connection-types (e.g. possession) by a mechanism similar to that of stereo-types in UML.

Aspects of an ontology that cannot be modeled using these notions are captured by (textual) **constraints**. Again these constraints are represented in glossaries. This is not very sophisticated, but allows the designer to specify various kinds of constraints (e.g. production rules, axioms etc.).

3.3 Structuring Ontologies

To structure an ontology KCPM provides the following notions: A **Universe of discourse (UoD)** is a certain part of an application domain for which an ontology is to be built (e.g. publishing, library, procurement, sales etc.). Several Universes of Discourse can be related to a **Domain** according to features which are shared by these UoD's. This can be seen as a clustering of a given set of UoD's to one or more domains to which they belong.

UoD's often are of concern for people (users) having a different educational background (e.g., engineers, accountants, salesmen) and thus speaking in different "languages" (in the sense of different terminologies and notions) based on different ontologies. In order to enhance the ontology development process from problems that might raise from that babel KCPM supports the splitting of UoD's into **Organizational Units** having an homogenous community of people concerned. A further splitting into **Task Areas** is offered for mastering complexity in cases of very large application domains. The same is true for the partition of a domain into sub-domains. Clearly, in subsequent steps, these isolated units should be systematically integrated to construct a whole domain ontology. Instead of or in addition to integration, specific ontologies could be introduced on each level containing common concepts of several other ontologies (usually of lower levels) thus supporting knowledge sharing (see next section). KCPM provides a platform to model these "islands", to merge them into domain models or to extract shared knowledge (see figures 4–6).

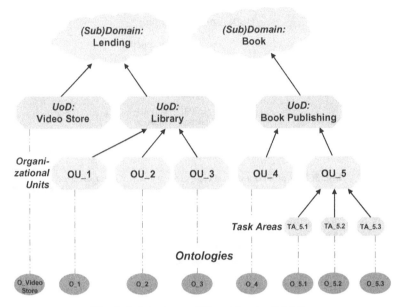

Fig. 4. Ontologies on different levels of detail

4   Integration, Sharing, and Re-use of Ontologies

It should have become obvious now, that KCPM glossaries representing ontologies may serve as an easy to understand basis for the communication between domain experts and ontology designers. Moreover, the tabular form also supports grouping of related concepts as well as consistency and completeness checks. In addition to that, they also prove to be appropriate for ontology integration and reuse analogously to the integration and reuse of conceptual schemas [1], [2], [8]. More generally, KCPM schemas act as containers of knowledge for sharing, discussion, reuse and reference.

Having KCPM schemas as a starting basis it suggests itself to choose, for their **integration,** a bottom-up approach along the hierarchy, i.e. from task areas via organizational units and UoD's to the root domain (see figure 5). At each integration step, the usual tasks have to be performed: conflict analysis, conflict resolution, merging and restructuring. Since KCPM provides only connected thing-types structural conflicts [1] are easier to detect than in the case of traditional conceptual models.

For **knowledge sharing,** sharable concepts are collected in a particular ontology (KCPM schema) which usually will be 'higher' in the hierarchy than the sharing ones. As an example, in figure 6, O_Book_shared would contain the shared concepts (shared terminology) w.r.t. 'books' of the UoD's library and book-publishing. Whereas it might happen, that ontologies on the task area and even on the UoD level might be completely shared and thus form what is usually called a *reference model,* this is not probable on the (sub-)domain level. The usual case will be that of the before mentioned example, namely the sharing of (invariant) parts:

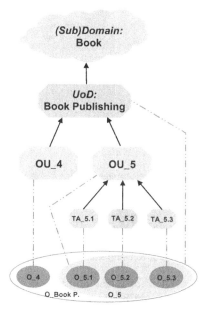

Fig. 5. Integration of task area and organizational unit ontologies

- single thing-types like "author", "person", "book", "ISBN",
- connection-types like 'ISBN identifies/is_identified_by book', 'author writes/is_written_by book', 'author is a person' as well as
- constraints.

It should be even possible to share meta attributes of thing-types or connection-types (e.g. examples that can be reused, min- and max cardinalities of perspectives etc.)

Sharing glossary contents can be based on either an expert's decision or on analogies derived from the different domains (e.g. the same thing-types, connection-types etc.).

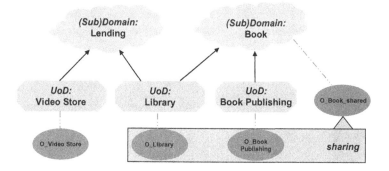

Fig. 6. Sharing notions of several UoD's

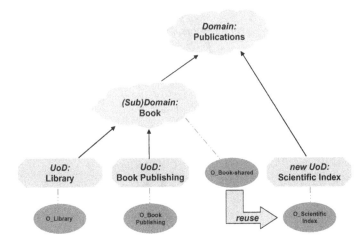

Fig. 7. Reusing shared knowledge

If an ontology is to be generated for a new domain, then it suggests itself to check, which pieces of existing ones might be shared and thus **reused**. E.g., concepts in O-Book-shared might be reused when developing a new ontology for the UoD "scientific index" (see figure 7).

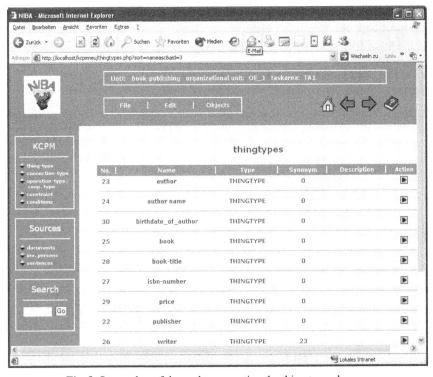

Fig. 8. Screenshot of the tool representing the thing type glossary

5 Summary

Currently KCPM is not completely formalized as is required by Knowledge Engineers. However it provides an interlingua and a first means of communication between domain experts (business owners) and designers which have to develop an ontology. In particular, KCPM comes with the following benefits:

Domain experts are not forced to make early decisions on what is a concept and what not, they simply have to collect domain specific notions and to specify these according to the KCPM meta attributes of thing-types. In other words, in a first step every thing which is relevant to a domain becomes a thing-type (i.e. is understood as a concept) although it may become a value type when mapped to a particular ontology language later on. This generalization is possible since the answer to the question of 'what is a concept and what is not' is encoded within the semantic network of thing-types related to each other by connection-types. For conceptual modeling it was shown in [10] that the answer can derived by applying heuristics on this network, first hints on how this could work for ontologies have been given in section 3.

Furthermore the glossary representation gives end-users a natural view on the schema which looks like a lexicon. For the domain expert, some extended views on such a lexicon support the check for completeness and consistency.

Actually we have developed a prototype to collect KCPM notions. This prototype is a web-application based on an Apache Web-Server and PHP Scripts. Figure 8 shows an example screen shot of that prototype. The idea of the prototype to present the ontology in a glossary. The main notions (thing-type, connection-type, constraints, cooperation-type, conditions are presented in a tabular form. For each entry, there are properties like meta attributes as well as other information like questions the designer has to answer, and answers to that questions. Each notion may be connected to a source (a document, a sentence, a reference to a person) from which the notion was retrieved. All sources again are presented in a tabular form. The prototype will be integrated into and uses components of the NIBA toolset[2] which is developed to support a user centred requirements analysis by using natural language processing techniques, KCPM and model mapping heuristics.

Acknowledgement. We thank the anonymous reviewers of the previously submitted version of that paper for their valuable comments and suggestions.

References

1. Batini, C.; Ceri, S.; Navathe, S. B.: Conceptual Database Design an Entity Relationship Approach, Benjamin Cummings Publ. Company, Redwood, Calif, Vol. 2. 1992.
2. Bellizona, R.; Fugini, M. G.; de Mey, V.: Reuse of Specifications and Designs in a Development Information System. In (Prakash, N. et al. eds.): Information System Development Process. Proc. IFIP WG8.1 Working Conf. on Information System Development Process; North Holland 1993, pp. 79-98.
3. Ceri, S. (ed.): Methodology and Tools for Database Design. North Holland, 1983.

4.   Cristani, M; Cuel, R.: A Comprehensive Guideline for Building a Domain Ontology from Scratch. In Proc. 4th International Conference on Knowledge Management I-Know 2004.
5.   Corcho, O.; Asuncion G. P.: A Road Map to Ontology Specification Languages. In (Dieng, R.; Corby, O. eds.): Knowledge Engineering and Knowledge Management – Methods, Models and Tools. Proc. 12th Int. Conf. EKAW 2000, Juan-les-Pins, France, LNAI, Vol. 1937, Springer, 2000, pp. 80-96.
6.   Fensel, D.: Ontologies: A Silver Bullet for Knowledge Management and Electronic Commerce. Springer Verlag, 2000.
7.   Halpin, T.: Business Rule Verbalization. In (Doroshenko, A. et al. eds.): Proc. 3rd Int. Conf. on Information Systems Technology and its Applications ISTA 2004, Salt Lake City, Lecture Notes in Informatics LNI-p48, GI-Edition, pp. 39-52.
8.   Kop, Ch.; Mayr, H.C.: Reusing Domain Knowledge in Requirement Analysis. In (J. Györkös et al. eds.): Proc. 3rd Conf. on Re-engineering, Reverse engineering and Reuse of Information Systems, ReTIS 1994, pp. 144-147.
9.   Kop, Ch.; Mayr, H.C.: Conceptual Predesign – Bridging the Gap between Requirements and Conceptual Design. In: Proc. 3rd International Conference on Requirements Engineering ICRE'98, April, 1998.
10. Mayr, H.C.; Kop, C.: A User Centered Approach to Requirements Modeling. In (Glinz, M., Müller-Luschnat, G. eds.): Proc. "Modellierung 2002". Lecture Notes in Informatics P-12 (LNI), GI-Edition, 2002, pp.75-86.
11. Nijssen, G.; Halpin, T. A.: Conceptual Scheme and Relational Database Design - A fact oriented approach. Prentice Hall Publ. Comp. 1989.
12. Noy, N. F., McGuiness, D.L.: Ontology Development 101: a guide to creating your first ontology.
     http://reliant.teknowledge.com/RKF/publication/Stanford/Ontology%20Tutorial.htm
13. Schreiber, G. et. al.: Knowledge Engineering and Management: The CommonKADS Methodology. Cambridge, Massachusetts: the MIT Press, 1999.
14. Sutcliffe, A.G.; Maiden, N.A.M.: Use of Domain Knowledge for Requirements Validation. In (Prakash, N. et al. eds.): Information System Development Process. Proc. IFIP WG8.1 Working Conf. on Information System Development Process; North Holland 1993, pp. 99-115.

Mobile Content Adaptation as an Optimisation Problem

Alexei Tretiakov and Sven Hartmann

Department of Information Systems, College of Business
Massey University, New Zealand
{A.Tretiakov, S.Hartmann}@massey.ac.nz

Abstract. We formulate an approach to adaptively structuring content for access via mobile devices, based on finding a global minimum of a cost function. The approach accounts for variations in communication channels, end-user device capabilities and user profiles, and can be easily extended to meet additional requirements by adding new terms to the cost function. In addition, we outline a simulated annealing algorithm for maintaining personalised views of a web site with continuously updated content.

1 Introduction

Within the last few years, the emergence of small, mobile and ergonomic devices such as PDAs or smart phones opens the market for a large variety of new information services. These devices enable mobile usage of digital information during mobility. Thanks to wireless networks, portable devices can connect to the Internet (the Mobile Internet) and thus allow users constant access to information services. At the same time, however, service providers offering such services for mobile clients have to consider a number of restrictions which exist due to both limitations of mobile devices (e.g. display properties, input methods, power consumption, varying standards) and of wireless networks (e.g. slow data transfer, connectivity).

Consequently, Mobile Internet poses a number of unique requirements to content services [3,4,7]. One option to cope with the new requirements is to redevelop existing services for each different portable device and environment. As pointed out in [3] this approach has been taken surprisingly often and is still rather popular in everyday practice. Providers offering services to heterogeneous mobile devices and with frequently if not steadily changing contents face a severe problem: keeping their services up to date and consistent binds resources in terms of time, intellectual man-power and money. This problem is even more severe as really innovative services for the Mobile Internet are often developed by small and medium enterprises which can typically not rely on exhaustless resources as global players can. To save maintenance costs and to ensure service consistency it would be preferable for them to maintain only a single description of the content they are providing which then can be automatically converted to the format most suitable for the current mobile environment.

[7] divides the requirements specific to mobile content services into three categories: adaptivity to communication channels, adaptivity to technical environ-

C. Bussler et al. (Eds.): WISE 2004 Workshops, LNCS 3307, pp. 201–210, 2004.

ments, and adaptivity to the user. Mobile devices present a much wider variety of device capabilities in terms of screen size, memory size, colours available etc., than personal computers. Thus, content has to be adapted to the client's technical environment. Also, different mobile devices may need to operate over a wide variety of bandwidths, leading to the requirement of adaptivity to communication channels. In addition, as mobile devices may be used under a wide variety of circumstances, there is a greater need (than with classical PC clients) to support customisation of end-user experience via user profiles - adaptivity to the user.

In this article, we propose a unified approach to achieving adaptivity to technical environments, communication channels and to the user, as far as the selection of media to be displayed on a single screen is concerned. Our idea is to model the adaptivity problem as a discrete optimisation problem that can be tackled using well-established heuristics the behaviour of which has been widely studied in mathematical optimisation. Taken that the diversity of mobile devices is rapidly increasing while the actual time frame for developing content services is steadily decreasing this approach should help to make adding adaptivity more independent from the particular content service to be enhanced.

2 Existing Approaches

The most straightforward approach to mobile content adaptation is re-authoring: manually redeveloping the web site for each target device. While guidelines such as [11] are available, considering the effort required, re-authoring is likely to attract significant costs. The alternative is to deploy adaptation logic server-side, and to automatically generate content suitable for the current combination of client device, connection and user type.

We distinguish two aspects of mobile content adaptation: adaptation within the existing web site structure, and adaptation involving re-allocation of content and the commensurate readjustment of the navigation graph.

Adaptation within the existing web site structure, or page-level adaptation, can be reduced to transforming media objects found in each page. Among the rather large number of publications devoted to page-level adaptation (see the review article quoted above), [8] stands out by providing a conceptual framework. According to [8], each media object can be rendered with different modalities (text, image, audio etc.) and fidelities (summarised, compressed etc.). The optimal combination of modalities and fidelities for media objects belonging to a page is obtained by minimising a cost function leading to a combination of high content value and low load time, under the preservation of device constraints reflecting the ability of the device to render media objects with given modalities and fidelities, and to fit their combination on a screen.

An approach to adaptation involving re-allocation of content is proposed by [7]. [7] introduces two algorithms for splitting a web page into smaller pages (possibly, with some common content). The algorithms ensure that media objects that need to be presented together (have a higher "proximity") are likely to remain on the same page. Proximity is formalised by defining cohesion order on possible combinations of media objects, or (alternatively) by specifying a proximity value for each pair of the media objects.

[7] uses the vocabulary of the media types theory [6], according to which the web page itself is a composite media object, an instance of a media type, and media objects such as images or text are basic media objects, instances of the corresponding basic types. We follow [7] by adopting the media types notation in this article.

Although the approach taken by [7] offers more flexibility than page-level adaptation, it does not allow for extensibility to incorporate tutoring strategy concerns. In the following section, we extend and generalise it to take account of the necessary trade-offs.

3 The Unified Approach

3.1 Formalising the Web Site Structure

Consider a set Ω of all base media objects belonging to a web site. A base media object is a media object that can not be subdivided, for example, an image, a chunk of text, or a sound track. Depending on the nature of the web site, base media objects may appear to have structure. For example, a decision can be made that a figure, composed of an image and a textual caption accompanying the figure should not be separated and displayed on separate pages. Then, in our terminology, a figure is a base media object.

We assume that each base media object ω can be attributed to some base media type, for example each image could be considered to be an instance of the PICTURE media type. We denote it as $\#\omega = \text{PICTURE}$.

We formalise web pages as sets of base media objects. We assume that a web page is small enough to be experienced at once, and that the actual layout can be determined by a layout algorithm. Then, following [6], a web page can be regarded as a composite media object, an instance of a composite media type structured as a bag of base media types. For example, a web page u containing two figures and some text can be described as $u = \{\omega_1, \omega_2, \omega_3\}$, where

$$\#\omega_1 = \#\omega_2 = \text{FIGURE}, \omega_3 = \text{TEXT} \tag{1}$$

and

$$\#u = \{\text{FIGURE}(2), \text{TEXT}(1)\}. \tag{2}$$

The web site structure is defined by assigning the base media objects belonging to the web site to web pages. We make an assumption that each base media object is assigned to one and only one web page. This is in the spirit of recommendations for mobile content adaptation given by [1], who suggest not using repeating elements such as navigation bars, to save bandwidth and screen space. Now, the assignment of base media objects to web pages can be formalised as a partition Ξ of Ω into non-intersecting, non-empty subsets:

$$\Xi = \{u_i\}, \tag{3}$$

so that

$$\Omega = \bigcup_i u_i, \text{ where } u_i \cap u_j = \varnothing \text{ for } i \neq j. \tag{4}$$

Obviously, Ω can be partitioned into web pages in many different ways. In the rest of this section we will build a cost function defined on the set of all possible partitions. The minimum of the cost function will correspond to a partition (and hence, to the web site structure), for which factors such as the necessity to keep certain base media objects together, the bandwidth and the screen size available, the user preferences, and the tutoring best practice considerations, are balanced against each other to form the optimal combination.

3.2 Minimising Separation

Let us assume that a non-negative function φ is defined on the power set (the set of all subsets) of the set of base media objects Ω :

$$2^{\Omega} \overset{\varphi}{\to} [0, +\infty) \tag{5}$$

The function expresses the importance for a set of base media objects to appear on the same web page. For example, to express that base media objects ω_1, ω_2 and ω_3 should (preferably) appear together, $\varphi(\{\omega_1, \omega_2, \omega_3\})$ can be defined to have a relatively large value.

We should note that while the domain of φ is rather large (2 in the power of the number of base media objects in the web site), we assume that the support of φ, defined as $\Lambda \equiv \{\chi \mid \chi \subseteq \Omega \text{ and } \varphi(\chi) > 0\}$ is relatively small. In other words, the number of subsets of Ω for which φ is greater than zero is relatively small, so that it is practical to consider algorithms involving enumerating all such subsets.

For web page u, a cost function describing how well the base media objects belonging to the page fit together can be defined as

$$\varepsilon_p(u) \equiv -\sum_{\xi \in \Lambda} \varphi(\xi). \tag{6}$$

The lower is the value of $\varepsilon_p(u)$, the better is the selection of base media objects. Now, the separation cost function for a partition Ξ of the web site into web pages is obtained by adding up cost functions for all pages:

$$E_p(\Xi) \equiv E_p(\{u_i\}) = \sum_i \varepsilon_p(u_i). \tag{7}$$

The lower is the value of the separation cost $E_p(\Xi)$, the better is the partition, as far as putting related base media objects on the same page is concerned (base media objects that should not be separated, are not separated). However, a partition corresponding to the minimum of the separation cost function would not produce a usable web site. Indeed, it is easy to see that the minimum can be achieved by putting all base media objects on the same page.

3.3   Adaptivity to Communication Channels

Let us denote time required to download a base media object ω to client device as $\tau(\omega)$. Time required to download a web page u can be estimated as

$$\tau(u) = \sum_{\omega \in u} \tau(\omega).$$

(8)

Let $\theta(x)$ be a step function:

$$\theta(x) = \begin{cases} 0 \text{ when } x < 0 \\ 1 \text{ when } x \geq 0 \end{cases}$$

(9)

Let τ_0 be an acceptable (from the user's point of view) download time for a web page. We define the communication channel cost function for a web page as follows:

$$\varepsilon_c(u) \equiv \theta(\tau(u) - \tau_0) \eta_c(\tau(u)),$$

(10)

where $\eta_c(x)$ is a function growing faster than linearly, for example one could take $\eta_c(x) \equiv x^2$.

The communication channel cost function for a partition Ξ is, again, obtained by adding up cost functions for all pages:

$$E_c(\Xi) \equiv E_c(\{u_i\}) = \sum_i \varepsilon_c(u_i).$$

(11)

By construction, for as long as all pages can be downloaded within the time given by τ_0, communication channel contributes no cost. Among the partitions with some of the pages with $\tau(u)$ greater than τ_0, partitions with "excessive" load uniformly spread between pages are favoured, because $\eta(x)$ grows faster than linearly with x.

Partition corresponding to a minimum of $\alpha E_p(\Xi) + \beta E_c(\Xi)$, with $\alpha > 0$ and $\beta > 0$, and $\alpha + \beta = 1$, corresponds to a balance of separation and communication channel costs. While minimising the separation cost function leads to larger pages, minimising the communication channel cost function leads to smaller pages, so that minimising a linear combination of both cost function is likely to result in reasonably sized pages, with base media objects that are particularly important to keep together (that belong together to sets with high values of φ) still staying together. The degree to which separation cost and communication channel cost influence the location of the minimum can be adjusted by setting the values of α and β.

However, if only separation cost and communication channel cost are taken into account, there is no way to assure that the resulting pages fit on the client device screen or to take into account user preferences and tutoring strategies / best practices. These factors are incorporated in the subsections to follow.

3.4 Adaptivity to Technical Environments

Technical environment of the target client device may be limited in a number of ways: it may have a limited memory, limited ability to display colours, fonts etc. Roughly, we divide the limitations in two categories: qualitative and quantitative.

Qualitative limitations are due to the inability of a device to render base media objects of a certain base media type. Qualitative limitations can be overcome in a straightforward manner, by either skipping the base media objects that can not be rendered or by transforming them into base media types that can be rendered. For example, when serving colour images to a device with a monochrome screen, they can be transformed (server side) to black and white images. In the following we assume that qualitative limitations are overcome by applying a suitable transformation, and do not consider them any more.

Quantitative limitations are due to the web pages served being "too large" for the device in some sense, for example, too large to be displayed on a single screen or to fit into memory. To adapt the web site to account for a quantitative limitation of the target device, it is of essence how base media objects are allocated to web pages, in other words, which partition is taken. Some partitions may result in web pages that are too large for the device (even if they are within the limits imposed by the communication channel). Here, we take the screen size limitation as an example of quantitative limitations of a device. Other quantitative limitations can be dealt with in a similar manner.

Let $s(u)$ be the size of a web page u. Size could be measured, for example, as the page height, with the page width fixed equal to the width of the target device screen. $s(u)$ is determined by the layout algorithm used and can be roughly estimated by associating size with each base media object, and taking a sum for all base media objects belonging to the page.

Let s_0 be the size of the screen. We define the technical environment cost function for a web page similarly to the communication channel cost function:

$$\varepsilon_d(u) \equiv \theta(s(u) - s_0)\eta_d(s(u)), \tag{12}$$

where $\eta_d(x)$ is a function growing faster than linearly (e.g., one could take $\eta_d(x) \equiv x^2$).

The technical environment cost function for a partition Ξ is obtained by adding up cost functions for all pages:

$$E_d(\Xi) \equiv E_d(\{u_i\}) = \sum_i \varepsilon_d(u_i). \tag{13}$$

3.5   Adaptivity to the User

We call a set of users with similar requirements for web site appearance a user type. We introduce a subtype relation and require it to be a partial order. In addition, we assume that all user types are subtypes of the **Generic User** type, which we denote as $\perp$. Each user belongs to the **Generic User** type $\perp$ (which, then, by construction, is a set of all users). In addition, a user may belong to any number of subtypes of $\perp$. We impose the following constraint, necessary to preserve the "is a" semantics of subtype relation: if a user belongs to user type P, he also has to belong to all supertypes of P. As an example, consider the diagram in Figure 1. A colourblind user accessing the system on-campus would be a member of **On-Campus User** and **Colorblind User** types, which automatically also makes him a member of **Disabled User** and **Generic User** types.

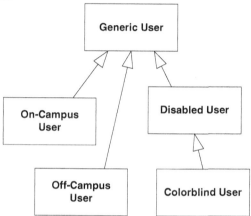

Fig. 1. An example of a user type structure. User types are shown as rectangles. The immediate subtype relation is indicated by arrows (UML notation).

The type system for user types outlined above is inspired by a type system for object-oriented databases introduced in [5]. However, it does not imply that the user model should be stored in an object oriented database. For as long as the properties postulated in the definitions given above are maintained, the type system could be a view over a traditional user model, for example, users with user model parameters falling within certain predefined ranges of values could be automatically assigned to a corresponding user type.

Let us assume that for each user type P, a cost function is defined on the power set of Ω (in other words, on all possible combinations of base media types that can be put on a web page). We denote it as $E_t^P(u)$, it should possess properties similar to the cost functions we defined for adaptivity to communication channel and to the technical environment. In particular, for a given user type, it should assume a global minimum for the selection of base media objects that is the most suitable for this user type. For practical reasons we again assume that the support of the cost function for a particular user type is relatively small.

The cost function for a particular user x (rather than for a user type), can now be defined as a linear combination of cost function for all user types the user belongs to:

$$E_u^x(v) = \frac{\sum_{x \in P} \lambda(P) E_t^P(v)}{\sum_{x \in P} \lambda(P)}, \qquad (14)$$

$$\text{where } \lambda(P) \geq 0.$$

Here, $\lambda(P)$ are positive numbers reflecting the relative importance of each user type. The adaptivity to the user cost function for the web site as a whole is obtained by adding up cost functions for individual pages:

$$E_u^x = \sum_v E_u^x(v). \qquad (15)$$

By construction of the type system for user types, the adaptivity to the user cost function is guaranteed to incorporate the component accounting for tutoring strategy. To make sure that tutoring strategy is properly represented one needs to set $\lambda(\perp)$, the weight of the **Generic User** type, to a sufficiently large value.

4 Unified Approach to Adaptivity

A unified cost function can now be constructed by taking a linear combination of cost functions for separation, adaptivity to communication channel, adaptivity to technical environment, and adaptivity to the user:

$$E(\Xi) = \alpha E_p(\Xi) + \beta E_c(\Xi)$$
$$+ \gamma E_d(\Xi) + \delta E_u(\Xi), \qquad (16)$$
$$\text{where } \alpha \geq 0, \ \beta \geq 0, \ \gamma \geq 0 \text{ and } \delta \geq 0,$$
$$\text{and } \alpha + \beta + \gamma + \delta = 1.$$

The minimum of $E(\Xi)$ corresponds to a balance of all adaptivity concerns. The degree to which various concerns are taken into account can be configured by assigning values to α, β, γ and δ.

5 Minimising the Cost Function

It should be noted, that there is no necessity to find an absolute minimum, but rather a good approximation would suffice. On the other hand, one needs to ensure, that the minimum found is a global minimum, over all possible partitions, rather than a local minimum, providing the best partition only for a small subset of all possible partitions. Here, we outline how the simulated annealing technique, known to allow finding an approximation to the global minimum without falling into local minima [2,9,10] could be applied to maintain personalised views of a continuously updated web site close the corresponding global minima with respect to the cost function $E(\Xi)$.

Consider a given combination of τ, τ_0, s, s_0, and a given assignment of the current user to user types. Clients corresponding to such a combination (essentially, similar users, using the same device over connections of the same bandwidth) share the same cost function $E(\Xi)$, and thus, should experience the web site via the same partition Ξ. If, as one would expect in a realistic environment, there are large numbers of similar clients, it is more efficient to constantly maintain an optimal partition as a customised view of the web site, rather than to create it in response to a user request. Such a view can be maintained by continuously executing the following algorithm:

At each step, choose one of the following updates with probabilities p_u, p_i or p_t, respectively:

- Fusion - combine two random web pages in one;
- Fission - split a random web page in two web pages (with base media objects distributed between the new pages at random);
- Transfer - remove a random base media object from a random web page, and put it into another (randomly chosen) web page[1].

Estimate the cost function $E(\Xi)$ after the update. If $E\left(\bar{\Xi}\right) < E(\Xi)$, where $\bar{\Xi}$ is the projected partition after the update, than execute the update. Otherwise, execute the update with probability $\exp\left[-\left(E\left(\bar{\Xi}\right) - E(\Xi)\right)/T\right]$, where T (the so-called "temperature") is a parameter controlling the speed of the algorithm divergence, and its precision: the higher is the value of T, the faster an approximate minimum is reached, but the precision is higher for smaller T.

The value of T is to be dynamically controlled as follows: every time the web site is updated (for example, by adding or removing base media objects), T is raised by the value of Δ, that may depend on the extent of the update (e.g., it could be linear in the number of added, removed or changed base media objects)[2]. Then, as the minimisation process continues, the value of T is gradually decreased (e.g., linearly in the number of steps) until a low enough (but non-zero) value T_0 is reached. The minimisation process may be stopped once $E(\Xi)$, on average, no longer shows a systematic change. However, in a system with relatively high rate of updates, the minimisation process may be executed continuously. The absolute minimum may

---

[1] It should be noted that transfer can be obtained as a combination of fusion and fission. However, the probability of such a transfer is rather low, so that the dynamics is different from a situation where transfer is included as an independent elementary step.

[2] The situation at time zero can be treated as the result of an extensive update, so that the minimisation starts with a relatively high value of T.

never be reached, however, at each moment of time, for an appropriate choice of the parameters controlling the minimisation process, a reasonably good (close to "optimal") view should be provided.

6 Resume

We introduced an approach allowing us to achieve adaptivity to communication channels, device technical environments and to the user within a single conceptual framework. In addition, we outlined a simulated annealing algorithm for maintaining personalised views of a web site with continuously updated content.

References

1. Chen, J., Zhou, B., Shi, J., Zhang, H., & Wu, Q. (2001). Function-based Object Model Towards Website Adaptation. In Shen, V.Y. & Saito, N. (Eds.), Proceedings of WWW10 (pp. 587-596). Hong Kong: IW3C2.
2. Ingber, L. (1993). Simulated annealing: Practice versus theory. Mathematical and Computer Modelling, 18, 29-57.
3. Korva, J., Plomp, J., Maatta, P., & Metso, M. (2001). On-line service adaptation for mobile and fixed terminal devices. In Tan, K.-L., Franklin, M.J., Lui, J.C.S (Eds.), Proceedings of the Second International Conference on Mobile Data Management (pp. 252-259).
4. Mantyjarvi, J. & Seppanen, T. (2003). Adapting applications in mobile terminals using fuzzy context information. Interacting with Computers, 15, 512-538.
5. Schewe, K.-D. & Thaleim, B. (1993). Fundamental Concepts of Object Oriented Databases. Acta Cybernetica, 11, 49-84.
6. Schewe, K.-D. & Thaleim, B. (2000). Theory of Media Objects for Internet Services. In Wittig, W. S. & Paul, S. (Eds.), Proceedings of LIT'2000 (pp. 67-78). Leipzig, Germany: FIT Leipzig.
7. Schewe, K.-D. (2002). Support of Integrated Wireless Web Access through Media Types. In Olivé, A. ,Yoshikawa, M., & Yu, E.S.K. (Eds.), Lecture Notes in Computer Science: Vol. 2784 (pp. 173 - 181). Berlin: Springer-Verlag.
8. Smith, J.R., Rakesh M., R., & Li, C.-S. (1999). Scalable multimedia delivery for pervasive computing. In Buford, J., Stevens, S., Bulterman, D., Jeffay K., & Zhang H.J. (Eds.), Proceedings of the seventh ACM international conference on Multimedia (pp. 131 - 140). New York: ACM Press.
9. Tsallis , C. & Stariolo, D.A. (1996). Generalized simulated annealing. Physica A, 233, 395-406.
10. Van Laarhoven, P. J. M. & Aarts, E. H. L. (1987). Simulated annealing: Theory and applications. MA, Norwell: Kluwer Academic Publishers.
11. World Wide Web Consortium (1999, March 15). HTML 4.0 Guidelines for Mobile Access. Retrieved February 15, 2004.

Applying Database Semantics to the WWW

Roland Hausser

Universität Erlangen-Nürnberg
Abteilung Computerlinguistik (CLUE)
rrh@linguistik.uni-erlangen.de

Abstract. Today's search engines build their indices on the basis of document mark-up in XML and significant letter sequences (words) occurring in the document texts. There are some drawbacks, however: the XML mark-up requires skill as well as tedious work from the user posting the document, and the indexing based on significant word distributions, though automatic and highly effective, is not as precise as required by many applications.

As a complement to current methods, this paper presents an automatic content analysis of texts which is based on traditional linguistic methods in conjunction with a comparatively new data structure ([6]) and algorithm ([3]). Having already presented the formal definitions elsewhere, we aim here at illustrating the system in action, based on an ongoing implementation in JAVA.

Database Semantics is the name of a computational system modeling natural language communication. DBS is designed for the construction of talking robots. Because of this background, applications of DBS to the internet will be presented by going from the agent's *hearer-mode* (interpretation of language) to the agent's *conceptualization* (choosing what to say and how to say it) to the agent's *speaker-mode* (production of language). Once the basic functioning of DBS has been explained, we will show how to incorporate its components into the internet and which www applications it improves.

1 Word Form Recognition in the Hearer-Mode

For the computer, the word forms in a text are merely sequences of letters. The first step towards computers *understanding* natural language is automatic word form recognition. This software component provides each word form in a sentence or text automatically with a lexical analysis.

Consider the following example of automatically recognizing the word form girl:

1.1 Example of Automatic Word Form Recognition in DBS

```
dbs2.DBS2-HEAR> -lex girl

[sur: girl ]
[noun: girl]
[cat: sn   ]
[sem: sg f ]
[mdr:      ]
[fnc:      ]
[idy: +1   ]
[prn:      ]
```

C. Bussler et al. (Eds.): WISE 2004 Workshops, LNCS 3307, pp. 211–220, 2004.

This lexical analysis has the form a feature structure, called *proplet*. Feature structures consist of a set of attribute-value pairs. Proplets are restricted, however, in that their attributes may not take feature structures as values, thus preventing a recursive embedding of feature structures in proplets.[1]

For better readability, the attributes of a proplet are displayed in a predefined standard order. The attribute sur contains the surface of the word as value. The attribute noun specifies the part of speech; its value is a concept which characterizes the core of the word meaning. The attributes cat (for category) and sem (for semantics) specify the morphosyntactic properties of the word.[2] The remaining attributes mdr (modifier), fnc (functor), idy (identity), and prn (proposition number) receive their values during syntactic-semantic parsing (see Section 2 below).

A system of automatic word form recognition provides much more detailed and reliable grammatical information than statistical tagging. Based on a finite lexicon and rules for inflection, derivation, and composition, the system recognizes a potentially infinite number of words. Furthermore, if a traditional lexicon is available on-line, a suitable system of automatic word form recognition can be built in a matter of weeks for any new language. Unlike statistical tagging, mistaken analyses can be precisely located and permanently corrected.[3] With the support of a reference corpus and a continuous sequence of monitor corpora, a system of automatic word form recognition can be maintained to provide near-perfect coverage, serving a wide range of applications.

2 Syntactic-Semantic Parsing in the Hearer-Mode

The next step in modeling the hearer-mode is syntactic-semantic parsing. It has the task of establishing the grammatical relations between the lexically analyzed word forms. In Database Semantics, grammatical relations are coded by *copying values* between proplets. Consider the following example of parsing the sentence the girl sleeps:

2.1 Building the Functor-Argument Structure

result of word form recognition   ⇒ *result of syntactic-semantic parsing*[4]

```
[sur: the  ] [sur: girl ] [sur: sleeps]        [sur:      ] [sur:       ]
[noun: _n1 ] [noun: girl] [verb: sleep]        [noun: girl ] [verb: sleep]
[cat: nn' np] [cat: sn   ] [cat: ns3' v]       [cat: snp   ] [cat: v     ]
[sem: def  ] [sem: sg f ] [sem: pres  ]        [sem: def sg f] [sem: pres ]
[mdr:      ] [mdr:      ] [mdr:        ]        [mdr:       ] [mdr:       ]
[fnc:      ] [fnc:      ] [arg:        ]        [fnc: sleep ] [arg: girl  ]
[idy: +1   ] [idy: +1   ] [ctn:        ]        [idy: 1     ] [ctn:       ]
[prn:      ] [prn:      ] [ctp:        ]        [prn: 1     ] [ctp:       ]
              [prn:     ] [prn:        ]        [wrdn: 1    ] [prn: 1     ]
                                                              [wrdn: 3    ]
```

---

[1] The attributes of proplets may take more than one value, however, as in a list.

[2] More specifically, the values sn stands for singular noun, sg for singular, and f for feminine.

[3] For a comparison of different approaches to automatic word form recognition see [4] and [5], Chapters 13–15.

[4] Once the values of the sur attributes have been used for automatic word form recognition, they are discarded during syntactic-semantic parsing, resulting in a more language-independent semantic representation.

The three proplets on the left result from automatic word form recognition and serve as input to the parser. The two proplets on the right are the output of the parser.

The parser reconstructs the functor-argument structure of the sentence by copying the noun value girl into the arg attribute of the verb, and the verb value sleep into the fnc attribute of the noun (bidirectional pointering).[5] Note that the input proplets *the* and *girl* are fused into a single proplet in the output (function word absorption), whereby the contribution of *the* is reflected by the value def in the sem slot of the resulting noun proplet. Furthermore, the valency position ns3' (for nominative singular third person) in the cat slot of the verb proplet in the input is being canceled in the output.

In addition to the intrapropositional functor-argument structure of isolated sentences, Database Semantics characterizes the concatenation of sentences in a text. There are two kinds of extrapropositional relations, (i) the conjunction between verbs and (ii) the identity between nouns. The following syntactic-semantic analysis shows the conjunction between the verbs of

The big girl has been sleeping. The young girl ate a big warm meal. The old girl is eating a big apple.

2.2 Result of Parsing a Short Text

```
[sur:         ] [sur:        ] [sur:          ] [sur:          ] [sur:         ] [sur:           ]
[noun: girl   ] [adj: big    ] [verb: sleep    ] [noun: girl    ] [adj: young   ] [verb: eat      ]
[cat: SNP     ] [cat: ADN    ] [cat: DECL      ] [cat: SNP      ] [cat: ADN     ] [cat: DECL      ]
[sem: def sg F] [sem: stand  ] [sem: hv-pres perf prog] [sem: def sg F] [sem: stand] [sem: past    ]
[mdr: big     ] [mdd: girl   ] [mdr:           ] [mdr: young    ] [mdd: girl    ] [mdr:           ]
[fnc: sleep   ] [idy: 2      ] [arg: girl      ] [fnc: eat      ] [idy: 3       ] [arg: girl meal ]
[idy: 2       ] [prn: 2      ] [ctn: 3 eat     ] [idy: 3        ] [prn: 3       ] [ctn: 4 eat     ]
[prn: 2       ] [wrdn: 2     ] [ctp:           ] [prn: 3        ] [wrdn: 2      ] [ctp: 2 sleep   ]
[wrdn: 1      ]               [prn: 2          ]                 [wrdn: 1      ] [prn: 3          ]
                              [wrdn: 4         ]                                 [wrdn: 4         ]

[sur:         ] [sur:        ] [sur:          ] [sur:          ] [sur:         ] [sur:           ]
[noun: meal   ] [adj: big    ] [adj: warm     ] [noun: girl    ] [adj: old     ] [verb: eat      ]
[cat: SNP     ] [cat: ADN    ] [cat: ADN      ] [cat: SNP      ] [cat: ADN     ] [cat: DECL      ]
[sem: indef sg] [sem: stand  ] [sem: stand    ] [sem: def sg F ] [sem: stand   ] [sem: be-pres prog]
[mdr: big warm] [mdd: meal   ] [mdd: meal     ] [mdr: old      ] [mdd: girl    ] [mdr:           ]
[fnc: eat     ] [idy: 4      ] [idy: 4        ] [fnc: eat      ] [idy: 5       ] [arg: girl apple]
[idy: 4       ] [prn: 3      ] [prn: 3        ] [idy: 5        ] [prn: 4       ] [ctn:           ]
[prn: 3       ] [wrdn: 6     ] [wrdn: 7       ] [prn: 4        ] [wrdn: 2      ] [ctp: 3 eat     ]
[wrdn: 5      ]                               [wrdn: 1         ]                 [prn: 4          ]
                                                                                [wrdn: 4         ]

[sur:         ] [sur:        ]
[noun: apple  ] [adj: big    ]
[cat: SNP     ] [cat: ADN    ]
[sem: indef sg] [sem: stand  ]
[mdr: big     ] [mdd: apple  ]
[fnc: eat     ] [idy: 6      ]
[idy: 6       ] [prn: 4      ]
[prn: 4       ] [wrdn: 7     ]
[wrdn: 6      ]
```

The concatenation of the three sentences in the sample text is coded by the values of the ctn (connection to next) and ctp (connection to previous) attributes of the verbs. More specifically, the ctp attribute of the verb proplet *sleep* has no value because there is no previous sentence, while the ctn attribute has the values 3 eat, representing the prn value and the verbal concept of the next proposition. Accordingly, the ctp attribute of the verb proplet *eat* has the values 2 sleep, while the ctn attribute has the values 4 drive, etc.

---

[5] Other values are provided by the control structure of the parser: the prn attributes receive a common number, the idy attribute receives a number, and the new attribute wrdn (for word number) is being added and supplied with suitable values.

Example 2.2 also shows the integration of the adjectives big, young, and old into the functor-argument structure (cf. values of the mdr and mdd attributes). It shows the handling of transitive sentences with the objects meal and apple. And it shows the complex verb constructions has been sleeping and is eating, which are each represented by a single proplet (another instance of function word absorption, cf. 2.1).

The syntactic-semantic parser producing the set of proplets in 2.2 is based on the time-linear algorithm of LA-grammar[6] ([3], [5], [7]). Extending the coverage of this parser is considerably more demanding than providing the lexical entries and rules for the automatic word form recognition of a natural language. This is because automatic word form recognition can be built on centuries of lexicographic work analyzing word forms grammatically, while no suitable[7] analyses are available for the grammatical relations between word forms in sentences and texts.

Nevertheless, near complete syntactic-semantic coverage of a natural language in the format shown in 2.2 can be achieved in a few years. Our strategy is as follows: Using automatic word form recognition in combination with a chunk parser ([1], [9]), the sequences of word forms in a corpus are boiled down to sequences of categories in phrases. After ordering these category sequences according to frequency and analyzing the most frequent ones first, the time-linear syntactic-semantic coverage of free text can be upscaled very efficiently.

3 Storage and Retrieval in a Word Bank

By coding the intra- and extrapropositional relations between the words in a text as attribute values, proplets are autonomous items which can be stored independently of any restrictions imposed by graphical representations such as trees. In other words, the storage of proplets is completely free and the principle for their storage can be chosen according to the needs of one's database.

In DBS, proplets are stored in the format of alphabetically ordered *token lines*. The first item of a token line is a concept; it is followed by all proplets containing this concept as the value of their second attribute. This data structure resembles a classic network database with its owner and member records, and is called a *word bank*. As an example, consider the following word bank storing the proplets derived in 2.1 and 2.2:

3.1 Illustrating the Data Structure of a Word Bank

```
Owner Proplets |-------- Token Line ---------->
--------------------------------------------------------------------------
[noun: apple] [sur:        ]
              [noun: apple ]
              [cat: SNP    ]
              [sem: indef sg]
              [mdr: big    ]
              [fnc: eat    ]
              [idy: 6      ]
              [prn: 4      ]
              [wrdn: 6     ]
```

---

[6] LA-grammar is named after its Left-Associative derivation order. LAG computes possible *continuations*, always combining a sentence start and a next word into a new sentence start.

[7] Most efforts in modern linguistics are not time-linear and therefore not input-output equivalent with the speaker-hearer. For further discussion see [5], Chapters 8 and 9.

```
[adj: big] [sur:      ] [sur:      ] [sur:      ]
           [adj: big  ] [adj: big  ] [adj: big  ]
           [cat: ADN  ] [cat: ADN  ] [cat: ADN  ]
           [sem: stand] [sem: stand] [sem: stand]
           [mdd: girl ] [mdd: meal ] [mdd: apple]
           [idy: 2    ] [idy: 4    ] [idy: 6    ]
           [prn: 2    ] [prn: 3    ] [prn: 4    ]
           [wrdn: 2   ] [wrdn: 6   ] [wrdn: 7   ]

[verb: eat] [sur:           ] [sur:                 ]
            [verb: eat      ] [verb: eat            ]
            [cat: DECL      ] [cat: DECL            ]
            [sem: past      ] [sem: be-pres prog    ]
            [mdr:           ] [mdr:                 ]
            [arg: girl meal ] [arg: girl apple      ]
            [ctn: 4 eat     ] [ctn:                 ]
            [ctp: 2 sleep   ] [ctp: 3 eat           ]
            [prn: 3         ] [prn: 4               ]
            [wrdn: 4        ] [wrdn: 4              ]

[noun: girl] [sur:          ] [sur:          ] [sur:          ] [sur:          ]
             [noun: girl    ] [noun: girl    ] [noun: girl    ] [noun: girl    ]
             [cat: SNP      ] [cat: SNP      ] [cat: SNP      ] [cat: SNP      ]
             [sem: def sg F ] [sem: def sg F ] [sem: def sg F ] [sem: def sg F ]
             [mdr:          ] [mdr: big      ] [mdr: young    ] [mdr: old      ]
             [fnc: sleep    ] [fnc: sleep    ] [fnc: eat      ] [fnc: eat      ]
             [idy: 1        ] [idy: 2        ] [idy: 3        ] [idy: 5        ]
             [prn: 1        ] [prn: 2        ] [prn: 3        ] [prn: 4        ]
             [wrdn: 1       ] [wrdn: 1       ] [wrdn: 1       ] [wrdn: 1       ]

[noun: meal] [sur:          ]
             [noun: meal    ]
             [cat: SNP      ]
             [sem: indef sg ]
             [mdr: big warm ]
             [fnc: eat      ]
             [idy: 4        ]
             [prn: 3        ]
             [wrdn: 5       ]

[adj: old] [sur:      ]
           [adj: old  ]
           [cat: ADN  ]
           [sem: stand]
           [mdd: girl ]
           [idy: 5    ]
           [prn: 4    ]
           [wrdn: 2   ]

[verb: sleep] [sur:          ] [sur:                    ]
              [verb: sleep   ] [verb: sleep             ]
              [cat: DECL     ] [cat: DECL               ]
              [sem: pres     ] [sem: hv-pres perf prog  ]
              [mdr:          ] [mdr:                    ]
              [arg: girl     ] [arg: girl               ]
              [ctn:          ] [ctn: 3 eat              ]
              [ctp:          ] [ctp:                    ]
              [prn: 1        ] [prn: 2                  ]
              [wrdn: 3       ] [wrdn: 4                 ]

[adj: warm] [sur:      ]
            [adj: warm ]
            [cat: ADN  ]
            [sem: stand]
            [mdd: meal ]
            [idy: 4    ]
            [prn: 3    ]
            [wrdn: 7   ]

[adj: young] [sur:      ]
             [adj: young]
             [cat: ADN  ]
             [sem: stand]
             [mdd: girl ]
             [idy: 3    ]
             [prn: 3    ]
             [wrdn: 2   ]
```

The reordering of a proplet sequence produced by the parser, e.g. 2.2, into the word bank format, e.g. 3.1, is automatic.

The word bank format has the advantage of easy storage and retrieval. The storage of a new sentence consists in adding its proplets at the end of their token lines. For example, a new proplet *girl* would be added at the end of the girl token line. The proplets in a token line reflect the temporal order of their arrival, by position and their prn number.

The retrieval of proplets is based on their concept value, their proposition number (prn), and their word number (wrdn), which jointly serve as the unique primary key. Proplet retrieval is needed by the following operations:

3.2   Operations Using Proplet Retrieval

1. *Internal navigation*
   For any proplet, a successor proplet may be retrieved. Repetition of this operation results in a time-linear navigation through the content of the word bank.
2. *External activation*
   For any concept provided by recognition, all proplets corresponding to this concept are retrieved by activating the concept's token line.

Both kinds of operations result in a selective activation of the content in a word bank.

The first type of operation is used to activate a sequence of propositions. For example, if we pick the second *eat* proplet in 3.1, the first arg value and the prn value tell the system to retrieve the *girl* proplet with the prn value 4. After returning to the verb, the second arg value is used to navigate to *apple*. After returning to the verb, the ctp value is used to navigate to the verb of the previous proposition, and so on.

The second type of operation is used to answer questions. For example, to answer the question *Which girl ate the meal?* based on the word bank 3.1, the system searches the token line of *eat* from right to left (i.e. going back in time), looking for the arg values *girl* and *meal*. The matching *eat* proplet has the prn value 3. Next, the system retrieves the *girl* proplet with the prn value 3 (first kind of 3.2 operation). Based on its mdr and prn values, the system determines that it was the *young girl* who ate the meal.[8]

This kind of retrieval is much more precise than a comparable full text search. For example, a Google search with the words *girl eat meal* currently results in 433 000 sites like the following:

> ... In fact, I had way too many for the whole of Mexico to eat. ... They make good apple sauce and they don't cost a dime. ... 2000-2003 You Grow Girl & Fluffco. ..

4   Semantic-Syntactic Parsing in the Speaker-Mode

In DBS, the production of language is based on an autonomous navigation through the content of the word bank. The navigation uses the relations between the proplets as a railroad system and an LA-grammar, called **LA-think**, as the motor-algorithm for moving the word bank's unique focus point along the rails.

Given that proplets usually provide more than one possible successor proplet, the system must make choices. The most basic solution are random choices. For rational behavior, however, the **LA-think** grammar must be refined into a control structure which chooses between continuation alternatives based on the evaluation of external and internal stimuli, the frequency of previous traversals, learned procedures, theme/rheme structure, etc.

---

[8] For a more formal description see AIJ'01.

Alternative navigations through the same propositional content are illustrated by the following set of proplets. It was generated automatically by **LA-hear** interpreting the sentence sequence The girl left the house. Then the girl crossed the street.

4.1 Proplets of *Girl Leave House. Girl Cross Street*

```
[sur:          ] [sur:              ] [sur:          ]
[noun: girl    ] [verb: leave       ] [noun: house   ]
[cat: SNP      ] [cat: DECL         ] [cat: SNP      ]
[sem: def sg F ] [sem: past         ] [sem: def sg   ]
[mdr:          ] [mdr:              ] [mdr:          ]
[fnc: leave    ] [arg: girl house   ] [fnc: leave    ]
[idy: 1        ] [ctn:              ] [idy: 2        ]
[prn: 1        ] [ctp: 1 leave      ] [prn: 1        ]
[wrdn: 1       ] [prn: 1            ] [wrdn: 4       ]
                 [wrdn: 3           ]

[sur:          ] [sur:              ] [sur:          ]
[noun: girl    ] [verb: cross       ] [noun: street  ]
[cat: SNP      ] [cat: DECL         ] [cat: SNP      ]
[sem: def sg F ] [sem: past         ] [sem: def sg   ]
[mdr:          ] [mdr:              ] [mdr:          ]
[fnc: cross    ] [arg: girl street  ] [fnc: cross    ]
[idy: 1        ] [ctn:              ] [idy: 3        ]
[prn: 2        ] [ctp: 1 leave      ] [prn: 2        ]
[wrdn: 1       ] [prn: 2            ] [wrdn: 4       ]
                 [wrdn: 3           ]
```

This data structure may be traversed forward, as in
   girl leave house | girl cross street
which is reflected by the English surface
   The girl left the house. Then she crossed the street.
It may also be traversed backwards, as in
   girl cross street | girl leave house
which is reflected by the English surface
   The girl crossed the street. Before that she left the house.
Furthermore, using the identity between the two *girl* proplets,[9] the navigation may enter the second proposition before finishing the first, as in
   girl | girl leave house | cross street,
reflected in English by the relative clause construction
   The girl who left the house crossed the street.
Using the conjunction between the verb proplets, the navigation may also produce adverbial subclauses such as
   After the girl left the house, she crossed the street. (forward)
   Before the girl crossed the street, she left the house. (backward)
An intrapropositional kind of backward navigation is passive, as in
   The street was crossed by the girl.
Each of these traversals is based on a particular rule sequence of **LA-think**.[10]
   The choice between these different traversals is motivated by how the agent views the content, i.e. from where the navigation enters the content (forward or backward), which

---

[9] Because identity-inference has not yet been implemented, the idy values of the two *girl* proplets were set to equal by hand.

[10] For explicit definitions of these rules see [5], [6], [7].

part is evaluated as foreground and which as background, etc. In addition to navigation merely activating the content contained in the word bank, there is also navigation which produces new content, called inference navigation. Like all kinds of navigation, inference navigation is controlled by the rules of a suitable **LA-think** grammar.

5   Word Form Production in the Speaker-Mode

A computational model of the speaker-mode raises the question of where the content to be uttered should come from. Intuitively, the answer is obvious: it should come from thought. But how should thought be modeled?

In DBS, thought is modeled as the time-linear navigation through the wordbank, controlled by LA-grammars for activating content, evaluating recognition, initiating action, planning, drawing conclusions, etc. In principle, any such navigation through the word bank is independent of language. However, in cognitive agents with language, the navigation serves as the speaker's *conceptualization*, i.e., as the speaker's choice of *what to say* and *how to say it*.

A conceptualization defined as a time-linear navigation through content makes language production relatively straightforward: If the speaker decides to communicate a navigation to the hearer, the concept names (i.e., values of the second attributes) of the proplets traversed by the navigation are translated into their language-dependent counterparts and realized as external signs. For example, traversing the proplets

eat girl young meal big warm

results in proplet sequences with the following sur values, depending on the language:

English: eat girl young meal big warm

French: mange fille jeune repas copieux chaud

German: essen Mädchen jung Mahlzeit groß warm

Korean: mek.ta so.nye e.ri.ta um.sik manh.ta tta.ttus.ha.ta

In addition to this language-dependent lexicalization of the universal navigation, the system must provide

1. language-dependent word order
2. function word precipitation
3. word form selection for proper agreement

For example, each of the above base form sequences must be mapped into

English: the young girl ate a big warm meal

French: la jeune fille mangeait un copieux repas chaud

German: das junge Mädchen aß eine große warme Mahlzeit

Korean: e.ri-n so.nye-ka tta.ttus.ha-n um.sik-ul manh-i mek-nun-ta

This process is handled by language-dependent LA-grammars, called **LA-speak**, in combination with language-dependent word form production systems. For example, the English word form ate is produced from an *eat* proplet the sem attribute of which contains the value past.

Given the time-linear derivation order common to **LA-hear, LA-think,** and **LA-speak,** one would hope that semantic-syntactic parsing and automatic word form production (speaker-mode) would reuse much of what has been built for automatic word form recognition and syntactic-semantic parsing (hearer-mode). The tasks of the two modes are quite different, however.

For example, automatic word form recognition disassembles a given letter sequence into a sequence of lexically analyzed allomorphs which are reassembled into a proplet, while automatic word form production selectively matches the values of a given proplet or set of proplets with lexically analyzed allomorphs which are assembled into a suitable letter sequence (surface). Nevertheless, the goal for designing the interpretation and the production system for a language must be to utilize the same data as much as possible.

6   Applying Database Semantics to the World Wide Web

The JAVA implementation of Database Semantics ([8]) is a prototype handling fragments of English, German, and Korean in the speaker- and the hearer-mode. Because there are presently no suitable robots available, the system runs on standard computers – which limits recognition and action to the language level.

Without the technology of robots recognizing their environment and acting in it autonomously, concepts cannot be defined in terms of recognition and action procedures, and thus are not available to be reused as the core of lexical meanings (word semantics). This happens to be a serious, though hopefully temporary, deficit for the software design of autonomous cognitive agents communicating in natural language. For the transfer of Database Semantics to the internet, however, it presents no obstacle. Consider the following www applications:

LA-hear grammars improve precision by parsing www documents, representing their content in the uniform format of a word bank (cf. 3.1). All that is required to utilize this giant index structure for document retrieval is one additional proplet attribute, called URL, for specifying the location of the proplet's document.

In this word bank, noun proplets specify their functors, verb proplet specify their arguments, modifier proplets specify their modified and vice versa, nouns specify identity with other nouns, and propositions specify their predecessor and and successor. For example, if the user is looking for documents on *professors driving BMWs*, the system would search through the token line of *drive*, collect all *drive* proplets with the arguments *professor* and *BMW*, and retrieve the associated documents by using the value of the proplets' URL attribute. In comparison, a free text search in Google using the words *professor drive BMW* currently returns 19 000 sites such as:

> ... Developing a hybrid vehicle that drives for long ... a realistic development
> proposition," emphasizes Professor Göschel. BMW has already played through
> an extreme ...

LA-think grammars improve recall by inferencing. For example, a search for *professors driving German cars* would initially overlook *professors driving BMWs*. However, based on the absolute propositions *BMWs are German cars, Mercedes are German cars, Porsches are German cars*, etc., the system infers that documents on professors driving BMWs are relevant for a query on professors driving German cars.

In addition, **LA-think** grammars can be developed into what Berners-Lee et al. [2] envisage as agents roaming the net to perform jobs for individual users. However, instead of being based on the railroad system of RDF, owner-coded in XML for each document, web agents based on **LA-think** use the relations between proplets, provided automatically by **LA-hear**. This kind of web application may utilize **LA-think** inferences developed independently for artificial cognitive agents as well as foster its own.

LA-speak grammars, finally, map content resulting from inferencing and represented as a sequence of proplets into natural language. Thus, in a web extended to DBS, the response to a query would not only be the retrieval of thousands of documents, but a selectively derived to-the-point answer using various resources and formulated in the user's chosen natural language.

7   Conclusion

This paper has described a general model of human-computer communication in natural language, called Database Semantics, and shown applications to the www such as the improvement of recall and precision, inferencing, and a user-friendly processing of answers. In the talk, the current JAVA implementation of DBS will be demoed in the speaker- and the hearer-mode.

References

[1] Abney, S.: Parsing by Chunks. In R. Berwick, S. Abney, and C. Tenny (eds.): Principle-Based Parsing. Kluwer Academic Publishers (1991)
[2] Berners-Lee, T., J. Hendler, & O. Lassila: The Semantic Web. Scientific American 284(5) (2001)
[3] Hausser, R.: Complexity in Left-Associative Grammar. Theoretical Computer Science, Vol. 106.2:283-308, Elsevier (1992)
[4] Hausser, R. (ed.): Linguistische Verifikation. Dokumentation zur Ersten Morpholympics. Max Niemeyer Verlag, Tübingen (1996)
[5] Hausser, R.: Foundations of Computational Linguistics, Human-Computer Communication in Natural Language. Springer-Verlag, Berlin, New York, 2nd Ed, (1999/2001)
[6] Hausser, R.: Database Semantics for Natural Language. Artificial Intelligence, Vol. 130.1:27–74, Elsevier (2001)
[7] Hausser, R.: Turn Taking in Database Semantics. To appear in H. Kangassalo et al. (eds.), Information Modeling and Knowledge Bases XVI, IOS Press Ohmsha, Amsterdam 2005
[8] Kycia, A.: Implementierung der Datenbanksemantik in JAVA. MA-thesis. Universität Erlangen-Nürnberg (2004)
[9] Vergne, J.: Une méthode pour l'analyse descendante et calculatoire de corpus multilingues: application au calcul des relations sujet-verbe, Actes de TALN 63-74, (2002)

X-Square: A Hybrid Three-Dimensional Bitmap Indexing for XML Document Retrieval

Jae-Min Lee[1], Byung-Yeon Hwang[1], and Bog-Ju Lee [2]

[1] Department of Computer Engineering, Catholic University of Korea, Korea
{likedawn, byhwang}@catholic.ac.kr
[2] Department of Computer Engineering, Dankook University, Korea
blee@dankook.ac.kr

Abstract. XML is studied and used as a key technology in many research and applications today. Accordingly there is an increasing need for the efficient XML document retrieval. Bitmap indexing is an efficient technique for determining true and false fast and it has been used mainly for reducing search extent rather than retrieving data. BitCube, an existing three-dimensional bitmap indexing for XML document retrieval, constructs bitmap from the entire index. In case high volumes of documents are loaded in a single cluster, however, this causes significant performance degradation in memory usage and operation speed. xPlaneb which is another bitmap indexing technique solves this problem by reconstructing three-dimensional bitmap index of BitCube using linked list. xPlaneb, however, has a high memory usage problem compared with BitCube when low volumes of documents are loaded because BitCube index consists of small field of one bits. This paper proposes X-Square which is a hybrid of Bit-Cube and xPlaneb. X-Square takes both advantages of BitCube and xPlaneb. Experimental results show that X-Square has better performance in memory usage than xPlaneb and BitCube although the operation speed is a bit worse than xPlaneb.

1 Introduction

XML(eXtended Markup Language) is studied and used as a key technology in many research and applications today. Especially XML plays a key role in the technologies such as multimedia data retrieval, e-commerce, e-books, and web services. Accordingly there is an increasing need for the efficient XML storage and retrieval [1, 2].

The technique of three-dimensional bitmap indexing appeared as a study for XML document retrieval. It retrieves information using three-dimensional bitmap based on the path while alternative techniques are tree-based. BitCube [3] is a representative three-dimensional bitmap indexing which is proved to be very fast in retrieving data. BitCube constructs bitmap from the entire index. In case high volumes of documents are loaded in a single cluster, however, the size of index increases rapidly and this causes significant performance degradation in memory usage and operating speed. XPlaneb [4] which is another three-dimensional bitmap indexing solves the problem

C. Bussler et al. (Eds.): WISE 2004 Workshops, LNCS 3307, pp. 221–232, 2004.
© Springer-Verlag Berlin Heidelberg 2004

of BitCube by reconstructing efficient nodes from the three-dimensional array index. xPlaneb, however, has higher memory usage when the document volume loaded in the cluster is small because it uses index consisting of nodes of 128 bits.

This paper proposes X-Square, a hybrid three-dimensional bitmap indexing, which adopts the advantages of both BiCube and xPlaneb. X-Square showed higher performance in the memory usage than BitCube and xPlaneb in the experimental results. In terms of operation speed X-Square was better than BitCube.

Section 2 describes the general of XML document retrieval techniques including BitCube and xPlaneb. Their problems are also discussed. X-Square and the idea of hybridizing BitCube and xPlaneb is introduced in the section 3. Section 4 illustrates the experimental results that are basically the performance comparison of BitCube, xPlaneb, and X-Square. Finally the conclusion and future work are discussed in the section 5.

2   Related Work

The research and effort to use XML more effectively are still continued. This research resulted in the standardization such as ebXML [5], MPEG-7 [6], and EBKS [7] and also the effort that the RDBMS vendors allow users to use XML on their system. Recent systems can specifically retrieve the semi-structural documents like XML.

The existing techniques for XML retrieval usually map XML documents to tree structure first, and retrieve the information or analyze the semantic based on the tree nodes. This is because the XML documents themselves are semi-structural trees. Recent indexing techniques include the hierarchical index [8] that split the tree partially. The method used in [9] saves the query as the view in the database and then retrieves the documents using the saved query. The techniques above are based on the tree structure and they all aim to search the tree nodes efficiently.

Three-dimensional bitmap indexing does not construct the index in tree structure as done in the other indexing methods. Unlike the alternative indexing techniques which retrieve the tree nodes, the three-dimensional bitmap indexing, for the fast retrieval, extracts the path of the XML documents and then performs the retrieval based on the path. Consequently the performance of three-dimensional bitmap indexing is better than the other techniques which suffer from the performance degradation due to node-based search.

2.1   BitCube

Bitmap indexing uses the operation of True and False to efficiently determine the range and the existence of the data. It is a lot faster than others because it operates on one bit basis. BitCube, three-dimensional bitmap indexing, also uses the traditional bitmap indexing. BitCube constructs three-dimensional array index which consists of documents in the cluster, their paths, and word identifiers to effectively extract information from XML documents. Each field is one bit so that the bit-wise operation can be performed on it. The documents which have similar structure are collected in one bitmap index. BitCube clusters the documents which have similar structures based on their paths. The criteria to determine the similarity is measured by how many documents have the same paths. Figure 1 shows the architecture of BitCube. BitCube consists of the documents loaded in the cluster, the paths, and the word name list. Each cell of in the architecture of BitCube is 1 bit-index fields which represent true or false. BitCube performs bit-wise operation using the index fields. BitCue also performs clustering with paths. The first plane used in the clustering is called the base bitmap.

BitCube supports three basic operations, e-path slice, word slice, and document projection, to extract information for user's query. BitCube generates the result very fast from the three-dimensional bitmap index by using bit-wise operations. BitCube already showed the better search speed in the performance comparison with existing systems such as XYZFind [10], XQEngine [11], and Xyleme [12].

BitCube, however, suffers abrupt increase in the size of index as the document volume increases. This also means the abrupt increase in the memory usage as the document volume increases. Consequently the operation speed is degraded.

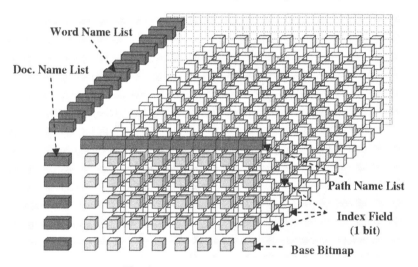

Fig. 1. The architecture of BitCube

2.2 xPlaneb

xPlaneb reconstructs the three-dimensional bitmap index using the linked list to overcome the problem of BitCube. xPlaneb reconstructs the planes of BitCube with the nodes of 128 bits so that better performance is guaranteed when high volumes of documents are loaded in a single cluster.

Figure 2 shows the architecture of xPlaneb. BitCube performs clustering with paths using the base bitmap as mentioned. Consequently, the base bitmap is filled mostly with true values. The other planes of BitCube, however, become the sparse matrices.

xPlaneb reconstructs the true valued-index fields with nodes. xPlaneb has the array of pointers which correspond to each field of base bitmap. This is called Document and Path Pointer Reference Map. xPlaneb also has the array of pointers which correspond to each field of word name list. This is called Word Pointer Reference List. Instead of performing bit-wise operations, xPlaneb accesses the index and produces the results using the two pointer reference indices.

xPlaneb employs three fundamental operations to extract information for user's query. These are the path linking, the word linking, and the document linking. xPlaneb does not perform the bit-wise operation. Instead, it prevents the performance degradation by eliminating False fields. xPlaneb showed better performance than BitCube in the situation that high volumes of documents are loaded in a single cluster.

In case the low volumes of documents are loaded in a cluster, however, the index size of BitCube can be less than that of xPlaneb because the field size of BitCube is one bit while the field of xPlaneb consists of fields of 128 bits. As the number of documents increase in the cluster, the memory usage of BitCube increases more rapidly than that of xPlaneb. However, during the intervals from the begining of the document loading to some specific point, the memory usage of BitCube is less than xPlaneb.

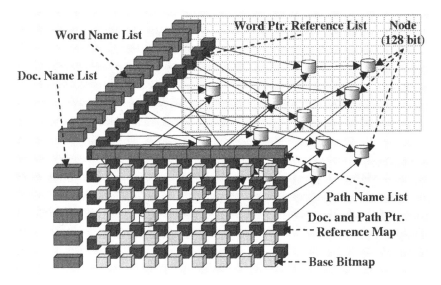

Fig. 2. The architecture of xPlaneb

3   Hybrid Three-Dimensional Bitmap Indexing

This section proposes X-Square which is a hybrid three-dimensional bitmap indexing that takes only the advantages of BitCube and xPlaneb. X-Square determines which indexing method is more effective between xPlaneb and BitCube through documents in the cluster, their paths, and the number of words. Consequently X-Square overcomes the problems of xPlaneb and BitCube and uses less memory than those two methods.

3.1 Design and Implementation of X-Square

xPlaneb solves the problem of abrupt increase in memory usage that can be found in BitCube when high volumes of documents are loaded in a single cluster. It also solves the performance degradation of operation speed. Although the index size of BitCube's depends on the size of a particular plane in the entire index, since the field that consists index is very small (one bit), small memory usage is required for the small document load. Therefore each cluster can have different indexing technique as for the memory usage.

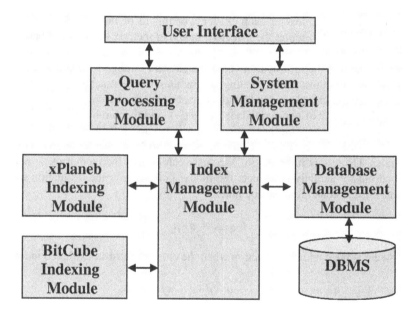

Fig. 3. The architecture of X-Square

X-Square determines which indexing method is better by looking the basic cluster information. X-Square creates different index in each cluster using the information. X-Square primarily consists of the Query Processing Module, the Database Management Module, and the Index Management Module. The Query Processing Module analyzes the query between the user interface and the system. It also returns the result to users by interacting with the Index Management Module. The Database Management Module interacts with the DBMS to load the updated information to the local databases when there is a change in the data. The Database Management Module also allows X-Square to use the information of BitCube and xPlaneb without having a special transformation. The Index Management Module interacts not only with the two modules mentioned above but also with the indexing module in BitCube and xPlaneb. The Index Management Module determines the most effective indexing module for each cluster based on the information that is provided by the Database Management Module. It actually creates the index using the determined index module. It also processes the user's queries that came from the Query Processing Module and pass them back to the Query Processing Module. If the query affects the data, the Index Management Module passes the information to the Database Management Module. Fig. 3 depicts the architecture of X-Square, the hybrid three-dimensional indexing method, which is proposed in the paper.

3.2 Selective Index Construction of X-Square

X-Square determines the more effective indexing method between BitCube and xPlaneb using the basic information of the cluster. By the selected index method it constructs individual index for each cluster. For this to be done, X-Square needs an evaluation function to predict the effective indexing method through the basic information of the clusters.

X-Square can get the information about the clusters through the Database Management Module without actually creating the indices. The extractable information includes the number of non-redundant documents (d), the number of non-redundant paths (p), the number of non-redundant words (w), and the number of whole words in the clusters (w_n). Some additional information is needed for the evaluation function. They are the size of integer data (a) and the size of node (b) that xPlaneb uses to construct index. Using this information, X-Square can predict the memory size when the individual cluster actually constructs the index. Following is the evaluation function when the clusters construct BitCube index.

$$F_{BitCube} = d \cdot p \cdot w$$

Following is the evaluation function when the clusters construct xPlaneb index.

$$F_{xPlaneb} = a \cdot (d \cdot p + w) + b \cdot w_n$$

When the system starts, X-Square calculates the two evaluation functions for each cluster. X-Square chooses the evaluation function which gives lower value and constructs the index with the corresponding method. While executing, if there are changes in the data, X-Square has to recalculate the evaluation functions. X-Square does not have to recalculate for the whole clusters. It is done only for the cluster which is affected by the data change.

X-Square must be able to decide that which indexing method to be used in the cluster when the operation for retrieving the information is done. X-Square also uses the bitmap index to minimize the operation time. The index has the value of True when a cluster consists of xPlaneb index while it has False for BitCube. Using this information, X-Square can determine fast which index method operation must be used when retrieves the cluster. Following is the algorithm of the X-Square for the selective index construction.

```
Method IndexSelection()
    cNumber=getClusterTotalNumber();
    mode=new bool[cNumber];
    for i=0 ~ cNumber
        mode[i]= getEstimatedSize(i);
        if mode[i]=true then X_Square.setCluster(i);
        else Bitcubes.setCluster(i);

Method getEstimatedSize(int id)
    d=getDocSize(id);
    p=getPathSize(id);
    w=getWordSize(id);
    wn=getNonDuplicatedWordSize(id);
    a=getIntSize(id);
    b=getNodeSize(id)
    esB=d * p * w;
    esX=(a * ((d * p) + w)) + (b * wn);
    if esB < esX then return false
        else return true
```

4 Experimental Results

The method proposed in the paper was implemented with MS Visual C#.NET, MS Windows 2000 Server operating system, and MS SQL Server 2000 database management system. The experiments were done on Intel Pentium III (1.0 GHz) personal computer with 256 MB main memory.

The experiment used a criteria called Duplication Rate. It is the probability that a word that is contained in a document in a cluster appears again in another document that has to be inserted into the same cluster. It is an important criterion because although there is a word that appears again in the documents, the memory usage does not increase at all in BitCube. The number of paths that are contained in a document is ten in average, the number of words in a document is 100 in average. The performance evaluation of X-Square should be based on the performance change as the average number of document change on the clusters. Two types of clusters were employed in the experiments. They differ in the number of documents loaded. One type of clusters has 100 documents in each cluster which represent "heavy loading". The other type of clusters has 10 documents in each cluster which represent "light loading".

Performance evaluation is done on two aspects. One is on the memory usage and the other is on the operation speed. The evaluation for the memory usage is measured by the amount of memory usage as the number of document increase in the situation that heavily loaded-clusters and lightly loaded-clusters are mixed. The evaluation for the operation speed is similarly measured by the operation speed as the number of document increase in the same situation.

4.1   Experimental Results of Memory Usage

Fig. 4 shows the memory usage of BitCube, xPlaneb, and X-Square in the situation that heavily loaded-clusters and lightly loaded-clusters are mixed. The duplication rates for the documents were all 45%. In the experiment, half of the clusters were the lightly loaded-clusters in which each cluster has 10 documents while the other half were the heavily loaded-clusters in which each cluster has 100 documents. The memory usage of BitCube, xPlaneb, and X-Square were measured as the numbers of documents increase from 1000 to 5000. As the result indicates, X-Square effectively selects the better indexing method for each cluster between BitCube and xPlaneb in the situation that the cluster sizes are diverse. Therefore the memory usage of X-Square for the entire index is always better than the other two methods.

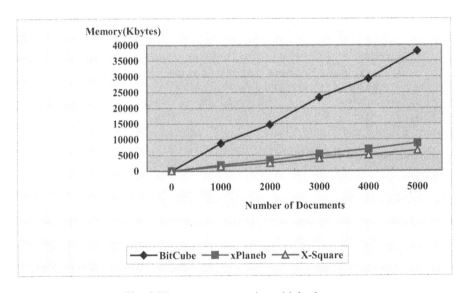

Fig. 4. The memory usages in multiple clusters

4.2   Experimental Results of Operation Speed

X-Square, as mentioned earlier, selectively constructs different types of index for each cluster. Therefore when retrieving is done in multiple clusters, determining the indexing method between BitCube and xPlaneb for each cluster should be done in actual operation time. X-Square, however, minimizes this operation time for the determination by using bitmap index. Due to this, X-Square does not show any performance degradation compared with the operations on the index only with either BitCube or xPlaneb.

Fig. 5 shows the speeds of path retrieval operation as various numbers of documents among BitCube, xPlaneb, and X-Square with the duplication rate 45%. The experiment was done in the same environment with the section 4.1 where various

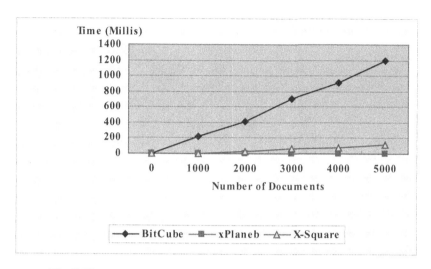

Fig. 5. The speeds of path retrieval when various types of clusters exist

types of clusters are mixed. The documents were increased by 1000. The paths which were retrieved in the experiment were included in all the documents. This means that the experiment was done in the worst condition. In case that the paths exist in some particular documents but do not exist in most of the documents, the performance will be always better than the result of Figure 5. As shown in the figure, the performances of xPlaneb and X-Square are always better than that of BitCube. X-Square shows a little bit worse performance than xPlaneb.

Fig. 6 shows the speeds of word retrieval of BitCube, xPlaneb, and X-Square when there are various types of clusters. As in the operation of path retrieval, the words which were retrieved were included in all the documents. Therefore the experiment was done in the worst condition. In case that the words exist in some particular documents but do not exist in most of the documents, the performance will be always better than the result of Fig. 6. xPlaneb and X-Square showed better performance than BitCube. With the same reason in the path retrieval, X-Square shows a bit worse speed than xPlaneb.

Fig. 7 shows the speeds of document retrieval of BitCube, xPlaneb, and X-Square when there are various types of clusters. In the operation of document retrieval, un-like the path retrieval or word retrieval, a document cannot exist in more than one cluster. The number of clusters that has to be retrieved to retrieve a document is always one. Since the documents are exactly divided in multiple clusters, the perform-ance degradation in the clusters with 100 documents is the same as in the clusters with 10 documents. The experiment measured the performance degradation for the clusters with 100 documents. As shown in the figure, X-Square and xPlaneb show less performance degradation than BitCube in the condition that various types of clusters exist. This is because the operations of BitCube and xPlaneb are affected by the operation time in heavily loaded-clusters rather than in lightly loaded-clusters.

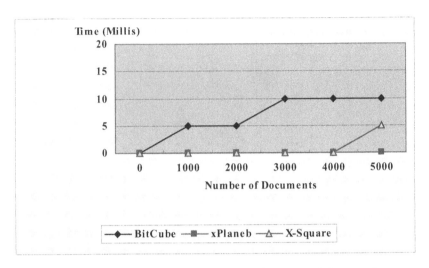

Fig. 6. The speeds of word retrieval when various types of clusters exist

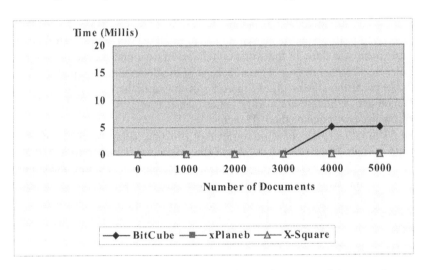

Fig. 7. The speeds of document retrieval when various types of clusters exist

BitCube and xPlaneb did not show any performance degradation when the number of documents loaded were low. Therefore xPlaneb did not suffer the performance degradation either in the condition with various types of clusters. BitCube, however, showed the performance degradation. Since X-Square selectively construct index for each cluster, it showed a bit less performance than xPlaneb, but much better performance than BitCube.

5 Conclusion

BitCube, the existing three-dimensional bitmap indexing method, has the problem of high memory usage and operation speed degradation when high volumes of documents are loaded in a single cluster. xPlaneb overcame the problem of BitCube by reconstructing three-dimensional bitmap index using 128 bit-nodes and showed better performance through the experiments. However, xPlaneb has a problem of higher memory usage than BitCube when low volumes of documents are loaded in a cluster by using relatively large size node of 128 bits.

In the paper, X-Square, a novel hybrid three-dimensional bitmap indexing method, is proposed which takes the advantages of BitCube and xPlaneb. The design, implementation, and experiment were shown in the paper. The experiment showed that X-Square has always better performance in memory usage than BitCube and xPlaneb, independent of cluster size. In terms of the operation speed, X-Square showed always relatively good performance, although it was a bit slower than xPlaneb. The reason that X-Square suffers from performance degradation earlier than xPlaneb is due to the effect of BitCube when retrieving the clusters with the low volumes of documents are loaded. However, this performance degradation is small because the performance degradation of BitCube is higher when high volumes of documents are loaded. Therefore the performance degradation of the proposed X-Square is small. In the experiment, the heavily loaded-clusters exist nearly the same portion with the lightly loaded-clusters. It is true that in the real situation this portion can be various. X-Square performs the retrieval regardless of this portion due to its "flexible" index construction.

Further research aims to the clustering method which can cluster the documents with various structures by using the characteristics of the propose method.

References

1. W3C.: Extensible Markup Language (XML) Version 1.0 (Second Edition). http://www.w3c.org/TR/ REC-xml (2000)
2. Lee, J.M., Hwang, B.Y.: A Space Compression of Three-Dimensional Bitmap Indexing using Linked List. Proc. of the 19th Korea Information Processing Society Spring Conference, Vol.10, No.1 (2003) 1519-1521
3. Yoon, J.P., Raghavan, V., Chakilam, V., Kerschberg, L.: BitCube: A Three-Dimensional Bitmap Indexing for XML Documents. J. of Intelligent Information System, Vol.17 (2001) 241-254
4. Lee, J.M., Hwang, B.Y.: xPlaneb: 3-Dimensioal Bitmap Index for XML Document Retrieval. J. of Korea Information Science Society, Vol.31, No.3 (2004) 331-339
5. ebXML. http://www.ebxml.org.
6. Manjunath, B., Salembier, P., Sikora, T.: Introduction to MPEG-7: Multimedia Content Description Interface, John Wiely (2002)
7. Electronic Book Korea. http://www.ebk.or.kr.
8. Cooper, B., Sample, N., Franklin, M., Shadmon, M.: A Fast Index for Semi-structured Data. Proc. of the 27th VLDB Conference, Roma, Italy (2001)

9.   Papakonstantinou, Y., Vianu, V.: DTD Inference for Views of XML Data. Proc. of ACM SIGACT-SIGMOD-SIGART Symposium on PODS (2000)
10. Egnor, D., Lord, R.: XYZFind: Structured Searching in Context with XML. ACM SIGIR Workshop, Athens, Greece (2000)
11. XQEngine. http://www.fatdog.com.
12. Rousset, M.: Semantic Data Integration in Xyleme. Presentation at INRIA (1999)

An Economy-Based Accounting System for Grid Computing Environments*

Jiadi Yu, Minglu Li, Ying Li, and Feng Hong

Department of Computer Science and Engineering, Shanghai Jiaotong University,
Shanghai 200030, P.R. China
{jdyu, li-ml, liying, hongfeng}@cs.sjtu.edu.cn

Abstract. Grid computing is the key technology of next generation Internet. A promising way of solving the problem of resource allocation in a Grid environment is an accounting procedure based upon a computational economy model. Charging and accounting is a base activity in an economy society, so it is an important part of grid computing system in computational economy environment. In this paper, we present firstly architecture of changing and accounting system, which support an economy-based approach to regulating the distribution of the resource. Afterward, we discuss briefly key technologies of the grid charging and accounting in a grid computing system, and accounting mechanism.

1 Introduction

Resources interconnected via the Internet with middleware supporting remote execution of applications constitute what is called the computational Grid [1,2,3]. The purpose of the computational grid is to provide dependable, consistent, pervasive, and inexpensive access to computational resources for the computing community in the form of a computing utility [1]. Grid infrastructures need support various services: security, uniform access, resource management, scheduling, application composition, computational economy, and accounting [5]. The grid will contain a large number of unconnected sites, and these sites will need to exchange accounting and information. Therefore grid economy and accounting have attracted more attention and research.

A charging and accounting service to be functional in a grid environment will manage the cost of usage of grid and support the economic activity according to the computational economy. It should be decentralized, scalable and flexible.

Charging and accounting for grid has been taken into account for some grid projects and researchers. DGAS [4] presented a accounting system for European DataGrid project; GridBank[5] was introduced as a grid accounting services architecture for computational grids; IBM's 'Extreme Blue' grid accounting project proposed a grid accounting framework GSAX [6] with dynamic pricing strategies independent of economic model. The problem of the accounting on a computational resource can be

---

* This paper is supported by 973 project (No.2002CB312002) of China, ChinaGrid Program of MOE of China, and grand project of the Science and Technology Commission of Shanghai Municipality (No. 03dz15026, No. 03dz15027 and No. 03dz15028).

C. Bussler et al. (Eds.): WISE 2004 Workshops, LNCS 3307, pp. 233–238, 2004.

faced in many different ways. The aim of this paper is not to describe analyze the details of all these approaches but to propose our vision of the problem.

In this paper, we will propose an economy-based accounting system for Grid Computing Environments. The paper is organized as follows. In Section 2, we describe the architecture of the grid computing system and interaction of various services in accounting system. Then, we briefly give an introduction to service elements to be charged and accounted in a grid computing system, and pricing and cost algorithms in Section 3. Finally, we give the conclusion of this paper and the future work in Section 4.

2   Changing and Accounting System

The choice of an adequate economic model has an important impact on the Workload Management. Accounting System that we designed is based on grid computational infrastructures, which accommodate different economic models used for resource allocation, and is able to support accounting of resources and service usage. Figure 1 shows architecture of Accounting System and Services Interaction.

- **Grid Resource Consumers (GRPs)** submit job and request resources; offer payment mechanism.

    Grid Payment Service (GPS) provides a service to a payment infrastructure. It can trade between Grid Resource Consumers and Grid Resource Providers, and include systems based around electronic cash, credit cards, pre-paid account, service tokens, etc.

- **Grid Resource Broker (GRB)** [7,8] is a mediator between the user and grid resources by using middleware services. It hides the complexity of resource management and scheduling. It is responsible for discovers resources, negotiates for service costs, performs resource selection, schedules tasks to resources and monitors their execution, stages the application and data for processing on remote resources, and finally gathers results and hands them to the user.

- **Grid middleware** offers services to connect grid user and remote resources through grid resource broker.

    Grid Account Server (GAS) provides a service to manage and maintains accounts and resource usage records of the Grid Resource Consumers and Providers. **GSI** provides a GAS interface to other services, and security mechanism; **GAS Manager** provides basic account operation and management such as open account, update account, close account, deposit, transfer, etc; **DB** is a database that stores account and resources usage information of the Grid Resource Consumers and Providers.

    Information Service provides a complete list of resources, and **Job Manage Service** deals with job submission to Grid Resource Provider.

- **Grid Resource Providers (GRPs)** advertise their services with the discovery service; negotiate service cost with Grid Resource Broker; offer pricing, accounting mechanism, and resource usage record.

Pricing Algorithms define the prices that resource provider would like to charge users. In order to maximize profit, resource provider may follow various policies to user, and the pricing can also be driven by demand and supply. **Grid Charging Service** calculates total cost of resources usage. **Resource Usage Service (RUS)** [9,10] provide a basic infrastructure to support the auditing and monitoring capability for the resources consumed by OGSA services in the grid and allows entities within the Grid to extract information from the service on potentially aggregated resource use.

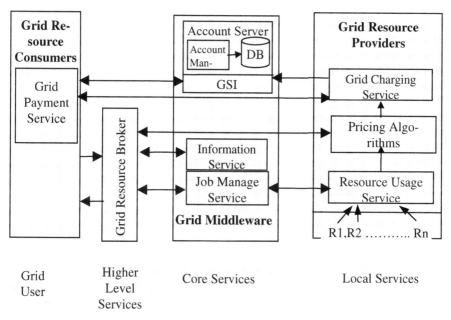

Fig. 1. Accounting System and Services Interaction

In Grid environment, Grid Resource Consumers and Grid Resource Providers open an account in account server. Then the user submits their applications with some parameters including budget and deadline to the Grid Resource Broker so that GRB may correctly choose resources, and estimation the application cost. The Information Service provides a complete list of resources to GRB, and then GRB selects suitable resources and Grid Resource Provider according to different scheduling criteria, such as data access times, estimated queue wait times, etc.

GRB interacts with Pricing Algorithms to consult acceptable price of services for both grid resource provider and consumer. If they come to an acceptable price, Pricing Algorithms informs Grid Charging Service about negotiatory price.

The GRB, having received the job description and select suitable resources for the given job, estimate the overall cost of the job by multiplying the corresponding resource prices with the resource usage expectations. Then, GRB needs to check the user accounts, in order to determine whether the user can afford the job to be computed or not. If the job cost exceeds the user's funds, the job is suspended. Otherwise, user job was submitted.

Then GRB submits user job to Grid Resource Provider via Job Manage Service. Grid Resource Provider provides the service by executing the user job and Grid Resource Provider's Resource Usage Service measures the resources consumed while the user job is executed. After the job finished, Resource Usage Service will obtains the usage statistics of the grid resources, and then generates a standard Resource Usage Record (RUR) [10]. Afterward, RUR inform Grid Charging Service about resource utilization.

Grid Charging Service receives the price from pricing algorithms, which negotiates with resource users, and the data from RUR. Then It calculates total cost based on the resource usage and pricing algorithms that the mutually agreed (Shown in Figure 2). Afterward, Grid Charging Service sent the total service cost and the resources usage statistics to Account Server.

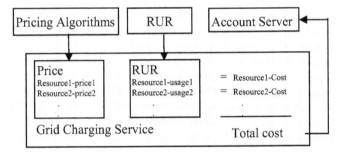

Fig. 2. Total Cost Calculate

The Grid Charging Service asks Grid Resource Consumer's Grid Payment Service to pay charge the user resource usage. Grid Resource Consumers will pay resource usage charge by using payment strategies of Grid Payment Service.

In the end, the Grid Resource Broker returns the results to the user.

3   Accounting Mechanism

3.1   Resources Elements to Be Accounted and Charged

It is necessary to decide for which resource elements one should pay. Any services invocation will consume a wide range of resources. However, a services provider may only be interested in a relatively small subset of these resources for the purposes of deciding a price to use a service. We have to correctly define how to implement the counters for each charged element. In addition, according to computations performed and algorithms used in solving problems, user applications have different resource requirements. Therefore, the consumption of the following resources may be accounted and charged [9]:

- CPU - User time (consumed by user App.) and System time (consumed while serving user App.)
- Memory
- Disc
- Wall Clock Time
- Node Count
- Network
- Processors
- Software and Libraries accessed.

3.2 Pricing Scheme and Calculating Cost

The pricing scheme to be adopted is still an open issue. In the grid computing environments, once a valid pricing policy has been established, a state of nearly stable equilibrium, which able to satisfy the needs of both resource consumers and resource producers, can be presented.

A simple pricing scheme is a fixed price model, which allows the resource owners to set the prices of the single resource elements, but it doesn't accord with QoS demands. In computational grid, the pricing depends on the resource supply and demand. Resource provider attempts to get maximal profit, and simultaneously user hope the price paid should as low as possible without failing to obtain the resource. Consumers and producers appeal to GBR to mediate resources price. We propose a pricing function for GBR: $P(t) = P \pm \varepsilon \Delta t$ where t is the time parameter. With time elapsing, GRB increases or decreases the price by a small amount ε after each negotiation. GBR sets a price for a resource and then queries both producers and consumers whether or not accept that price. If producers and consumers agree to this price, resources price are set. Otherwise, if resources consumers unsatisfied, resources price will be decreased a small amount ε by GRB, namely $P(t) = P_0 - \varepsilon \Delta t$; if resources producer unsatisfied, resources price will increased a small amount ε, namely $P(t) = P_0 + \varepsilon \Delta t$.

The calculating cost is a procedure that calculates the price of the resource, which depends on the user's resource usage and pricing algorithms. The computing usage is defined as the product p • u, where p is a performance factor and u is the amount of usage of that resource element [11]. For example if p refers to the CPU power, u should be the amount of CPU time used by the job. We define resource cost as a • (p • u), where p and u are defined above, a is weight factors used to image the price of resource, which was get according to the chosen pricing algorithm. The cost of the whole job can be obtained from cost of every resource by computing:

$$C = \sum_{i=1}^{n} a_i \cdot (p_i \cdot u_i)$$

The i index runs over the resource elements (i.e. CPU, RAM, Disk, etc...).

4 Conclusions and Further Work

We have shown that an economy-based accounting system for Grid Computing Environments, which is a complex system that involves many services interaction. Then, we briefly describe accounted and charged resources elements, and discuss pricing and cost algorithms. The system we discuss in this paper will apply to ShanghaiGrid.

Other works that will need to be considered and need further investigation include:

- Detailed pricing algorithms that depends on the supply and demand
- Devise accounting policies and payment policies
- Increase reliability and fault tolerance of the released services;
- Study the related economic model that suitable for our grid.

Moreover, the interaction of this system with other services of Grid needs to be analyzed in further.

References

1. Foster, I., Kesselman, C.(eds.).: The Grid: Blueprint for a New Computing Infrastructure. Morgan Kaufmann (1999)
2. Foster, I., Kesselman, C., Tuecke S.: The Anatomy of the Grid: Enabling Scalable Virtual Organizations. International Journal of High Performance Computing Application, 15(3) (2001)
3. Foster, I., Kesselman, C., Nick, J., Tuecke, S.: The Physiology of the Grid: An Open Grid Services Architecture for Distributed Systems Integration.
4. A. Guarise et al.: DataGrid Accounting System Architecture- v 1.0. Technical Report DataGrid-01-TED-0126-1 0. INFN Turin, Italy, February 2003.
5. Alexander, B., Rajkumar, B.: GridBank: A Grid Accounting Services Architecture (GASA) for distributed systems sharing and integration. In 17th Annual International Parallel and Distributed Processing Symposium (IPDPS 2003) Workshop on Internet Computing and E-Commerce (2003)
6. Magowan, J.: Extreme Blue Grid Accounting Project (Grid Service Accounting Extensions–GSAX). GGF Resource Usage Service Working Group (2003)
7. Buyya, R.: Economic-based Distributed Resource Management and Scheduling for Grid Computing, PhD Thesis. Monash University, Melbourne, Australia, April 12, 2002. http://www.buyya.com/thesis/
8. Buyya, R., Abramson, D., and Giddy, J.: An Economy Driven Resource Management Architecture for Global Computational Power Grids. The 7th International Conference on Parallel and Distributed Processing Techniques and Applications (PDPTA 2000), Las Vegas, USA, June 26-29, 2000.
9. Global Grid Forum: GridEconomic Services Architecture (GESA). http://www.gridforum.org/3_SRM/gesa.htm
10. Global Grid Forum: RUR - Resource Usage Record Working Group. http://www.gridforum.org/3_SRM/ur.htm
11. C.Anglano, S.Barale, L.Gaido, A.Guarise, S.Lusso, A.Werbrouck: An accounting system for the DataGrid project -Preliminary proposal. draft in discussion at Global Grid Forum 3, Frascati, Italy, (October, 2001). http://server11.infn.it/workload-grid/docs/DataGrid-01-TED-0115-3_0.pdf

Track2: Web Services Quality (WQW)

QoS-Based Message-Oriented Middleware for Web Services

Piyush Maheshwari, Trung Nguyen Kien, and Abdelkarim Erradi

School of Computer Science and Engineering
The University of New South Wales, Australia
{piyush, trungnk, aerradi}@cse.unsw.edu.au

Abstract. The emergence of Web services has promised to IT industry a technology that provides the ability to establish integration standards and therefore to evolve and integrate business-to-business (B2B) applications effectively in a platform-neutral and language-neutral fashion. Consequently, quality of service (QoS) has become a significant factor for this promising technology. The question is "How to provide accessible, reliable, secured, and trustworthy Web services?" Since the nature of communication of Web services is based on exchanging messages, therefore message-oriented middleware (MOM) is often seen to be the first solution to promote the quality of service for Web services. Web Services Message Queue (WSMQ), a MOM, has been designed at the University of New South Wales to answer some of the above questions. In this paper, we summarize WSMQ features and functionalities, and describe new extensions in order to further augment the quality of service support in WSMQ.

1 Introduction

W3C defines a Web service as "a software system designed to support interoperable machine-to-machine interaction over a network. It has an interface described in a machine-processable format (specifically WSDL). Other systems interact with the Web service in a manner prescribed by its description using SOAP-messages, typically conveyed using HTTP with an XML serialization in conjunction with other Web-related standards." [3]. This definition gives us a closer look on the approach of how Web services operate over the Internet (e.g., definition, description, and discovery via the Internet-based protocols) and what makes Web services interoperable (e.g., XML-based messages).

Web services stepped into distributed computing whilst there have already been number of prior technologies like EDI (Electronic Data Interchange), CORBA (Common Request Broker Architecture), DCOM (Distributed Component Object Model) and Java RMI (Remote Method Invocation). But neither of the existing technologies could gain broad industry supports and acceptance due to their complexities (e.g., CORBA, DCOM), cost factors (EDI), or platform/language specifics (e.g., RMI). Moreover, these attempts have yielded tightly coupled systems that are not suitable for B2B communications [4]. Web services promises to overcome

C. Bussler et al. (Eds.): WISE 2004 Workshops, LNCS 3307, pp. 241–251, 2004.
© Springer-Verlag Berlin Heidelberg 2004

these limitations by promoting standards-based interoperability and loose coupling [12].

Along with the emergence and widespread proliferation of Web services, Quality of Service (QoS) has been seen as a significant factor in determining usability, utility and trustworthiness of a service. The major requirements for supporting QoS in Web services are as follows [2]:

- *Availability*: Readiness of a Web service for immediate use.
- *Accessibility*: Capability to scale and serve increasing number of requests.
- *Integrity*: Correctness of the interaction in respect to the response.
- *Performance*: Measured on the basis of throughput and latency of services.
- *Reliability*: Assured and ordered delivery for messages being sent and received by service requesters and service providers.
- *Security*: Authenticating, encrypting messages for providing access control to Web services to maintain confidentiality and prevent unauthorized access.

The rest of this paper is organized as follows. In Section 2, we present a short overview of Message-Oriented Middleware (MOM) and its relationship with Web Services. Section 3 describes the functionalities and features of existing Web Service Message Queue (WSMQ), whilst QoS, which it offers, is presented in Section 4. Section 5 presents the motivations of enhancing WSMQ, some extensions and implementation at glance. Section 6 finally concludes the paper.

2 Message-Oriented Middleware

MOM was one of the first technologies to develop the concept of a common communication mechanism allowing applications to exchange data in terms of messages across the network [6]. The interesting idea about this approach is that it lets the system to be loosely coupled - messages can be sent asynchronously without the destination is to be available, and it coordinates traffic in network communications – to provide reliable message delivery in point-to-point or publish/subscribe fashion [7, 12].

2.1 MOM and Web Services

Web services interactions are based on exchanging of standards-based XML documents, i.e. SOAP messages. This is called message-based interoperability, the natural interaction paradigm of MOMs [12]. And also because message-based systems are loosely coupled and document-oriented, they fit well with Web services.

On the other hand, providing reliable and secured Web services determines largely the success of service providers and the popular of Web services whilst Internet protocols, like HTTP, on which Web services are based, are definitely unreliable medium of communication and not to mention that there is absolutely no assurance that a server would be able to handle possibilities of a load of myriad requests per second. Especially those are significant issues that must be resolved to survive in a distributed computing environment. We will show that a MOM plays important roles to address these necessities.

2.2 Related Works and Technologies

There are number of industrial MOM products available such as IBM WebsphereMQ [15] (previously known as MQSeries), SonicMQ [13], Sun One MQ [14], etc. Those messaging systems are built on different technologies and having their own unique features. For example, SonicMQ is a standards-based enterprise messaging system, and supports SOAP, both publish/subscribe and point-to-point messaging, guaranteed message delivery, dynamic routing and security with SSL, LDAP, etc. IBM WebsphereMQ supports for industry standard communication protocols, including HTTP, TCP/IP and Java protocols. Security is enhanced by built-in security, apart from SSL option.

3 WSMQ – Functionalities and Features

3.1 Functional Overview

WSMQ includes a number of components aiming to improve the reliability of Web services, to strengthen the operation of Web services with prioritizations, to increase the performance under certain circumstances, and to provide a set of administrative tools [1].

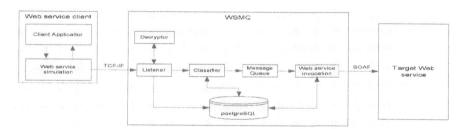

Fig. 1. WSMQ functional overview

Figure 1 illustrates a good picture of WSMQ functional and operational overview. The colored rectangles indicate components controlled by WSMQ. Observably, there are two main components:

- The simulation of Web service invocation library provides the communication between clients and WSMQ by creating a message object that contains the necessary details to invoke a Web service as well as additional information required by WSMQ such as user name, password, client connection details, etc.
- The messaging service component contains a number of sub-components through which an incoming message is required to undergo in order to be successfully processed:
    - **Listener**: through which incoming messages arrive at WSMQ as Java objects, and threads are created to handle these requests.
    - **Decryptor**: is responsible for decrypting messages that were encrypted by the Web service client.

- **Message backup**: the message is then saved into permanent storage database for future use (re-invoke if target Web service is not available, maintain persistence if server is down…).
- **Message classification and prioritization**: Figure 2 shows the functions of the Classifier component. The owner of the message can be authenticated upon entering the Classifier. Once authentication is completed, the status of the message would change. Then relevant information is retrieved from the message. This includes details of the clients that would be needed to complete the messaging service. Finally, the message is prioritized under certain scheme specified at the configuration of the system.

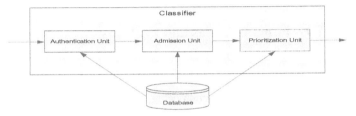

Fig. 2. Classifier component

- **Message queue**: After being assigned a priority in the Classifier, message is forwarded to a message queue that is responsible for the specified priority. For example, a message with priority 5 would be queued in internal queue number 5. An algorithm is in place such that messages in higher prioritized message queues are fetched more frequently than those with lower priority.
- **Message relay**: The working mechanism in message relay component is to ensure that the invocation is done with maximum possibility of success. Indeed, if the target Web service is offline, then it will look up in the database for a backup Web service that provides equivalent service. If found, the message will be transferred to the corresponding WSMQ (could be itself or another remote WSMQ) and start the entire process again. If not, the message is suspended and its status is updated. Periodically, number of attempts will be executed until target is available or the client time out occurs.
- **Message completion**: The status of message is updated, appropriate results from target Web service is returned to the client.

3.2   Message Status

The key idea of WSMQ in order to achieve reliability feature is managing *message status*. There are five different statuses throughout a message lifecycle:
- **Processing**: The first status for any message arriving at WSMQ.
- **Completed**: is assigned to the message after processing successfully.

- **Clustered**: is assigned to the message when the invocation of the target Web service fails and the request is routed successfully to an alternative service.
- **Zombie**: is assigned to the message when the first invocation fails.
- **Dead**: is assigned to the message when the response can not be delivered to the client (e.g., timeout or erroneous connection).

When messages obtain the status of 'completed', 'clustered' or 'dead', no further messaging services is performed on such messages. Diagram in Figure 3 expresses status transition of a Web service during its lifetime.

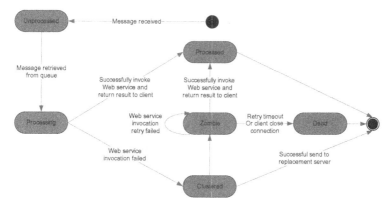

Fig. 3. Messsage status transition

3.3   Communication Between WSMQ and Target Web Services

Any Web service must first be registered in WSMQ in order to use messaging service. The registration involves associating Web services with one or more queues that can reside locally or remotely.

The cost of this decision is that in the case where a target Web service is unavailable and an alternative is found, it would probably be more efficient to invoke the alternative Web service directly. However under this scheme, WSMQ sends the message to the corresponding queue of the alternative Web service and the queue would repeat the whole process as it has received a new message. There are reasons why this decision was made:

- **Consistency**: Each service invocation can be tracked through its request message in the corresponding queue.
- **Fair**: Does not allow single message to consume large amount of resources by repeated invocation. This reduces the probability of starvation particularly in a system where prioritization of messages exists.
- **Efficiency**: Allow implementation of load balancing.

4 WSMQ – Quality of Service

Fundamentally, QoS is a combination of various quality criteria to which a good service must comply. There are number of approaches to achieve QoS, and they usually depend on type of service offered. In the case of congestion-management, one tries to raise the priority of a flow or limiting the priority of another by queuing and servicing queues in different ways. If the objective is to achieve reliable data flow, different reliability mechanisms may be considered. The scalability of a system may be obtained by balancing the load in the system, forwarding requests to other relatively remote systems.

WSMQ provides several QoS features. The most important approaches include message prioritization, message reliability and Web services innovation performance enhancement with load balancing. We now examine each feature in the following sections.

4.1 Message Prioritization

WSMQ implements two schemes of prioritizing Web service executions:

- **User prioritization** – A user may wish to pay more to complete its usage of a service before other users; WSMQ allows this by assigning the service request message of that user with a higher priority. The higher priorities messages own, the more often they get executed.
- **Web service prioritization** – Upon registration, each Web service is assigned a priority. Under this scheme, as each service request message enters the Queue server, it is prioritized according to its target Web service. Again, highly prioritized messages are executed more frequently.

The two approaches for prioritization cannot guarantee the timely completing certain service requests. There are many reasons that are beyond the control of WSMQ, for example, the unavailability of Web services, inundated requests for certain services, etc. The prioritization mechanism does however greatly improve the probability of completing highly prioritized messages within a short time. Logically, the cost is the longer processing time for messages with lower priorities. In most cases, this is not an issue as long as we can avoid starvation and promote accessibility of Web services.

4.2 Reliability and Fault Tolerance

WSMQ provides fault tolerance by using three different approaches:

- **Guaranteed delivery**: If a message is not delivered, the system is able to identify the error, and try to recover from the error and redeliver the message; otherwise error notification is reported to the requester.
- **Restart mechanism**: In case of failure, WSMQ has the ability to recover from errors and continue processing pending messages without affecting the clients.
- **Clustering Web services**: Clustered service improves the probability of Web service completion by allowing similar Web services to form a cluster upon

their registration. In case of failure, WSMQ will dynamically swap the target Web service with an equivalent backup service from the cluster.

To evaluate the reliability introduced by WSMQ, we conducted a series of tests to compare direct Web service invocation – using Apache Axis client libraries and through WSMQ. In this implementation, we generated 20 concurrent clients invoking a simple Web service; each client sent 50 messages continuously. This scenario is meant to attempt to overload the target Web service. Figure 4 summarizes the test results (zero response time means that the client failed to invoke the Web service).

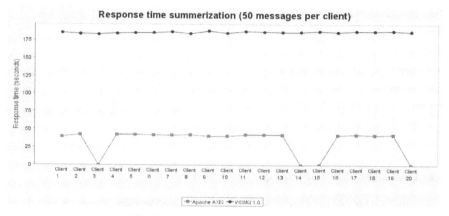

Fig. 4. Message reliability with WSMQ

Though there is a weak performance observed for WSMQ but since it is adding new values to provide QoS to invocation requests before doing the actual Web service invocation, the degradation on performance is trivial. Later on, in section 5, we will present a new implementation in order to leverage the performance of WSMQ.

4.3 Load Balancing

There exists a situation that some queue servers may be inundated with service requests while few others are idle. Load balancing reduces the severity of this situation by attempting to distribute the message load from congested queue servers to some other queue servers, which are at rest. Each queue server is associated with a number, called load factor, in order to measure the percentage of the total capacity. Numerically, it is linearly proportional to the product of the number of internal priority queues and the highest level of priority. Anytime the queue server accepts a new message, the load factor is checked to make sure it does not exceed 75% otherwise load balancing will take place.

4.4 Security

WSMQ provides the built-in security functionalities with authentication/authorization and encryption algorithm DES/MD5. Clients are able to use the simulation library in order to perform encryption. Additionally, they are assigned user names and passwords bundled within sent messages, which will be authenticated at queue servers.

5 WSMQ – Extensions

As a messaging system dedicated for Web services, WSMQ plays an important role in leveraging Web services in real settings. It is specifically designed to address some of the major issues relating to Web services and offers a number of significant QoS features, namely reliability, scalability, security and performance; therefore trying to achieve all of them in one attempt cannot be done without compromises and inconclusive features.

WSMQ has achieved some success in adding more values to QoS for Web services such as guaranteed delivery and recovery mechanism, but since this is the first design iteration of WSMQ, essentially there is a need for improving the system towards industry standards. Few ideas to enhance WSMQ are discussed below to make it more robust framework for future developments.

5.1 Interoperability with Multiple Transport Protocols

Currently, WSMQ accepts Java objects generated using the simulation library. This is proprietary and not compliant with any standard messaging protocols. The suggested enhancement is to provide multiple channels to reach WSMQ by supporting various transport protocols such as HTTP, JMS, TCP, etc. In order to accept SOAP messages over different transport protocols, WSQM will provide a flexible framework that allows plugging transport handlers to extract the coming SOAP message and dispatch it to the appropriate queue for processing. The idea is depicted in Figure 5.

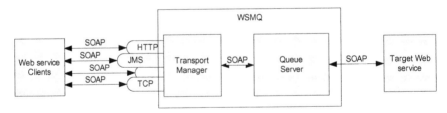

Fig. 5. Supporting Multiple transport protocols

5.2 Scalability and Performance

As highlighted in section 4.2 the QoS features of WSMQ comes at the cost of poor performance compared with direct invocation. This section discusses various strategies that will be used to improve the performance and scalability of WSMQ. They are summarized below:

5.2.1 Improve the Scheduling Algorithm for Message Processing

WSMQ prioritizes messages and processes them on the basis of their priorities *(Fixed-priority scheduling)*, but for messages with the same priority, WSMQ operates on first-come-first-serve (FIFO) basis. One of the problems is that one request may be stuck behind another one that requires a long time to generate a response. The scheduling algorithm will be enhanced to take consideration of the approximate execution time for Web service invocations. Initially, upon Web service registration, the queue server can estimate invocation time of Web services, and this estimate will be revised on the basis of subsequent invocations. At runtime the scheduling algorithm will dynamically assign higher priority to requests for Web services with shorter execution time. This enhancement will improve WSMQ throughput and reduce congestion by first serving requests for fast services.

5.2.2 Optimize WSMQ Server Resources Usage

Our analysis of the reasons of poor performance points to the high number of threads being created by WSMQ. When a message arrives at the Listener component, a thread is created to serve the request, and this will not scale with high number of requests. We plan to enhance the scalability of WSMQ by extending the ideas developed by SEDA (Staged Event-Driven Architecture) project [17]. SEDA proposes staged event driven architecture for highly concurrent Internet applications to overcome the limitations of traditional thread based Web Services Engine. The issues with threading, including cache and TLB misses, scheduling overheads, and lock contention, can produce poor performance when there are large numbers of threads that have been created.

Another cause of poor performance is the PostgreSQL database used for queues persistence, we plan- to replace it with YFilter [18], a highly scalable XML query processing system, and this will also improve the performance of cache lookup.

5.2.3 Shorten Response Time with Caching

The service responsiveness is one of performance measurement for the success of a Web service. There are number of solutions which have been investigated to define protocols, operating between service requesters and service providers, ranging from network protocols enhancement to mechanisms running on end systems such as caching, prefetching, etc. [10].

Caching is one of the standard techniques employed in distributed systems to reduce the latency [10]. The idea of caching has been successfully applied to Web contents and it will still be an ideal solution in caching Web services which have been recently invoked. Each time there is a request for invoking a Web service, WSMQ would look up the cache and return the results to clients without communicating to target Web service, thus reducing the response time and increasing throughput significantly.

To cache Web services efficiently, we will implement the architecture of a response cache for Web services client middleware [11], as shown in Figure 6.

Although caching may affect the performance of the queue server but it is worthy a trade-off for faster response time to clients and higher throughput that WSMQ will provide.

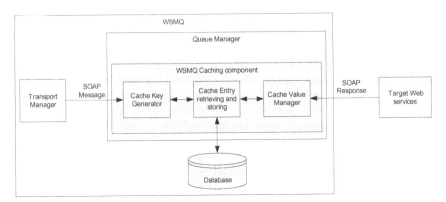

Fig. 6. Responsive caching component

6 Conclusions

In this paper, we first presented WSMQ, a MOM-based queue implementation for Web services, which has achieved a number of QoS features for services such as reliable messaging, recovery mechanism, and security. We also discussed weaknesses of existing WSMQ in terms of interoperability, which is the dependence on the simulation libraries, and serious performance degradation comparing with direct Web service invocation, therefore proposed two essential extensions to overcome these limitations and to strengthen the QoS offered by WSMQ. They are:

- **Interoperability enrichment**: Web services interoperability is achieved mainly because of SOAP. By accepting SOAP messages directly from clients over various transport protocols, WSMQ can provide services to client applications in a platform and language independent manner, and the simulation library is disregarded from the system.
- **Scalability enhancement**: Improving scheduling algorithm for message processing, applying ideas of staged event-driven architecture and caching Web services are three potential strategies to promote scalability of WSMQ.

At the time of writing this paper, the implementation of the above extensions is underway and the results will be reported in the coming months.

References

1. Piyush Maheshwari, Hua Tang, and Roger Liang: Enhancing Web services with message-oriented middleware, *Proceedings of the IEEE International Conference on Web Services*, San Diego, July 2004 (ICWS 2004).
2. Anbazhagan Mani and Arun Nagarajan: Understanding quality of service for Web services (January 2002). IBM Developerworks.
   http://www-106.ibm.com/developerworks/webservices/library/ws-quality.html
3. W3C Web Services Glossary (11 February 2004). http://www.w3.org/TR/ws-gloss/
4. IBM Web Services Architecture Team: Web Services Architecture Overview.
   http://www-106.ibm.com/developerworks/library/w-ovr/ (accessed June 2004).

5. Jim Fisher: Augmenting EAI with Web services. Web Service Journal Magazine, Vol. 3, Issue 1, January 2003, p.16.
6. Daniel Serain, Iain Craig(translator): Middleware. Springer 1999.
7. Chris Britton: IT Architectures and Middleware. Addison-Wesley 2000.
8. Brian D. Goodman: Accelerate your Web services with caching (December 2002). IBM Developer Works. http://www-106.ibm.com/developerworks/library/ws-cach1/ (accessed June 2004).
9. James McGovern and Sameer Tyagi: Java Web Services Architecture. Morgan Kaufmann Publishers 2003.
10. Marco Conti, Mohan Kumar, Sajal K. Das, and Behrooz A. Shirazi: Quality of Service issues in Internet Web Services. *IEEE Transactions on Computer*, Vol. 51, No. 6, June 2002. pp.593-594.
11. Takase, T., Tatsubori, M.: Efficient web services response caching by selecting optimal data representation, *Proceedings of the 24th International Conference on Distributed Computing Systems*, March 2004. pp.188-197.
12. Gustavo Alonso, Fabio Casati, Harumi Kuno, Vijay Machiraju: Web Services concepts, architectures and applications. Springer 2004.
13. Sonicsoftware: SonicMQ Datasheet. http://www.sonicsoftware.com/products/docs/sonicmq.pdf
14. Sun Microsystems: Sun Java System Message Queue PE Datasheet. Sun Microsystems. http://wwws.sun.com/software/products/message_queue_pe/ds_message_queue_pe.pdf (accessed August 2004).
15. IBM Corp: Websphere MQ Overview. http://www-306.ibm.com/software/integration/wmq/?S_TACT=103BGW01&S_CMP= campaign (accessed August 2004).
16. Sun Microsystems: Java Message Service specification version 1.1. Sun Microsystems April 12, 2002. http://java.sun.com/products/jms/docs.html
17. Matt Welsh, David Culler, and Eric Brewer: SEDA – An Architecture for Highly Concurrent, Well-Conditioned Internet Services. *Proceedings of the 18th ACM Symposium on Operating Systems Principles*, October 21-24, 2001, Chateau Lake Louise, Banff, Canada, ACM Press, 2001.
18. Diao Y. and Franklin M. J: High-Performance XML Filtering: An Overview of YFilter, *IEEE Data Engineering Bulletin 2003*. http://www.cs.berkeley.edu/~diaoyl/publications/filtering-overview.pdf

Incorporating QoS Specifications in Service Discovery

V. Deora, J. Shao, G. Shercliff, P.J. Stockreisser, W.A. Gray, and N.J. Fiddian

School of Computer Science
Cardiff University
Cardiff, UK
v.deora@cs.cf.ac.uk

Abstract. In this paper, we extend the current approaches to service discovery in a service oriented computing environment, such as Web Services and Grid, by allowing service providers and consumers to express their promises and requirements for quality of service (QoS). More specifically, we allow service providers to advertise their services in an extended DAML-S that supports quality specifications, and we allow service consumers to request services by stating required quality levels. We propose a model here for incorporating QoS specifications and requirements in service discovery, and describe how matchmaking between advertised and requested services based on functional as well as quality requirements is supported in our model.

1 Introduction

There is a growing interest in service oriented computing (SOC) in recent years [1,2,3,4]. Central to SOC is the notion of a *service* which can broadly be considered as a software component that represents some computational or data-offering capability. By allowing services to be advertised declaratively, discovered dynamically and invoked remotely, SOC makes it possible for users to locate, select and execute services without having to know how and where they are implemented. As such, this new computing paradigm offers great potential for distributed applications in an open environment and on a large scale.

In this paper, we consider the problem of how to support dynamic service discovery within an SOC environment. This is an important issue because an SOC environment can potentially contain thousands of autonomous services which may come and go at any time. It is desirable therefore that the user is able to request a service by stating declaratively what is required, rather than having to specify how to obtain or access a specific one at a pre-determined location. In other words, discovering which services are available to meet the requirement of a specific service request should be performed dynamically at the time the request is made.

A general approach to supporting this type of service discovery is based on the *register-find-bind* model [5] outlined in Figure 1. Here, service providers (SPs) make their services available by registering their capabilities in a centralised

C. Bussler et al. (Eds.): WISE 2004 Workshops, LNCS 3307, pp. 252–263, 2004.
© Springer-Verlag Berlin Heidelberg 2004

service registry. Service requesters (SRs) then locate their required services by sending their requirements to the registry. A matchmaking component is often implemented as part of the registry to match an incoming service request with those available in the registry. If a match is found, the details of the advertising SP are returned to the requesting SR. The SP and SR are then said to be *bound* to complete their task.

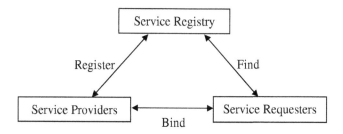

Fig. 1. A Generic Service Discovery Model

Currently, matchmaking between requested and registered services is largely based on their functional attributes. To illustrate this, consider the following example. Suppose that there are several SPs who offer multimedia services to PDA or mobile phone users, and we have an SR who wishes to purchase a monthly subscription package for science-fiction movies and news services, including 30 free text messages and at least 50 free talk minutes. This service request may be represented abstractly as follows:

subscription_type = monthly
+ Video_Content where media_style = science_fiction
+ Html_content where html_content_type = news
+ text_messages where number_of_free_messages = 30
+ Phone_Calls where number_of_free_minutes ≥ 50

Fig. 2. A Request for Service

Here, the request is made in terms of the required functions, for example, the qualifying SP must offer `science fiction` movies. To determine which SP(s) can offer the required service, the matchmaking component searches through the registry, typically using a string comparison method, to see if any registered services match some or all of the functional attributes listed in the request. If, for example, SP1 has advertised that it offers `science fiction` movies or cartoons, then SP1 is identified as a potential provider for the required service and its details are returned to the SR.[1]

The above model works fine if we assume that the SR is only interested in the functional aspects of a service. In practice, however, it is quite possible that we may have several SPs offering the same service, and just like in a common marketplace, an SR may wish to select a service based on functional as well as other attributes such as quality and cost. Thus, it would be desirable that the SR can pose the following request, where frame rate = 24 and availability = 7 days/week are QoS requirements:

---

subscription_type = monthly
+ Video_Content where media_style = science_fiction
  (frame_rate = 24 & availability = 7 days/week)
+ Html_content where html_content_type = news
+ text_messages where number_of_free_messages = 30
+ Phone_Calls where number_of_free_minutes ≥ 50

Fig. 3. Service Request with QoS Requirements

The current function-based approaches are not sufficient to support this more advanced form of service discovery. In this paper, we extend the existing approaches to service discovery by incorporating QoS specifications and requirements into matchmaking. That is, we let SPs advertise their functional capabilities and QoS promises to the registry, and monitor the actual quality of the services offered by the SPs. An SR can then request a service by specifying not only functional requirements, but also QoS expectations. We propose a two-step service discovery model here, and describe how matchmaking between advertised and requested services based on functional as well as QoS requirements is supported in our model.

The rest of the paper is organised as follows. Section 2 discusses the related work. Section 3 introduces our service discovery model. We will explain how service advertisement, request and matchmaking are supported in our model. Section 4 presents conclusions and discusses future work.

2   Related Work

The progress on supporting dynamic service discovery in SOC is largely represented by the development of UDDI [6], which is currently a *de facto* standard for service advertisement and discovery. The standard UDDI does not offer any

---

[1] Note that it is not necessary to find a single SP who can satisfy the SR's request completely, and the matchmaking component will search for all the SPs who can serve any part of the request.

support for QoS specification and relies largely on keyword matching for service discovery. Recently, some extensions have been made to UDDI to allow inclusion of QoS in service specifications [7], but they support only a very limited set of specific attributes, for example, network response time. Our approach differs from these extensions in that we employ a QoS ontology in service specification. This allows richer semantics of services to be specified and more sophisticated matchmaking between advertised and requested services to be performed, using a wide range of QoS attributes that require different means of representation, monitoring and assessment.

Integrating QoS with service description has also been considered by the work on deriving service level agreement (SLA) for web services. IBM, for example, has recently introduced a framework which allows SRs to form contracts with SPs using an XML-based language [8]. This framework also allows a representation with which the QoS provision agreed by the SPs can be monitored. While these works also attempt to integrate QoS with service descriptions and store such extended service descriptions in a repository for reference, they differ from our work in that they consider QoS representation and integration for services after they have been discovered, rather than in the initial discovery of relevant services. In other words, we attempt to use QoS information as part of a service-selection process, whereas the works on SLA consider it from the service provision perspective.

Various service description languages, such as WSDL [9], DAML-S [10] and OWL-S [11], have been proposed. WSDL is used currently in conjunction with UDDI as a standard for describing web services. This is a low level mechanism which does not support semantic description of services. DAML-S, and its newer version OWL-S, are developed by the semantic web community for describing services at a higher level. They support the use of service ontology in service description and allow some form of reasoning in service discovery [12,13]. Although these languages are quite powerful in describing the functional aspects of a service, they offer little support for specifying the non-functional aspects. We also use DAML-S for service descriptions, but extend it to include explicit, separate QoS specifications.

3   QoS-Based Service Discovery

In this section we introduce our QoS-based service discovery model. Our approach is outlined in Figure 4, which is an extension to the generic service discovery model given in Figure 1.

The service registry in our model consists of two components: the Yellow Pages (YP) component and the QoS component. The YP component is similar in purpose to the matchmaking component that we described in Section 1, and is used to determine which advertised services match the requirements stated in an incoming service request. Note however that in our model both functional and quality properties may be specified. The QoS component, on the other hand, is used to calculate the quality of a service on demand, using the QoS ratings

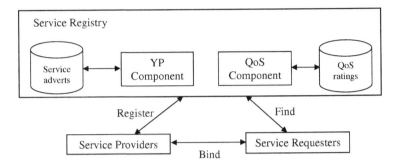

Fig. 4. QoS based Service Discovery

collected from the previous uses of the service. By interacting with these two components, an SR can find a required service in two steps:

- **Searching.** In this step, the SR sends a service request containing functional and/or QoS requirements to the YP component. For example, SR1 may request a service that can offer `science fiction` movies (a functional requirement) and the `frame rate` of movie delivery is required to be 24 frames per second (a QoS requirement). The SR uses this step to search for SPs who *claim* to be able to offer the required service. The YP component will return a list of SPs whose advertisements match what is required in the SR's request.

- **Evaluation.** Following the searching step, the SR can ask the QoS component to assess *how well* each SP returned by the YP component can actually provide the service in this step. This is necessary because service advertisements can not entirely be trusted, and some SPs may not honour what they have promised. For example, the YP component may find, from the advertisements, that SP1 can provide the movie service that SR1 has requested, but the past experience by other users may suggest that SP1 is more likely to provide, on average, 22 instead of 24 frames per second for its movie delivery. Allowing QoS assessment by the QoS component in this step therefore gives the SR the opportunity to establish what can really *be expected* from a particular SP.

We consider this two-step service discovery model being a significant improvement over the existing approaches. By allowing QoS attributes of a service to be specified (by SRs and SPs), searched (by the YP component) and evaluated (by the QoS component), our approach supports a more meaningful, accurate and relevant service discovery in SOC. In the rest of the paper, we will primarily consider the searching step, and will discuss how service advertisement, request and matchmaking are supported in our model. The reader is referred to [14] for a detailed description of the evaluation step.

3.1   Description of Services

To support dynamic and automatic service discovery, it is first necessary to be able to describe services in a machine-processable way. To enable this, we need an expressive service description language and some ontologies for common terminology. In our model, we use DAML-S [10] for service description. We choose DAML-S because it allows us to describe not just the low-level service functionality and requirements in terms of message format, data types and protocols, but also attach semantic information, such as service classification and descriptions, to the services. For standardising terminology in service description, we create two ontologies. The *service ontology* provides SPs and SRs with a common terminology for advertising and requesting services, and enables the YP component to match advertisements with requests. The *quality ontology*, on the other hand, specifies what QoS attributes are and how they are related to the services.

Creating a service ontology is supported by DAML-S and is relatively straightforward, but is domain dependent. Thus, different service ontologies are needed for different domains. For a simple **media** application, for example, a sample service ontology is given in Figure 5 (for simplicity of presentation, we have expressed the ontology here as a class diagram, rather than its implementation in RDF).[2]

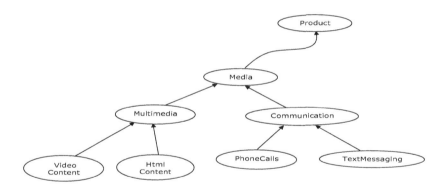

Fig. 5. A Service Ontology for a Simple Media Application

Creation of a quality ontology is, however, not currently supported by DAML-S, and requires some explanation. For different classes of services, a large number of attributes may be used to describe their QoS properties. Some are domain dependent and will only be relevant to a specific class of services. For example, **frame rate** is only relevant to a movie service. Others are domain independent and are applicable to all types of service. For example, **availability** [15] is applicable to movie as well as other services.

---

[2] Note that due to naming conflicts with DAML-S our top-level service is of class **Product** – DAML-S itself defines **Service** as a class from which all services inherit.

Thus, it is important that our quality ontology distinguishes between these two types of QoS attributes, so that we do not repeat ourselves in specifying service independent QoS for each individual service. Motivated by this observation, we group all QoS attributes into *service specific* and *service independent*, as shown in the example ontology given in Figure 6 for the simple `media` service. As can be seen, a service must include a service specific QoS attribute explicitly (e.g. `VideoContent` has `FrameRateCategory` as one of its QoS property), but will include service independent QoS attributes implicitly (e.g. `VideoContent` also has `AvailabilityCategory`, `PerformanceCategory` and `ReliabilityCategory` as its QoS attributes).

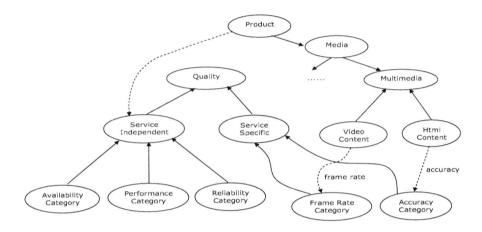

Fig. 6. A Quality Ontology for the Simple Media Application

The two ontologies are then integrated with DAML-S to facilitate service description. This is achieved by making our `Product` class to inherit from the `ServiceProfile` class provided by DAML-S. This is illustrated in Figure 7. Note that DAML-S defines its `Service` class in terms of `Service Profile`, `Service Model` and `Service Grounding`. For our work, we have only used `Service Profile` as this is sufficient for service discovery purposes.

It is worth noting that in the extended service description in DAML-S, we have also included the `QualityPreference` class. This is to allow an SR to specify preferences in searching for the required service. By stating whether it wishes to maximise service quality or perform some user specified tradeoff between quality and cost, a flexible service discovery can be supported. More detailed discussion on this is, however, beyond the scope of the current paper.

SPs and SRs can then advertise and request services using the extended service description facilities given in Figure 7. To ensure that service advertisements and requests adhere to the service and quality ontologies, we introduce advertisement and request schemas. Due to space restrictions we will not dis-

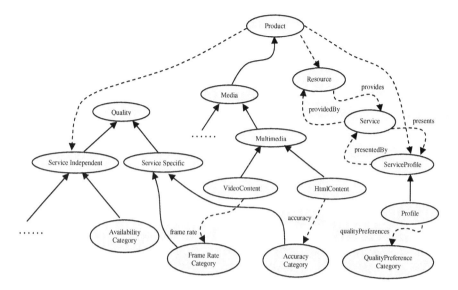

Fig. 7. The Extended Service Description in DAML-S

cuss these schemas further. However, it is worth noting that SPs and SRs do not have to specify values for all QoS properties that are listed in the quality ontology. If some QoS property is unspecified, we will treat it as *unknown* (if it is in an advertisement) or *uninterested* (if it is in a request). Once created, service advertisements and requests are sent to the YP component for registration and matchmaking, respectively.

3.2   Matchmaking

Matching a service request with the advertised ones is performed by the YP component. In this section, we explain how this is done. Suppose that we have a set of advertised services A and a service request R, respectively, as follows

$$A = \{s_1^a, s_2^a, \ldots, s_n^a\} \qquad R = \{s_1^r, s_2^r, \ldots, s_k^r\}$$

where each s_i^a $(1 \leq i \leq n)$ is an advertised service and each s_j^r $(1 \leq j \leq k)$ is a requested service. Note that a single service request may ask for several services.

For matchmaking purposes, we assume that an advertised service (s^a) and a requested service (s^r) are represented as follows:

$$s^a = \langle sn, sp, fs, qs \rangle \qquad s^r = \langle sn, fs, qs \rangle$$

where sn is the service name, sp is the service provider, fs is the set of functional specifications and qs is the set of QoS specifications. We refer to these components using the "." notation, that is, $s^a.sn$ refers to the service name of s^a.

Our matchmaking task is to find a set of SPs who offer services that will match any subset of R. That is, we search for

$$M = \{s_i^a \mid s_i^a \succeq R' \subseteq R, 1 \leq i \leq n\}$$

where $s_i^a \succeq R'$ denotes that s_i^a provides a service that satisfies the functional and QoS requirements of each $s^r \in R'$. The following steps describe how M is found.

1. *Determine which advertisements are relevant to R.* This is not simply a process of comparing $s_i^a.sn$ to $s_j^r.sn$. Since our service ontology organises classes of services as a hierarchy, it is necessary to traverse the service ontology too. For example, the example ontology given in Figure 5 defines VideoContent and HTMLContent as two sub-classes of Multimedia. If an SP advertises to offer Multimedia service, then this SP is considered to offer *both* VideoContent and HTMLContent services together. Thus, to search for SPs who can provide VideoContent and HTMLContent services, it is necessary to consider the advertisements that offer Multimedia services too. The following procedure explains how this is performed by the YP component:

---

input $A = \{s_1^a, s_2^a, \ldots, s_n^a\}$, $R = \{s_1^r, s_2^r, \ldots, s_k^r\}$, ont = service ontology
output $Rel \subseteq A$

1 $Rel = \emptyset$
2 for each s_j^r $(1 \leq j \leq k)$
3      $Rel = Rel \cup \{s_i^a.sp \mid s_i^a.sn = s_j^r.sn, 1 \leq i \leq n\}$
4      $p = s_j^r$
5   while $(p \neq null)$
6          $p = getParentClass(p, ont)$
7          $S = \{s_i^a \mid s_i^a.sn = p, 1 \leq i \leq n\}$
8   for each $s \in S$
9              $c = getComponentServices(s)$
10             $Rel = Rel \cup \{s_i^a.sp \mid c \subseteq R, s_i^a.sn = p\}$
11 return Rel

The YP component will first find all the advertisements that have the same service names as those requested (line 3). Then, the YP component recursively traverse the service ontology up (line 6) to find those services that are more general than s_j^r, but contain no component services that are not requested in R (lines 9 & 10). This "no more than required" restriction is necessary because currently we assume that an advertised service must be taken in its entirety. For example, one is not allowed to take the HTMLContent service alone from an SP if it has advertised to offer Multimedia service. Clearly, SPs who offer more than necessary (and perhaps will charge more) are undesirable.

2. *Determine which advertisements meet functional requirements.* In this step, the functional requirements specified in each $s^r \in R$ are used to determine

which advertised services that the YP component discovered in Step 1 must not be returned to the SR. That is, the YP component performs the following:

```
input Rel = {s₁ᵃ, s₂ᵃ, ..., sₘᵃ}, R = {s₁ʳ, s₂ʳ, ..., sₖʳ}
output RF ⊆ Rel

1   RF = ∅
2   for each sⱼʳ (1 ≤ j ≤ k)
3       RF = RF ∪ {sᵢᵃ.sp | sᵢᵃ.sn = sⱼʳ.sn, sᵢᵃ.fs ≥ sⱼʳ.fs, 1 ≤ i ≤ m}
4   return RF
```

where $s_i^a.fs \geq s_j^r.fs$ expresses that advertised functionality $(s_i^a.fs)$ must be equal to or better than the requested $(s_j^r.fs)$. For example, if the SR requires Media style = science fiction, then movie services advertisements that offer cartoons will be disregarded at this stage. This is a fairly straightforward process. If no advertisements can be found, the YP component will send failed message to the SR.

3. *Determine which advertisements meet QoS requirements.* This is similar to Step 2, except that the conditions for matching are different. Assume that $qa \in s_i^a.qs$ is one of the advertised qualities for s_i^a and $qr \in s_j^r.qs$ is one of the requested qualities for s_j^r. The YP component will match qa with qr according to the following:

advertised (qa)	requested (qr)	matching condition
specified	specified	$qa \geq qr$
specified	unspecified	matching
unspecified	specified	matching

That is, if either qa or qr is unspecified, then the YP component considers the two qualities unconditionally matching. This is justified because they represent the cases where either the SR is not interested in some QoS properties or whether its QoS requirements can be met or not cannot be verified. At the end of this step, any advertisements that do not meet the required QoS properties will be dropped from RF, and the details of SPs for the remaining advertisements are returned to the SR.

The above description explained how the YP component performs matchmaking between advertised and requested services during the searching step. As we have outlined earlier in this section, our service discovery model also has a second step – the evaluation step. The SR may decide to use the QoS component in the evaluation step to establish what can really be expected from the SPs returned by the YP component. This is particularly useful in cases where some SPs cannot be trusted or some QoS requirements specified by the SR are unspecified by the SPs. The QoS component can in such cases help to establish some "facts" about the "unknowns", based on other users' experience with the services. We have developed an expectation-based QoS calculation model and for details of our algorithm, the reader is referred to [14].

4   Conclusions and Future Work

In this paper we presented a framework for incorporating QoS specifications in service discovery. The proposed service discovery model is currently being implemented as part of the CONOISE project [16], which aims to develop agent-based technology for forming and managing virtual organisations (VOs) in an SOC environment. In our model we extended the standard DAML-S to allow SPs and SRs to advertise and request services with both functional and QoS requirements, and described our matchmaking mechanism. It is important to note that the service and quality ontologies developed here are not fixed schemas. They can be created and modified as required, without affecting the underlying service discovery mechanism. Thus, our model provides a scalable, dynamic service discovery in an open, distributed computing environment.

We also introduced a two-step QoS-based service discovery model in this paper. With this model, we distinguish between what might be expected of a service (derived from advertisements, previous experiences or recommendations) and what might be materialised (calculated from previous uses of the service). We see this distinction being significant, as it mirrors service discovery in the real world and allows meaningful service discovery to be conducted.

There are several issues which will need further studies. Currently, we use a single YP component. It will be interesting to consider the case where multiple YP components, either distributed or working as a cluster, are used, and study how they may collaborate, especially if we allow each YP component to have its own local domain service and quality ontologies. It will also be useful to consider service composition, that is, to allow SRs to request composition of services, and to extend our matchmaking with a similar capability. Finally, our matchmaking mechanism is rather basic at the moment. There is a need to consider a more powerful matchmaking mechanism whereby ontological reasoning is fully exploited.

Acknowledgments. This work is supported by British Telecommunications plc, and we would like to thank the members of the CONOISE project team for their constructive comments on this work.

References

1. Casati, F., Shan, M.C.: Definition, execution, analysis, and optimization of composite e-services. IEEE Data Engineering Bulletin. Vol. 24(1) (2001) 29–34
2. Leymann, F.: Web services: distributed applications without limits. In: Proceedings of Tenth Conference on Database Systems for Business, Technology and Web. (2003)
3. Piccinelli, G., Stammers, E.: From e-processes to e-networks: an e-service-oriented approach. In: Proceedings of Third International Conference on Internet Computing. Vol. 3 (2002) 549–553
4. Rust, R.T., Kannan, P.K.: E-service: a new paradigm for business in the electronic environment. Communications of the ACM Vol. 46(6) (2003) 36–42

5. Kreger, H.:   Web services conceptual architecture (WSCA).   (http://www-4.ibm.com/software/solutions/webservices/pdf/WSCA.pdf) (2001)
6. Belwood, T. et al: UDDI Version 3.0.1 Specification. (http://www.uddi.org/)
7. Chen, Z., Liang-Tien, C., Silverajan, B., Bu-Sung, L.: Ux: An architecture providing qos-aware and federated support for uddi. In: Proceedings of the First International Conference on Web Services. (2003)
8. Ludwig, H., Keller, A., Dan, A., King, R.P.: A service level agreement language for dynamic electronic services. In: Proceedings of Fourth IEEE International Workshop on Advanced Issues of E-Commerce and Web-based Information Systems. (2002) 25–32
9. Christensen, E. et al: Web services description language (WSDL). (http://www.w3.org/TR/wsdl)
10. Ankolekar, A., Burstein, M., Hobbs, J., Lassila, O., Martin, D., McIllraith, S., Narayanan, S., Paolucci, M., Payne, T., Sycara, K., Zeng, H.: Daml-s: Web service description for the semantic web. In: Proceedings of First International Semantic Web Conference. (2002)
11. Web-Ontology Working Group: Web ontology language - services (OWL-S). (http://www.daml.org/services/owl-s/1.0/)
12. Dogac, A., Cingil, I., Laleci, G.B., Kabak, Y.: Improving the functionality of uddi registries through web service semantics. In: Third International Workshop on Technologies for E-Services. (2002) 9–18
13. Dogac, A., Kabak, Y., Laleci, G.: Enriching ebxml registries with owl ontologies for efficient service discovery. In: Fourteenth International Workshop on Research Issues on Data Engineering. (2004)
14. Deora, V., Shao, J., Gray, W.A., Fiddian, N.J.: A quality of service management framework based on user expectations. In: Proceedings of the First International Conference on Service Oriented Computing. (2003) 104–114
15. Mani, A., Nagarajan, A.: Understanding quality of service for web services. (http://www-106.ibm.com/developerworks/library/ws-quality.html) (2002)
16. Norman, T.J., Preece, A., Chalmers, S., Jennings, N.R., Luck, M., Dang, V.D., Nguyen, T.D., Deora, V., Shao, J., Gray, W.A., Fiddian, N.J.: Conoise: Agent-based formation of virtual organisations. In: The Twenty-third SGAI International Conference on Innovative Techniques and Applications of Artificial Intelligence. (2003)

QoS Based Pricing for Web Services

George Eby Mathew, Joseph Shields, and Vikas Verma

IT Strategy & Management Research Center,
Software Engineering & Technology Labs,
Infosys Technologies Limited,
Electronic City, Hosur Road,
Bangalore – 560 100, India.
{george_mathew, joseph_shields, vikas_verma02}@infosys.com
+91-80-51163896

Abstract. Web Services technologies have over a period of time replaced expensive EDI links and have come to stay as the backbone for collaboration between various enterprises. While currently majority of Web Services are available free, over a period of time increased business dependencies of customers on Web Services are resulting in demands for better Quality of Service. Investments in newer technologies to improve Quality of Service results in increasing Cost of Service, which needs to be offset by revenues. While service providers seek predictability in revenues, customers and users of the Web Services seek flexibility in pricing by not being charged for services not used and service features that are not provided. QoS thus becomes a key determinant of pricing in Web Services. This paper attempts to define a framework for pricing Web Services based on the QoS features provided, the underlying Cost of Service and the level of predictability of revenues that accrue to the service provider based on the transaction volumes of various services. The proposed framework suggests a *Subscription-based Pricing* for Commoditized Web Services, *Transaction-based Pricing* for Channelized Web Services and *Risk-Based Pricing* for Customized Web Services.

1 Introduction

The use of Web Services both in B2B and B2C transactions is maturing and evolving. At current levels of maturity, Web Services technologies are used to replace expensive EDI links, design application that connect legacy applications to advanced web based frontend applications, link applications, data and systems over intranets, and in some cases over public Internet. These applications are predominantly used within the boundaries of the enterprise, and at most available to their extranet users. For instance, Dell Computer sees Web Services as a cost effective way to connect with suppliers and third-party logistics providers. General Motors uses Web Services to coordinate its interactions with dealers and auto purchasers [1].

C. Bussler et al. (Eds.): WISE 2004 Workshops, LNCS 3307, pp. 264–275, 2004.
© Springer-Verlag Berlin Heidelberg 2004

Apart from these Web Services enabled business functionalities are also being harnessed and subscribed to by end users over the internet. The market for such services are emerging and evolving. Due to low entry barriers in producing and publishing Web Services, there are a plethora of services that are available, majority of them available free of charge. These include services such as SMS text messaging, stocks update, and faxing services [2]. While this helps promote a new technology and educate customers, companies are learning from their experiments and evolving viable business models so as to aggregate value to be offered at a price. As the market for smaller applications gets saturated and more customers hook on to Web Service applications, large scale implementations are expected to kick in. In some respects these will change the course of Web Services development, and make paid Web Services offerings available to large corporations. Web Services vendors will then begin to look for designing newer services demanded by educated customers and scientific means of pricing the same.

A price of a service can be set by two fundamental methods namely a cost based approach or a value based approach. All other factors affecting pricing, such as setting competitive expectations or considering elasticity of the market to determine the maximum profit at a given price and volume function leads to one of the two approaches [3]. Our approach to addressing the issue of pricing for Web Services is the cost based approach or the "cost-plus" approach, as it is traditionally known and modeling it around the Quality of Service, Cost of Services sold and transaction volumes.

The paper first illustrates the impact of Quality of Service, Cost of Service sold and transaction volumes on pricing. We then define the types of Web Services and modes of Web Services delivery that have implications on Quality of Service, Cost of Service sold and transaction volumes. We then propose three types of pricing models that can be employed, establish links between the types of Web Services and these pricing models.

2 Pricing Web Services

Web Services pricing can be complex due to non-standardization across the industry and the emergence of changing business models and architectures for deployment [4]. However, pricing is critical for value recognition and value aggregation for the services consumers are willing to pay for. In today's freeware domain, it will bring in legitimacy by ensuring high standards of quality, content and reliability. Web Services are not the first of its kind to charge for technology delivered functionality. For many years Application Service Providers (ASP) have supplied and charged for functionality available over the Internet [2]. Both Web Services and ASPs are similar in that they both charge for business functionality serviced (Table 1) using technology but there are differences.

While traditionally ASP pricing is done based on pay-as-you-go models with a subscription fee plus a transaction based charge, the variations in pricing have been dependant on the variations in volumes of transactions. For example SAP uses a role-based pricing for blanket subscription to all of its products under mySAP.com in addition to transaction based pricing for usage of specific components. JD Edwards uses a pricing model for its JDe.sourcing program, wherein as part of the contract companies pay an initial implementation fee and then a monthly per-user charge.

Web Services however are relatively complex when compared to ASP models as they offer dynamic and random configurability of services delivered. ASP is context dependant. While both enable subscription based and transaction based pricing, the ability to configure and customize the services delivered by Web Services demands that the pricing needs to take into account the Quality of Service. Unlike the ASP pricing models which are predominantly based on volume variations, Web Services pricing models need to be based on QoS variations.

Table 1. Web Services and ASP models – key differences

Web Services	ASP Models
1. Automate dynamic connections across applications/data eliminating human intervention or the need to lay expensive plumbing	1. Make traditional application software available to a broader range of customers and relies on very traditional software technology
2. Offers flexible service delivery capability.	2. Service delivery is pre-defined and context specific.
3. Technology independent. Uses standards oriented architecture.	3. Technology dependant.
4. Still emerging. Low entry barrier.	4. Has a clearly defined business model.
5. Caters to both B2B for B2C.	5. Caters to B2B.
6. Technology driven: Web Services leverages on technology to deliver variability in services	6. Business driven: ASP model decides on the service to be delivered and leverages appropriate technology to deliver it.

3   Impact of QoS, Cost of Service, and Transaction Volumes on Pricing

Quality of Service is an important consideration in B2B and B2C transactions [5]. Rajesh Sumra et al [6] listed out various QoS properties that need to be addressed in the implementation of Web Service applications. These, according to them, are availability, accessibility, integrity, performance, reliability, interoperability, and security. These QoS features need investments in technologies. Varying demands on QoS levels lead to the service providers incurring variations in Cost of Service. In the cost based pricing approach, the Cost of Service which is dependent on the demands of QoS will become an essential criterion in deciding the pricing of a Web Service. More specifically, cost of technology types associated with providing specific QoS functionality are described in Table 2.

Table 2. QoS induced Technology Investments and Cost of Service

QoS Parameter	Derived QoS benefits	Associated Technology Investment Areas
Availability	Readiness for immediate execution	Sequential and parallel processing capability
	Time taken to recover from service failure	Systems, storage, network infrastructure redundancy
	Capability of systems to meet variable load	Scalable infrastructure, Loose coupling, Web Services Management & Clustering
Accessibility	Capability to serve multiple clients and diverse requests.	Data Formats, Network/ system throughput, Load balancing capabilities
	System/location independence	Platform/device independent
Integrity	Prevent unauthorized access to, or modification	Encryption, Intrusion detection
	Transactional integrity	Identity and Information Lifecycle Management
Performance	Number of requests executed, time needed to complete transactions	Variable load capacity, Robustness of application logic, protocols
Reliability	Ability to maintain Web Service quality	Robustness of asynchronous messaging systems
	Assured and ordered delivery	Reliable transport protocols
Interoperability	Robustness of interfacing standards	Standardization of interoperability framework
Security	Providing non-repudiation and confidentiality	Reliable security standards and management systems
	User authorization	Encryption, Access control

Gunjan Samtani et al [7] in their paper on Web Services ROI list some of the non-QoS specific cost elements that need to be considered while costing for services sold. These elements have been listed below:

- o   Operational costs
- o   Vendor consulting fees and retainer fee
- o   Hardware and Software requirements
- o   Training requirements
- o   Network bandwidth requirements
- o   Monitoring tools

There is also a relationship between Quality of Service and transaction volumes. The ability of the Web Services Infrastructure to bear the varying load (aka transaction volumes) affects the Quality of Service delivered to the customer [8]. There are cost implications associated with managing transaction volumes while delivering requisite QoS. For example, load balancing prioritizes various types of traffic and ensures that uptime of the Web Service is ensured. This needs to be executed both at the web server level and at web application server level implying that there are cost implications both at the vendor and customer end. Loads or transaction volumes also help in understanding the capacity of the asset that will be required to provide QoS for a defined volume of service demanded. Hence the need for vendors to understand the volumes when aggregating the cost of services sold. Therefore pricing will be a function of transaction volumes (or load), which has a direct bearing on both the QoS as well as the cost of services sold. It is incumbent therefore to have various pricing models depending on the load expected on the system as discussed in subsequent sections.

While a method for pricing Web Services is still evolving, the premise of this paper is Quality of Service being a fundamental expectation [9] from a Web Service offering, provides a good starting point for evolving a pricing mechanism.

Service providers can provide differentiated servicing by modelling the demand on the infrastructure capacity for different customers and service types and define appropriate QoS levels for different applications and customers.

For example, a multimedia Web Service might require good throughput, but a banking Web Service might require security and transactional QoS. The former requires an engaged experience for the user while the latter is transaction oriented. Therefore it is imperative that pricing models be contextualized to the Web Services Delivery model and customer types [10] as detailed in the subsequent sections.

4   Three Types of Web Services

Depending on the cost of service, which is directly correlated with the number of features in the QoS demanded by a customer, service providers adopt either a cost plus approach or a value based approach for pricing their services. However, such pricing is dependent on the volume of transactions, the number of customers subscribing for the service and the demands for customization.

4.1   Commoditized Web Services

Commoditized services are those where standardized functionality is needed by all customers over a defined period of time. These may be based on critical data which changes continuously and is of critical use for a large base of customers. Such services are further characterized by high volume transactions with very low customization. Service providers offering commoditized web services need to deliver standard services to a large group of buyers. Web Services providers who cater to such a demand thrive on high volumes and the ability to pass on the costs to multiple users through standardized pricing of their offerings. To deliver such services vendors require highly available and scalable delivery capabilities.

A bundled Web Service of stock quotes which provides news along with currency exchange rates is an example of this. The pricing model is based on the nature of Web Service delivered which in this case is characterized by well defined packaging that appeals to a large number of customers, rapid request fulfillment, and large volumes both for the vendor as well as the user. Being a commodity service, the service provider needs to assure a high degree of availability, accessibility, very high performance and high degrees of reliability, interoperability and security. The Cost of Service for providing such features would be high and hence the service provider looks for predictability of revenues by seeking to spread such costs over large volumes.

4.2   Channelized Web Services

Channelized services are those which are standard, but offered only on an on-demand basis to selective users. The volume of usage of such applications is very user specific. There could be a few number of users with high levels of usage of certain services. However, the service provider needs to possess an array of such offerings in order to spread the costs over a larger market base. Here the services are designated to similar customer profiles, depending on their specific level of utility.

A good example of such services is an equity research firm providing customized client specific quotes and analysis for various customers. Not all the customers have access to all the quotes. By subscribing to a set of quotes, the customers get customized in-depth analysis of these stocks (more rigorous than the commoditized services). Unlike the customized services which are useful for all, these services are useful for only a few. Hence customers have a choice of not subscribing to services which are not of use to them. This helps the buyer to keep costs low by not procuring information which is not needed and information when it is not needed. Thus service providers need to charge the customers only for the services used by them. For delivering such services they need to invest in technologies which ensure a very high degree of availability, accessibility and integrity compared to commoditized services, high levels of performance and reliability, very high levels of interoperability and security compared to commoditized services. Such investments for assured QoS would result in very high Cost of Service. However, since the utility of these services is not uniform across the customer base, the customers seek flexibility in choosing only those they value and do not mind paying a premium for the same.

4.3   Customized Web Services

A customized web service is delivered to a specific end user. This calls for investment in relation-specific assets, as the vendor needs to cater to client specific requirements. These types of services are typified by low customer and vendor volumes. Web services vendors who offer brokering services between firms or those that form collaborative exchanges are examples of these. End users are attracted to such models because of prohibitive costs associated with EDI and extranet pipes. Customized Web Services are characterized by both low vendor and customer volumes and are driven by specific vendor offering that meet specific user need.

For example, General Motors uses Web Services to coordinate its interactions with dealers and auto purchasers. Over time, GM plans to use a consortium it established with Ford and Daimler-Chrysler to extend this technology architecture to its relationships with suppliers. Such a network is characterized by high levels of availability and accessibility, very high levels of integrity, medium levels of performance, high levels of reliability and interoperability and very high levels of security. Such QoS features require large investments which are relationship specific. Thus the Cost of Service per customer is high.

Table 3 outlines the characteristics of various types of Web Services which are categorized based on QoS, Cost of Service and transaction volumes. The other features like relation specific investments and customization have also been taken into consideration while justifying the three categories which we defined, as we found that they really determine nature of web services pricing. These features together have been called as business features.

Table 3. Types of Web Services

	Commoditized Web Services	Channelized Web Services	Customized Web Services
Business Features			
Volume	High	High	Low
Cost of service per user	Low	Medium	High
Relation-specific investments	Low	Medium	High
Customization	Low	Medium	High
QoS Features			
Availability	High	Very High	High
Accessibility	High	Very High	High
Integrity	High	Very High	Very High
Performance	Very High	High	Medium
Reliability	High	High	High
Interoperability	High	Very High	High
Security	High	Very High	Very High

5 Three Pricing Models

5.1 Subscription-Based Pricing for Commoditized Web Services

The subscription-based pricing is an often used model in the information services industry wherein the user of the service pays a time bound subscription fee during which the service provider provides unlimited access to the resources subscribed for. There would be no restrictions on the number of transactions. A stock quote service is a typical example of this.

Service providers need to invest high amounts in the infrastructure for parallel processing, storage, redundant systems, network infrastructure, fault tolerance logic, load balancing capabilities etc., in order to provide QoS features of high availability, accessibility, integrity, performance, reliability, interoperability and security. Such high investments add to the Cost of Service. These investments being very high in their order of magnitude, service providers need to spread them across a large market base for achieving an effective ROI. The service providers can also hedge their risks by planning for assured returns by prescribing pre-calculated prices of their services. The standardized nature of the service helps in arriving at a pricing model helping a well defined packaging that appeals to a large number of customers, rapid request fulfillment, and large volume both for the vendor as well as the user. This ensures predictability of revenues for the service provider. Since the services are standardized the customers do not have much of flexibility in choosing a pricing scheme.

5.2 Transaction-Based Pricing for Channelized Web Services

Transaction based pricing is a combination of cost-plus and value-based pricing relying on the number of web service transactions requested and executed. Services that fall into this category are those that are packaged for a finite number of similar customers who might be willing to pay on an ad hoc basis. The cost of providing the services is divided among the number of customers through a retainer fee mechanism and customers are charged on per use basis. Such models are applicable to scenarios where there are customers whose demands are not pre-defined or pre-known.

In order to meet the QoS demands of buyers and to facilitate an effective access to services on an 'on-demand' basis, the service providers need to invest in robust asynchronous messaging systems, reliable transport protocols etc., which facilitates effective selective access of services, while not compromising on the basic QoS features. Such risks can be offset by pricing the service with an assured revenue by providing for a fixed component as a retainer fee and also providing the benefit to the buyer of not getting charged for services not used, by incorporating a variable component which is dependant on the usage. This ensures predictability for the service provider as well as flexibility to the customer.

5.3 Risk-Based Model of Pricing for Customized Web Services

This model is an exception as the customer defines the Quality of Service required from the vendor and is willing to pay the price for ensuring this. This model is employed when a customer is outsourcing a non-core functionality but requires SLAs. The customer may also stipulate that the vendor service only one customer at a time.

Such model is also applicable for scenarios where in the service provider needs to invest in relationship-specific assets for assuring buyer-defined QoS. Such investments focus on security and user-defined performance while ensuring the basic quality parameters like availability, accessibility, integrity, reliability and interoperability. The risks and costs are shared by the buyer and the service provider, with the buyer investing in some of the relationship specific assets and assuring a predictable stream of revenues to the service provider. The Web Services types and pricing models are as summarized in table 4.

6   Application and Conclusion

Using these considerations Web Services can be priced using context specific models which allow for flexibility for the customer and predictability for the service provider. Services which require high transaction volume, at high quality of service, incurring higher Cost of Service sold are at best commoditized offerings The pricing for such

Table 4. Web Services types and pricing models based on transaction volumes and cost of services

Web Services Type	Suggested Pricing Model	QoS Features	Stakeholder Impact				Pricing Model Description
			Transaction Volume		Cost of Service		
			Vendor	Customer	Vendor	Customer	
Commoditized Web Services	Subscription-based Pricing Model	Standardized functionality needed by all customers. High volume transactions with very low customization.	High	High	Low	Low	A customer pays for unlimited use of a defined set of services over a specified period of time
Channelized Web Services	Transaction-based Pricing Model	Select services for select customers available on "on call" basis. Packaged services designated for similar customers.	High	Low	Medium	High	Customer pays by the number of transactions using Web Services within a defined period of time.
Customized Web Services	Risk-based Pricing Model	Services delivered are specific to an end user. These types of services are typified by low customer and vendor volumes.	Low	Low	High	High	The customer makes a one-off payment.

offerings are relatively lower compared to the other pricing options which helps encourage the volumes required to sustain the pricing model.

Services that are needed on an ad hoc basis such as prices of automotive parts for example, can be offered on a pay per use basis as the service may not be needed by all the customers of the vendor but clusters of customers such as the automotive manufacturers. The Cost of Service sold may not be as low as the subscription based model since there is some element of "channeling" involved in the creation of the service and an element of unpredictability in demand. Such services are best priced on a per transaction basis in addition to a retainer fee.

Customers may also require very focused and customized services for which they are willing to pay a premium. These are low volume transactions which entitles the customer to a certain set of Web Services that may be generically available and a set of premium services on an additional payment basis. Such a model can also be used in situations wherein the Web Services firm provides the collaborative exchange and user participants pay an enrollment fee to join in. A specialized application of this model can be applied to outsourced functionalities to a Web Service vendor which offers customers stricter SLAs and QoS guidelines.

7 Further Research

The authors are conceptualizing models to enumerate ROI as the basis for pricing of Web Services. The ROI approach will use the cost based pricing approach for the cost side of ROI and use value based pricing approach for benefits realization beyond QoS including parameters such as production efficiencies in case the customer firm is a manufacturing firm and transaction efficiencies in the case where the customer firm is a service firm. Such a model extends the value of QoS based pricing to real industry contexts.

References

1. Hagel, J. lll., Technology as a Catalyst for Strategic Thinking, Harvard Management Update, Vol. 7 Issue 12, 3-4 (2002)
2. Clark, M., Making Money out of Selling Web Services – Part I, Show me the Business Model, Web Services Architect Website at http://www.webservicesarchitect.com (2004)
3. Dolan, R.J., How do you know when the price is right? Harvard Business Review, Vol. 73 Issue 5, 194-200 (1995)
4. Poynder, R., New delivery methods are embraced, but old pricing problems remain, Information Today, Vol. 14, Issue 2, 11-12 (1997)
5. Yates, S., Kafka, S.J., and Hurd, L., Web Services Payoff, Forrester Research (2001)
6. Sumra, R., and Arulazi, D., Quality of Service for Web Services—Demystification, Limitations, and Best Practices, Developer.com Website at http://www.developer.com (2004)
7. Samtani, G., and Sadhwani, D., Web Services Return on Investment, Working out what you're Getting out of Web Services, Web Services Architect Website at http://www.webservicesarchitect.com (2004)

8. Siddhartha, P., Ganesan, R., and Sengupta, S., Smartware – a Management Infrastructure for Web Services, 1st Workshop on Web Services: Modeling, Architecture and Infrastructure (WSMAI-2003), ICEIS Press, (2003)
9. Ran, S., A model for Web Services discovery with QoS, SIGecom Exchange Newsletter, Vol 4.1, ACM (2003)
10. Lim, B., Web Services: The Next Dimension in e-Business Computing, 7th Asia-Pacific Decision Science Institute International Conference, Bangkok, 136–142 (2002)

Author Index

Lecture Notes in Computer Science

For information about Vols. 1–3207

please contact your bookseller or Springer